# Exploring Spiritual Naturalism

## Year 1

An Anthology of Articles from the
Spiritual Naturalist Society

# Exploring Spiritual Naturalism

## Year 1

An Anthology of Articles from the
Spiritual Naturalist Society

Edited by DT Strain

Spiritual Naturalist Society

2014

**Exploring Spiritual Naturalism, Year 1: An Anthology of Articles from the Spiritual Naturalist Society**

Edited by DT Strain. Articles written by Arthur G. Broadhurst, Michel Daw, Michael Dowd, Sigfried Gold, Jennifer Hancock, Rick Heller, Ted Meissner, B. T. Newberg, Thomas Schenk, and DT Strain. Foreword by Susan Blackmore. Cover art by Sharmon Davidson.

© 2013 Spiritual Naturalist Society, Inc.
ISBN 978-1-304-43516-3

Published 2014 by Spiritual Naturalist Society

www.spiritualnaturalistsociety.org

# TABLE OF CONTENTS

FOREWORD ................................................................1

**PART I INTRODUCING SPIRITUAL NATURALISM ........5**

What is Spiritual Naturalism? .................................7
Six reasons you will see more of Spiritual Naturalism
in the future ........................................................15
The Other Resource................................................21
What Do All Spiritual Naturalists Have in Common?............25
Is Spiritual Naturalism an Oxymoron? .........................29
Top 10 Signs of Good Spirituality .............................33
Compassion as Foundation .......................................39

**PART II REASON & PERSPECTIVE ...................................43**

Embracing A Natural Life.........................................45
A New (old) Skepticism...........................................55
The New Copernican Shift: How Science is
Revolutionizing Spirituality ....................................59
Beauty in the Equation ...........................................63
Real Religion?......................................................69
Big History: The Heart of Spiritual Naturalism.................73
How Do You Understand Nature? ..................................77
Saving the Marriage of Science and Myth .......................85
Three Transcendents ...............................................89

**PART III PRACTICE & RITUAL...................................103**

Naturalist Practice: The Big Picture..........................105
Meditation 101 ...................................................113
Bicycle Meditation ...............................................125
Love Naturally ...................................................127
What is Spiritual Transformation?..............................129
Working Ritual with the Center .................................149
Spiritual Naturalist Drumming..................................157
Something Special May Happen....................................163
Distractions to Spiritual Practice.............................167
Happiness Upon Reflection.......................................177

How to Stay Mindful .............................................................. 179
Daily Fruit ............................................................................ 183
Working Toward Liberation .................................................. 185

## PART IV SPIRITUAL NATURALISM IN
## TOUGH TIMES.......................................................... 191

The Power of Gratitude ........................................................ 193
A Spiritual Naturalist Take on Tragedy .............................. 195
Last Hum of the Cicada: Death for Naturalists ................... 199
When Love Seems Absent.................................................... 203

## PART V APPLIED ISSUES ......................................... 207

Religious Freedom from the Inside Out .............................. 209
Do Spiritual Naturalists Believe in God? ............................211
Do You Believe in Love?.....................................................213
Managers of Human Nature: A Job Description for
Spiritual Naturalists ............................................................217
What "Death is a Part of Life" Means.................................223
Wisdom Hides in Plain Sight ..............................................227
Marriage and Spirituality....................................................229

## PART VI NATURALIST APPROACHES TO
## SPECIFIC TRADITIONS............................................ 235

Christianity Without God .....................................................237
Evolutionary Christianity ....................................................241
Naturalistic Paganism..........................................................265
About Stoicism ....................................................................273
Stoicism as a Spiritual Path ................................................281
The Big Deal About Complexity..........................................285
Taoism and Naturalism........................................................291
Naturalistic Buddhism .........................................................295
Living Life Intentionally .....................................................301

## ABOUT THE SPIRITUAL NATURALIST SOCIETY...... 303

## AUTHOR BIOGRAPHIES.............................................. 307

# FOREWORD

*Dr. Susan Blackmore is a writer, lecturer, broadcaster, Zen practitioner, and Visiting Professor at the University of Plymouth. Her research includes memes, evolutionary theory, consciousness, and meditation. Susan is author of over sixty academic articles and about eighty book contributions. Her books include* The Meme Machine, Conversations on Consciousness, Zen and the Art of Consciousness, *and the textbook,* Consciousness: An Introduction.

\* \* \*

I welcome being a 'spiritual naturalist', even if I'm not entirely sure what that means or how a spiritual life is possible within a natural world view.

During my lifetime, need for such a concept has become ever more pressing. Accelerating science has not only revealed our humble origins in the wider scheme of life, but shown the harm we are doing to our planet and our apparent inability to face up to it. Our delusions about self, consciousness and free will have been profoundly challenged and our mechanistic mental processes exposed. And yet … and yet …

Many of us who accept a fully naturalistic view of the world - a world without spirits and spooks, a world without mysterious mental forces or other realms beyond this one – still yearn for something that we have no better word for than 'spiritual'. It's a terrible word. It implies the existence of 'spirits' which have no place in a naturalistic world view. But I have no better word for what I think of as my 'spiritual practice', and I know that many of you feel the same. So – inadequate as it is – we call ourselves 'spiritual naturalists'.

How did I get this way? Like so many things in my life, it began with an extraordinary experience I had as a student in 1970, over 40 years ago. Completely out of the blue, unexpected and unasked for, I was thrust into more than two hours of an extraordinary, unfolding series of experiences. At the time I called it 'astral projection', the only relevant word I knew from my teenage readings in Theosophy and occultism. Later the term 'near-death experience' was coined and I realised that I had encountered almost all the features of a classic NDE – travelling through a tunnel, emerging into the light, seeming to leave my body and travel far and wide, meeting other beings, and facing a decision to return. Yet other aspects still did not fit any category – becoming tiny, becoming vast, falling out of time and space, struggling through indescribable challenges. Later still I came to think of it as a mystical experience in which self dissolved into everything else and there was no more duality.

My response immediately afterwards was – I suppose understandably – a dualist one. This must prove, I thought, that there are spirits or souls, that I can live without my body, and even survive after death. I jumped to the conclusion that these spiritual realms entail telepathy and clairvoyance, and all manner of psychic phenomena. This is why I decided to devote my life to parapsychology and to proving to all those closed-minded scientists around me that their materialist view was wrong.

Some years later, after numerous failed ESP experiments and lots of research into ghosts, poltergeists, Tarot cards, near-death and out-of-body experiences, I concluded that I had been wrong. Mind is not something apart from matter. There probably are no paranormal phenomena, nothing leaves the body in an OBE, and the amazing experiences so many people have can be explained in naturalistic terms. And yet … and yet …

What about those experiences? In a naturalist worldview they must be explicable in terms of bodies, brains and normal physical processes. So how do we fit them into our lives? Do we seek them, value them, or dismiss them as hallucinations? My own response has been two-fold. On the one hand I launched myself into learning to meditate and began on what has become more than thirty years of Zen training. On the other I moved away from parapsychology, realising that the real mystery was the nature of consciousness – of subjective experience. How can we be conscious beings in a natural nondual world? What kind of sense does that make? What on earth can consciousness be? Or – as I would now prefer to ask – how and why are we so deluded as to imagine ourselves as separate conscious beings living in an external world?

Many great questions arise when we throw out the supernatural and yet refuse to throw out what, for lack of any better words, we call our 'spiritual life', 'spiritual practice' or 'spiritual path'. And many of those questions are tackled in this collection. How does compassion arise in a natural world? What does wisdom mean? How can we share and respect spirituality without falling into dogma and religion? How can we understand the transformations that take place in those who practice meditation and mindfulness? Where does human happiness fit in? And gratitude, and death, and love?

This great collection of articles is just the beginning of what must become a deep exploration of the challenges and potential of what we now call spiritual naturalism.

# PART I
# INTRODUCING SPIRITUAL NATURALISM

Spiritual Naturalism has been described as 'science with awe', but a true spirituality has to be more than that. Awe and wonder are important parts of spirituality. They inspire us to undertake the journey, but they are only the 'window dressing' of spiritual naturalism. A robust spiritual path will have the natural world revealed by science as its worldview, but it will also consist of a set of profound perspectives and wise values. It will include specific contemplative practices designed to instill that philosophy into our intuitive way of being. It will be a lifestyle that allows us to make progress. This progress will be a steady and measurable cultivation of a character that is more enlightened, more in tune with the way of the universe, more virtuous, more compassionate, and therefore more capable of experiencing the flourishing, good life. This is nothing less than a path to *freedom* – freedom from fear and from the bonds of circumstance as a condition for happiness.

# What is Spiritual Naturalism?

*DT Strain*

*Spiritual Naturalism* (also called religious naturalism) is a worldview, value system, and personal life practice. A religion to some, philosophy to others, Spiritual Naturalism sees the universe as one natural and sacred whole – as is the *rationality* and the science through which nature is revealed. It advocates principles and practices that have *compassion* as their foundation, and it finds wisdom and inspiration in innumerable rich traditions and ethical philosophies from around the world.

The focus of Spiritual Naturalism is *happiness*, contentment, or flourishing in life, and a relief from suffering. It is a spirituality whereby we work to become wiser and to live better over time through continued learning, contemplative practices, and character development. It is by walking such a path that we become more capable of helping to make the world a better place, and in so doing, come closer to the flourishing 'good life'.

To explain in more detail, it is helpful to take each word separately:

> **Naturalism** is a view of the world that includes those things which we can observe or directly conclude from observations. Naturalists' conception of reality consists of the natural world as outlined by the latest scientific understanding. As for claims for which we have no evidence, we do not hold any beliefs in these and do not make any other claims about them. It is quite possible, even likely, that many things exist which we cannot detect, but we believe in a humble approach to knowledge. With humility, we can recognize that human beings are imperfect in their ability to know all things. Therefore, we are careful to limit our claims about reality to what we can experience and measure, as well as

7

reproduce and show to others. On all else, we are content to admit "we don't know".

***Spirituality*** is the other word in Spiritual Naturalism. For many, the word 'spirituality' has an association with the supernatural. However, we mean the term in its more general and original sense. The Latin root word *spiritus* meant 'wind' or 'breath', or the essence of something. As we might speak of the 'spirit of the law' or 'school spirit', the spiritual is that which is concerned with the *essence* of life – or the *essential* things in life. Thus, a person with no sense of spirituality would be a person that lives on the surface, always dealing only with the shallow or the mundane; perhaps even a materialistic person. But to have spirituality is to be concerned with the larger, deeper, and essential matters of life and to apply ourselves consciously toward them in a committed practice or 'walk'. This includes, as Socrates put it, the 'examined life', and this is what we mean by *spirituality*.

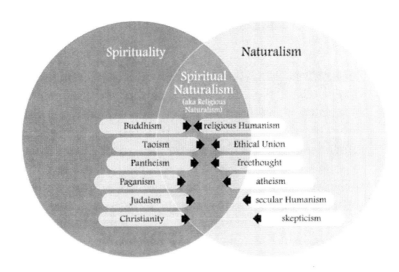

*Many communities now have subsets growing toward a common naturalistic spirituality.*

Because it is a general term that overlaps with many viewpoints, it is possible for a person to be a Spiritual Naturalist and several other things simultaneously. Spiritual Naturalism cuts across traditional or familiar categories. Many Humanists, Unitarians, Freethinkers, Jews, Pagans, Buddhists, skeptics, atheists, agnostics, and others may also be Spiritual Naturalists, though not all of them.

It may help to compare Spiritual Naturalism to other belief systems you may have heard of:

## Christianity, Islam, and Judaism

The chief difference between Spiritual Naturalists and Christians is the former's naturalist worldview and approach to knowledge. Spiritual Naturalists prefer the methods of empiricism, logic, reason, and observation for determining what is true about our world, while Christians usually also include faith, revelation, communion, scripture, and such means as sources of knowledge. This is why naturalists do not share Christian beliefs regarding the existence of God, other supernatural entities, or an afterlife. It is also why most Christians would not consider Spiritual Naturalism compatible with their beliefs. However, when it comes to other virtues, ethics, and values, the two find many things in common. Like Christians, Spiritual Naturalists also believe in loving your neighbor, treating others as you would be treated, forgiveness, mercy, and charity. There is also a contemplative and meditative thread within the Christian tradition that can be similar to Spiritual Naturalist practices. There should be many worthy projects and causes which Christians and Spiritual Naturalists can work together on, in mutual love and respect for one another. The other Abrahamic faiths of Islam and Orthodox Judaism compare to Spiritual Naturalism in similar ways as Christianity, and for similar reasons. Judaism in general, because of its intimate expression within culture, tradition, and ritual, consists of many Spiritual Naturalist people that yet consider themselves Jewish. Lastly, there is a small but vibrant and growing movement of Christian naturalists, and we have at least two such people on our Advisory

Board and feature descriptions of this view in our Resources and Member Archives.

## Atheism / Agnosticism

Since Spiritual Naturalists do not have supernatural beliefs, this would make many of them either atheist and/or agnostic on the subject of gods (with exceptions mentioned below). But while all Spiritual Naturalists are atheists or agnostics, not all atheists and agnostics are Spiritual Naturalists. To be such, they would also have a focus on the principles and practices of Spiritual Naturalism, and be interested in those kinds of pursuits. Also, Spiritual Naturalists are not generally concerned with telling believers they are wrong or with religious criticism, while this may be a concern of some atheists. For those atheists and agnostics that do share its values and concerns, they could easily be Spiritual Naturalists simultaneously. Having said this, some Spiritual Naturalists may find metaphorical personifications or archetypes useful. Those who engage in this kind of deity practice may be naturalists and yet not count themselves as atheistic.

## Humanism

Humanism is very similar to Spiritual Naturalism, such that nearly all Spiritual Naturalists would fall under the definition of Humanist. The modern conception of Humanist since the first Humanist Manifesto in 1933 has been those who are (a) naturalistic and (b) have a concern for their fellow human being. So, there is certainly a great deal of overlap and compatibility. However, there are some individuals for which overlap may not apply. While Humanism has a strong tradition of supporting and even helping to birth the animal rights movement, some Spiritual Naturalists may not prefer the term 'Humanist' because of their concern for all beings. Some Humanist gatherings may also tend to be more academic and secular in feel for other Spiritual Naturalists. On the other side, many Humanists relate more to the strictly *secular humanist* tradition, whereby they find words like 'spirituality' and the rituals and practices of Spiritual Naturalists to be too religious in tone. Further, many Humanist organizations focus on worthy social issues, political activity, and religious criticism, whereas Spiritual Naturalism begins with living rightly by example and with *inner* development as a starting point. The founder of the Spiritual Naturalist Society, Daniel Strain, is a past president of Humanist organizations, and currently a Humanist minister certified by the American Humanist Association.

## Unitarian Universalism (UU)

Many of Spiritual Naturalism's modern outlooks, tolerant dispositions, ritual and spiritual practices, and tendency to take wisdom from many traditional sources may seem very UU. Indeed, many Unitarians are Spiritual Naturalists and vice versa. However, one difference with UU congregations is that they also include supernaturalists and are not expressly naturalist and empiricist in their worldview. In that regard Spiritual Naturalism is not as broad as Unitarianism, but a good number of Unitarians are also Spiritual Naturalists and certainly a very welcome part of the Society.

## Freethought / Skepticism / Rationalism

Spiritual Naturalism includes a reverence for rationality – both the rational order on which the universe operates, as well as the human capacity for reason. This certainly includes freethinking, rationalism, and a healthy skepticism (not cynicism). Like these groups, we believe that extraordinary claims require extraordinary evidence. However, Spiritual Naturalism goes further by including a focus on personal practices and wisdom teachings designed to enhance happiness in life. This additional content may not be of interest to some freethinkers, skeptics, or rationalists, but could easily be of interest to many of them. Again, in these cases there would be simultaneous overlap.

## Buddhism

In a way, Spiritual Naturalism could be looked at as a form of philosophical Buddhism. There are many schools and ways of conceiving of Buddhism and practicing it. Some very much include the supernatural and some are more of a 'secular Buddhism'. Many of Buddhism's concepts can be interpreted in naturalistic terms. Buddhism has certainly inspired the Spiritual Naturalist practices of meditation, mindfulness, compassion, and more. Therefore, there is much overlap and many people are both Buddhists and Spiritual Naturalists.

## Paganism

Like Buddhism, there is a spectrum of interpretation regarding many Pagan paths. On one end is a literal interpretation whereby gods and spirits are believed in supernatural terms, and on the other end, they may be seen as metaphoric personifications of fully natural forces or aspects of nature, or as useful archetypes. There could therefore be a good deal of overlap for at least some Pagans, with *Naturalistic* Paganism or Humanistic Paganism even being considered a type of Spiritual Naturalism. Indeed, there is a historic thread in Paganism that has seen the universe as one integrated natural whole, with a value on experience as the means for learning about it.

## Pantheism

Pantheists also have a range of interpretation for their concepts. For those who are naturalist in their approach, they will find consistency with Spiritual Naturalism as well.

**In conclusion, many varieties of Humanism, Buddhism, Paganism, Unitarianism, Freethought, skepticism, atheism, agnosticism, and pantheism fall under the realm of Spiritual Naturalism and would be very much at home at the SNS.**

Other varieties of these which tend to either believe in the supernatural or – on the opposite end – are adverse to anything with a 'religion-like' feel, would be less compatible. In either case, these groups would still be those with which Spiritual Naturalists would be happy to live and work compassionately and respectfully on common causes.

# Six reasons you will see more of Spiritual Naturalism in the future

*DT Strain*

Many may not have heard the term yet, but Spiritual Naturalism is going to be something you'll probably hear more about in the future. Also called *Religious Naturalism* by some, it's basically a way of life that is spiritual in its tone, its practices, its ethics, and its focus – but which is based on a naturalist worldview – in other words, a view of the world either disbelieving or agnostic regarding the supernatural. Here are six reasons Spiritual Naturalism, of many varieties, will be big in the future especially in the Western world...

## 1. The rapid growth of non-religion and non-belief

Secularism and irreligion have been more prominent in Europe for some time. For example, the British Social Attitudes Survey shows a sharp decline in the dominant religion in the area (Christianity) from well over 65% in 1983 to below 45% in 2009. Over that same time, those with 'no religion' went from a little over 30% to over 50%. In Norway a 2006 survey found 48% said they either didn't believe in God or were in doubt. In France only 12% attend a religious service more than once per month[1].

The U.S. had been the oddball among Western nations, with its greater religiosity, but since the 1990s the number of non-religious and non-believing has about doubled. The Pew Forum indicates that 25% of 18-25 year olds are nonreligious[2]. In every branch of the U.S. military, those with 'no religious preference' are second only to Protestants, outnumbering Catholics and every other religious designation[3].

Of course, simple irreligion, non-belief, atheism, or agnosticism alone doesn't get us to Spiritual Naturalism, which is where the other reasons come in...

## 2. The inevitable search for meaning in later life

It's a pattern seen on the individual, as well as on a cultural level historically. The rise of religious conservatism in the 1980s consisted of many of the same individuals who had been highly liberal 20 years prior in the 1960s. These changes were likely influenced by the changing conditions and concerns of people as they enter different phases of life.

The young people currently leaving their family's belief systems aren't going to stay young and rebellious forever. Eventually, they'll settle into more traditional roles and when that happens they're going to start looking for something more than merely, "not that". Will these people fall back into traditional faith-based religion in droves? There's reason to suspect it won't happen just that way this time around.

Unlike the 80s, we now have a thriving and robust internet community constantly exposing us directly to people of diverse beliefs. This casts doubt on older dogmas, even for an older person looking for community. Further, churches with their lower attendance today, aren't the community fellowships they used to be. Meanwhile internet communities and internet tools for finding alternatives provide many more options than were available in the 70s and 80s.

Lastly, in general, our culture in the U.S. is simply more diverse. Many of us interact directly with people of all kinds of beliefs all the time, either because of immigrants from other cultures, or the greater acceptability of voicing divergent views. Many atheists come out of households of two different religions, and our American household is now that, on overdrive. So, unconvinced of faith-based cosmologies and claims, if other spiritual paths can provide what these groups will be looking for without demanding their intellectual integrity, those approaches will be in a good spot for growth.

## 3. Greater access to pre-supernatural philosophy

And what are those alternative approaches? There is a wealth of philosophy about 'how best to live' in fulfilling ways that are what one might call 'pre-supernatural'. These include the atomist and materialist philosophies of ancient Greece, as well as many interpretations of early Buddhism and Taoism. While these have been around forever, the difference is that more people have access to these alternatives than they did before, and they are generally more known. Not only that, but these ideas have found their way into modern health guides. For example, the medical community has fully incorporated Yoga and is in the process of both studying and incorporating meditation into its programs. Meanwhile in the therapy field, things like Rational Emotive Behavior Therapy (REBT) can be drawn directly back to many ideas in ancient Stoicism. All of these represent different ways of looking at the world, finding meaning, and guiding our behavior than systems which required belief in the supernatural, and they all form a solid foundation to Spiritual Naturalism.

## 4. The overlap of modern science and ancient philosophy

Not only are the practical methods and practices of ancient philosophy finding their way into modern fields, but their worldviews are looking very compatible with some of the perspectives of modern science in their essential aspects. For several hundred years, many of the fields of science had become highly specialized and segregated. But in more recent times with movements like the founding of the Santa Fe Institute and other multi-discipline endeavors, these very different departments are starting to look for overlap and more large-scale syntheses that look at the big picture. Complex Systems Theory brings together fields as diverse as economics, environmental science, computer science, biology, cognitive science, and cosmology. They study the commonalities in these systems like brains, societies, ant colonies, storm systems, and more. In the process, they talk about things like bifurcation, emergence, indeterminacy, and so on. Oddly, many of these kinds of observations run highly parallel to the observations made by ancient philosophers as they studied nature around them. Taoists describe the 'flow' of natural systems. *Autopoeisis* is the concept in complexity science whereby systems can eventually replace all of their components while the overall systems' structure remains. This is, quite literally, what Heraclitus observed when he stated, "A man cannot step twice into the same river".

Why does that matter? Because these kinds of observations about nature formed the basis upon which the ethics of Taoist, Epicurean, Buddhist, and Stoic philosophy were based. As these concepts become more central to the thrust of the scientific perspective, the same kinds of life principles will naturally begin to follow more prominently. Ancient philosophers were not like the academic philosophers of today. Even in the West, they were more like monks – producing guides to happy living and practicing what they preached. This is a spirituality, and it will be no wonder if similar orders begin to emerge, based on the latest scientific understanding – not a distortion of it or in opposition to it.

## 5. Spiritual Naturalism crosses traditional boundaries

Many different traditions and faiths have within them subsets which are drawn toward Spiritual Naturalism. The Center for Naturalism and the author's own Humanist Contemplative efforts reflect one end of the Humanist and atheist spectra which, though naturalist, reach out for more ritual and spiritual practices in both function and flavor. Unitarian Universalists, though they are not exclusively naturalist, have long had many similar members in their fold. Many Buddhists have among them those who have very empirical and naturalistic views, but find Buddhist principles and practices to be true and useful. In fact, Buddhism has a skeptical heritage in the Kalama Sutra, which instructs us to investigate for ourselves rather than accept things based on dogma, tradition, or authority. Further, Buddha himself is said to have specifically avoided questions about the 'beyond' saying that true religion is about how to live happy and productive lives and escape suffering now.

Pagans of various sorts are rising up all over the country as well, and many of these look at their pagan cosmology in very metaphoric ways, essentially accepting the naturalistic view of the universe. Many Pantheists also have naturalistic interpretations for their pantheism which are consistent with empirical methods.

*Cultural Judaism* has been a phenomenon for quite some time now. Here we have people who may have discarded the supernatural aspects of belief, or are at least agnostic to them, but who still practice the rituals and traditions of Judaism as an important part of their culture. Meanwhile, a 'cultural Christianity' is forming by which many call themselves Christian but in actuality have much different beliefs. There has even been a substantial case made by Lloyd Geering for a non-theistic form of Christianity in his book, *Christianity Without God*. This, in fact, may not be a new idea when we look at Thomas Jefferson, who considered himself a Christian in the sense that he followed the ethical teachings of Jesus, but did not see him as divine.

So it is that, across many demographic pigeonholes as they are currently drawn, there are people on the naturalistic ends of their respective communities. Many of them are beginning to see more kinship with their counterparts across those traditional labels than with those they are currently grouped. You can recognize the consistency of their 'spirituality minded' demeanor, the way they try to live their lives, the tolerance, the openness, and the joint partnership of both compassion *and* reason as a goal. These people gravitate toward a spirituality based on one whole natural universe accessible by our senses and reasoning minds, and seen as wondrous and awe inspiring in its own right. When people from these different traditions come together, there will be the potential for a new and exciting project of thought and discovery in Spiritual Naturalism.

## 6. The strength of the positive over the negative

Ultimately, the more substantial of traditions are those that answer questions for their adherents in a way that makes sense to them, but also offers them positive hope and practical ways of living more happy and compassionate lives. This cannot be accomplished through mere *anti-ism*. Carl Sagan was a master at illustrating the grandeur and beauty of our natural universe, and the inspiring effort to learn more about it. These kinds of thoughts can induce something akin to a religious experience, and form a superior foundation for meaning and living. Philosophies that rely on and build on that inspiring foundation, and go further to mine the treasures of our collective history for wisdom will comprise the many shades of Spiritual Naturalism. If such a philosophy can emerge, there is good reason to expect it will grow considerably in the coming century.

**Notes:**
1. http://en.wikipedia.org/wiki/Demographics_of_atheism
2. http://hpronline.org/religion-in-america/rise-of-the-nonbelievers
3. http://www.beliefnet.com/Faiths/2003/04/Faith-In-Combat.aspx

# The Other Resource

*Thomas Schenk*

A spirited discussion about the relationship of science and religion has been going on for a long while. This discussion has largely focused on questions of cosmology and the ultimate nature of our world. I would like to suggest that another, perhaps more important, component of this discussion has received far less attention: the valuation of our *internal* resources.

Science has been brilliant in helping us exploit external resources. This brilliance has often blinded us to the availability of internal resources. The development of one's inner resources is an integral part of spirituality. While the wisdom of inner resources is not religious by itself, it has long been associated with religious traditions. Further, it is one of the few things that the world's major religions have in common.

What are inner resources? There is an old saying that "the best things in life are free." These superlative *freebies* are the more prominent products of inner resources such as love, friendship, religious experience, and the contemplation of beauty, truth, and goodness.

Of course, in recent times we have managed to make the pursuit of love and friendship rather expensive. Religious experience is scoffed at, even by many who proclaim they are religious. Contemplation of beauty, truth, and goodness has slipped from being the meat and potatoes of a higher education to being but crumbs upon its table. Yet, for all that, many people still recognize these as the things that can make life richer and more fulfilling.

Many scientists pursue their disciplines as much, or more, out of curiosity and a love of knowing as out of a desire to make money. Many of them have described a scientific "aha moment" as among the happiest in their life. Such scientists understand that there is a truth in that adage about the best things in life. Yet science as a discipline tends to be wary of the internal, which is not a ready object for empirical study.

Inner resources remain mysterious, even with recent advances in the study of the brain. While there have been exponential gains in our understanding of brain chemistry and even the chemical pathways of happiness, the question of how these chemical reactions translate into the existential experience of joy still eludes us. Meanwhile, evolutionary theory helps us understand why certain human activities might be rewarded by the experience of joy, as they serve the survival of the species. But why something like the contemplation of beauty should be so rewarded is much harder to explain. Despite its being difficult, there is no reason to think that, at least in principle, this could not be explained in naturalistic terms.

Though a certain line of religious thought has relegated the spiritual to a supernatural sphere accessible only in death, a perennial line of religious thought provides an alternative understanding. "The kingdom of heaven is within you" states the evangelist Luke. "Samsara and Nirvana are one and the same," adds the Buddha. In this view heaven/nirvana is an internal resource accessible here and now. There is nothing supernatural about it.

Accessing the kingdom of heaven is an extreme of the notion of the internal good. A simple walk in the woods, however, if we go our way with a caring heart and focused attention, can become, at least briefly, a visit to that kingdom. I suspect that most people who adhere to naturalism yet also cultivate spirituality, do so because of such an experience of the simple joy of being in the world.

Billions of dollars are spent each year around the world to pay for market research and the effective promotion of commercial products. The market economy would certainly not favor people learning to find joy and fulfillment in the freeness of their hearts and minds. This is for us, however, a genuine alternative. Let me hasten to add that this is not an either/or choice – external goods and internal goods are both goods. There is no reason not to pursue both. It is only to say that, if like so many of us Westerners, our life is filled with purchased things but we still feel a bit empty, maybe it is for want of those very things that cannot be purchased – that can only come from the cultivation of the soul.

We naturalists well understand that the cosmology presented by science is more accurate than the various mythic cosmologies of religion. But religion offers people many values besides cosmology. The cultivation and harvesting of internal goods is such a value. There is no reason why spiritual naturalism cannot be as effective, indeed more effective, than any religion in promoting and aiding in the cultivation of internal goods. I do not think that we are there yet, but perhaps it is time we move forward in this direction.

# What Do All Spiritual Naturalists Have in Common?

*B. T. Newberg*

The Spiritual Naturalist Society brings together naturalistic strands from a wide variety of traditions, from Buddhism to Christianity to Atheism. Is there really anything shared in common by these strands?

I think there is. What's more, I suspect it's not just loose resemblance, but something absolutely fundamental. What is it? It's simply the fact that…

### …we explain everything in terms of *nature*.

Mainstream forms of religions may understand the world in terms of God's will, tao, dharma, etc. But naturalistic forms all understand it in terms of nature. For most of us today, that usually means a modern scientific view of nature.

In order to unpack that idea, let's take a quick crash course in root metaphors.

## What is a root metaphor?

All explanations rely on metaphors, explaining one thing in terms of another. A *root metaphor* is one by which virtually everything else is explained.

According to Loyal Rue, the root metaphor fuses ideas about what's real and what matters:

> *"The root metaphor renders the real sacred, and the sacred real."* (Rue, 2005)

For example, the mainstream Judeo-Christo-Islamic traditions, which use the root metaphor of *God-as-person*, ground all ideas about how the world came to be and how we should behave in the creative will of God.

Other traditions use other root metaphors. According to Rue, ancient Greek philosophy uses *logos*, Hinduism and Buddhism *dharma*, Chinese religion *tao*, and so on.

What I'm proposing is that naturalistic forms of traditions reject these other root metaphors in favor of *nature*. This root metaphor may have replaced the others, or always existed side-by-side with them. It may be visualized like this...

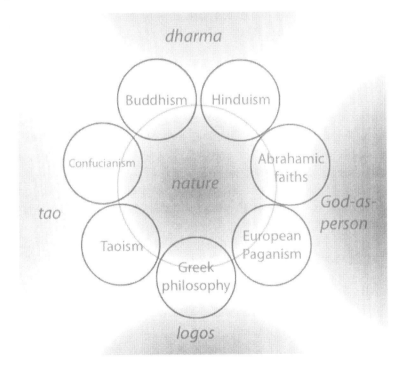

## *Nature* the explainer

Evidence for this claim is demonstrable by differences in how we explain things.

The role God plays in the Abrahamic mainstream is *explanandus*, or explainer (Rue, 1989):

- Why is the sky blue? Because God made it that way.

- Why should we love each other? Because God wants us to.

The metaphor of *God-as-person* succinctly explains how things are (God willed them so) and how we ought to live (according to God's will).

For naturalists, such a metaphor is no longer credible. Instead, we have come to a point where God is the *explanandum*, or what needs to be explained:

- Why does God never mention kangaroos in the Bible? Because the authors of the Bible, all too human, didn't know about Australia.

Here, a natural explanation illuminates the nature of "God." Nature has become the explainer.

In Eastern traditions, the conversation gets more challenging, but still works. Here's a dharmic version from Buddhism:

- How do we know karma conditions rebirth after death? Because that is the nature of the dharma, which the Buddha perceived.

And a naturalistic version:

- How do we know karma conditions rebirth after death? Because we experience one moment of consciousness "dying" and conditioning the "birth" of another (*birth* and *death* have been redefined in naturalistic terms).

Nature is the explainer, and that's what we all have in common.

Would you agree? Or is there something else more fundamental that we share?

# References

Rue, L. (1989). *Amythia.* Tuscaloosa, AL: University of Alabama Press.

Rue, L. (2005). *Religion Is Not About God.* New Brunswick, NJ: Rutgers University Press.

# Is Spiritual Naturalism an Oxymoron?

*Thomas Schenk*

Over the years, I have encountered people who believe that spirituality and naturalism are incompatible and think the term 'Spiritual Naturalist' is something of an oxymoron. Here is my personal statement on this.

Is Spiritual Naturalism an Oxymoron? Like many philosophical questions, the answer depends upon how we define the terms. Some people define "spiritual" as dealing with something called 'spirits', immaterial beings; defined thus, it is necessarily at odds with naturalism. Others define the spiritual as a particular mental perspective, a way of seeing, and as such it is quite compatible with naturalism. So the simple answer to the question posed is that "spiritual naturalism" is not an oxymoron if it is defined as a particular way, we'll call it an alternative way, of perceiving and being in this world.

So what is this alternative way of perceiving and being in this world? In the Gospel of Luke, Christ says: "The Kingdom of Heaven is within you." This singular statement is rather at odds with much of the rest of the Bible and what the Jewish and Christian traditions say about "the kingdom of heaven," but is a good starting point for answering our question. In the mainstream tradition, God and heaven are transcendent from the world and from our experience while we are alive. In short, God and heaven are supernatural. But if the Kingdom of Heaven is within, then it is a part of our world and a part of our self. It is something that each of us potentially can experience and even live from right here and right now. It is a part, a mysterious part, of the structure and working of the brain.

Is there any evidence that we can actually have such an experience? The answer to this is unequivocally yes. Through all of recorded history in each of the major civilizations, writers have spoken of this experience. One famous example from the

West comes from the poet Blake who in describing this experience wrote:

> *To see the world in a grain of sand,*
> *And a heaven in a wild flower,*
> *Hold infinity in the palm of your hand,*
> *And eternity in an hour.*

A rather literal naturalist might complain of the obvious: one can't literally hold infinity in the palm of one's hand, and an hour by definition is not an eternity. What Blake is referring to here is an experience where the mental calculations through which we mark time and space and other proportions simply cease to matter; an experience of boundlessness.

In the Eastern traditions this experience of boundlessness is often referred to as the experience of non-duality. In the experience of non-duality, subject and object, experiencer and experience are one and the same. Since our ordinary way of experiencing usually includes a sense of a distinction between the self and its world, to see in this way is certainly a different way of seeing.

While the Eastern spiritual traditions and some in the West systematically pursue this way of perceiving and being (with its sense of a greater depth of being and connectedness), many come across at least a taste of it through love, through ordinary religious practice, through the experience of wild nature, and in many other ways. While it is the rare human who is able to permanently transform his or her being through the experience of boundlessness, it is quite common for people to have, and be deeply affected by, this experience.

There is little that the various religious and spiritual traditions throughout the world have in common. One element that many do have in common is a concern with both the ultimate context of existence (a concern with cosmology) and with the ultimate internal good (a form of which I have described above). In the traditions, these two elements are always interrelated, even integral. Modern science has brilliantly expanded our

30

understanding of the first of these concerns. The modern world in general has increasingly lost touch with the second of these concerns. And as far as the relation between them, Steven Weinberg's statement that, "the more the universe seems comprehensible, the more it seems pointless," rather sums it up. In short, we no longer sense a connection between our inner lives and the mindless swirling of the stars.

In my opinion, a primary goal of Naturalist Spirituality is to recognize and articulate the wonder of the comprehended cosmos that comes to us from science, while re-discovering the boundless inner cosmos that the spiritual traditions had opened up ages ago. Finally, it is to reconnect the relationship. From within the experience of boundlessness the inter-relationship, indeed the integrity, of self and world is simply what one knows for sure.

# Top 10 Signs of Good Spirituality

*DT Strain*

Over the course of my comparative studies, there are some general traits I've noticed which seem to be shared between those wisdom streams and I thought it could be helpful to point them out. Here are some traits that are a sign of a good and healthy spiritual path…

## 10. Aim of True Happiness

Good spirituality will have as its aim the happiness of the practitioner. Of course, deep understanding of what this entails is essential. By 'True Happiness' we mean something more than mere pleasure associated with one's conditions. Rather, the kind of happiness a good spirituality will pursue will be a deeper sense of contentment that transcends circumstance. It will be a source of inner strength in the face of adversity and humble appreciation in the face of fortune. Such a happiness is also not selfish in the shallow sense of the word, in that the practitioner will come to see that mere self interest is not always a path to it.

## 9. Humble approach to knowledge

A good spirituality will engender humility in the practitioner when it comes to beliefs. It will produce a practitioner that is careful about making claims that cannot be substantiated. The practitioner will appreciate their limitations as a human being, not assuming they have more ability to 'know' things than they do. They would learn to be comfortable with a state of 'not knowing' all things. Such an approach will guide the practitioner in their own assumptions, as well as in accepting the claims of others without good reason. A good spiritual path will encourage doubt, asking questions, etc. It will not encourage the practitioner to accept claims on the basis of authority, or tradition, or faith, or any other means than good sense and self experience. But at the same time, this principle will not be one that encourages the practitioner to spend their time telling others what they should or shouldn't believe. Rather, its focus will be on helping the practitioner in their own walk.

## 8. Holistic, not dualistic

A good spirituality will inspire appreciation of the interconnectedness of all things. Dualistic thinking, whether it comes to nature, ourselves, us/them mentalities, and so on, will be anathema to a sound spirituality. Such a spiritual path will, in part, help to guide the practitioner to operate more effectively in an interconnected universe; appreciating subtle cause and effect, and acting more wisely in such a system. This 'skillful means' will be a way for the practitioner to see the big picture – to handle the complexities of life more like a surfer on ever-changing waves, moving in a dance with the universe, rather than stubbornly trying to move against the grain.

## 7. Acceptance of impermanence

The ever-changing flux of the universe, and the impermanence in which that results, has always been obvious to any observer. Nearly all worldviews, philosophies, traditions, or religions can be grouped into two categories regarding how they handle impermanence. One group will try to claim that there really is some permanent phenomenon to which we can attach our hopes and secure our philosophy (an afterlife, a deity, a 'salvation', magic powers, etc). While this may or may not be true, #9 (a humble approach to knowledge) suggests that we cannot know for certain whether it is. For that reason, a good spirituality will belong to the second category, which instead helps the practitioner to come to terms with impermanence; to accept it and learn to live effectively and happily in an impermanent universe. Spirituality, at its best, even helps to grow a sense of awe and wonder at such a grand flux, as we come to realize that impermanence means not merely death, but birth as well, and makes possible everything we love and experience.

## 6. Motivation-focused, not consequentialism

While much philosophy is often concerned with elaborate logical models to define the ethical, based on actions, consequences, and outward results, a good spirituality will know the limitations of these approaches. In the face of highly complex situations we rarely know all the variables, let alone their values and the results of our actions. But a good spirituality will emphasize the importance of good motivation on behalf of the practitioner. It will direct the practitioner to that inner motivation in all actions. Surely, it is important to use our reason as best we can to take responsible action, but in the end, if we have good motivation and take that due diligence, outcomes are not entirely within our say, as the rest of the universe will play its part as well. A good spirituality engenders a deep appreciation and intuitive-level knowledge of that truth. In this way, our deeper happiness in life begins to divorce itself from circumstantial outcomes.

## 5. Practice-centered

A good spirituality will be more than merely intellectual teachings or academic philosophy or a 'world view'. It will not be merely centered on intellectual assent to a certain set of beliefs. Rather, its true power will be in its practice. That is, it will be a system of disciplines one can apply and become more skillful at over time. Its wisdom and its practices will be integrated and support one another. In this way, one's spirituality will not merely be a label – it will be an activity; and the practitioner will have a sense of making continual progress, day by day, as they walk that path.

## 4. Changing self instead of others or the world

A legitimately spiritual person will certainly be found taking positive action to help others and help make positive change in the world, but these are merely symptoms of the spiritual life. A good spirituality will help the practitioner always to focus on changing what they have the most capacity to change: the person in the mirror. Understanding that we live in an impermanent and interconnected world, the practitioner will understand that all of their efforts may or may not come to fruition. Therefore, a good spirituality will help us to change our focus from "I must change the world" to, "I must be the kind of person that seeks positive change in the world". Thus, when we adopt this focus we have already succeeded, regardless of outcomes. This focus not only helps against 'burn out' in activist efforts, but it helps us avoid the pitfalls of focusing too much on how others ought to be acting without tending to our own shortcomings.

## 3. Transcending the ego

A sign of a poor spirituality will be that it coddles the practitioner and makes all things about them. Perhaps it promises wish fulfillment and certain externals such as wealth, health, reputation, etc. It fools us into thinking we have more control than we do. These claims to empower the practitioner appeal to the practitioner's shallow and mundane self interests and reinforce the ego. A good spirituality will be ego-busting. It will help to free the practitioner from the prison of the ego, expanding one's sense of self and concern outward to include others. Only through such a liberation from the ego can we begin to see what had been consuming distress for what it is, and begin to know a larger world. Healthy spiritual paths will help us in this process.

## 2. Wisdom, not –ism

Good spirituality will not be about labels, or a particular people or culture, or particular brands, or personalities. It will inspire the practitioner to seek out and respect wise notions and practices wherever they can be found. It will not inspire the practitioner to defend their 'ism' as though holding a flag, but rather to seek truth first with an open mind. Such a practitioner will not care too much whether this or that is considered a religion by some or a philosophy by others, or what titles by which they may or may not be called. They will be adept at exchanging lexicons to suit the context and the conversant, keeping in mind the meaning behind that language is what is important. They will not turn away from certain sources because of bias, ignorance, or reactionary tendencies. Good spirituality encourages the practitioner not to form attachments to the trappings of its own form.

## 1. Compassion as foundation

Most importantly, a good spirituality will have compassion at its core. Even the pursuit of truth is only worthwhile because of the good it makes possible for all people and is thus secondary to compassion. Good spirituality will help to expand one's sense of empathy and compassion, ultimately toward all beings. It will teach forgiveness and reject retributive approaches toward dealing with human conflict. Even when action against others is necessary, it will help the practitioner maintain compassion even for enemies. A good spirituality will reject the notion that compassion and pragmatism are at odds – that the virtuous and the advantageous can be exclusive to one another. Ultimately, the practitioner of a good spiritual path will come toward greater perception that virtue (including compassion) and wisdom are synonymous.

# Compassion as Foundation

*DT Strain*

Compassion is under assault in our media, entertainment, and politics. Meanwhile the faceless nature of the internet often encourages even greater levels of meanness and vitriol than would normally occur in human interactions, and this negativity unavoidably spills into other parts of our lives.

Yet, compassion is an essential part of our nature as social animals and moral beings. Thomas Merton wrote that compassion is, "the keen awareness of the interdependence of all things". Called *Rahmah* in Islam, compassion is considered a major trait of God, who they call *"the merciful and compassionate"*. Hinduism has a principle of doing no harm called *Ahimsa* and their word for compassion is *Daya*. In Buddhism, you have the notion of wishing a release from suffering in others, called *Karuna*, and the notion of wishing happiness for others – loving kindness – called *Metta*. When asked if cultivation of compassion and loving-kindness is part of their practice, the Buddha replied, 'no... [it is] all of our practice." The life of Jesus exemplifies the very essence of compassion to Christians. Judaism lists 13 attributes of compassion and leading Rabbi Hillel the Elder in the 1st Century stated that the whole Torah could be summed up as, "That which is hateful to you, do not do to your fellow" adding that all the rest is merely commentary on that principle.

This emphasis on compassion as key to a healthy life and happiness is also supported by the latest science in the fields of psychology, sociology, and neurology. Even computer science has discovered the role of forgiveness, empathy, and mercy in its simulation studies of which behavioral rules seem to rise to the top in naturally selective environments. Clearly, compassion is so central to humanity that it has found its way into the great streams of wisdom throughout history and across the globe. All wisdom begins with compassion, all reason requires it, and all healthy discipline serves it. All other principles of natural spirituality – the application of reason, the pursuit of a flourishing life, the function of ethics, and our role in society – spring from this foundation and serve its ends.

Compassion means love, concern, and caring for self, our fellow human beings, and life in general. We recognize that compassion is natural to our healthy development as interconnected social beings. When we nurture our compassion, we live more fulfilled and meaningful lives because we act in accordance with our best nature as human beings.

Compassion includes love and caring for the well-being of everyone, which results in several things. For one, this compassion includes ourselves. When we use compassion it does not imply allowing ourselves to be dominated or abused by others. Caring for everyone also implies that we attempt to have compassion, even for our enemies. Some people who act poorly or heinously may be victims of their own histories and delusions and they suffer greatly for their deeds, even if they do not realize the source of their suffering. When we try to help our enemies improve, we are improved.

Being compassionate means more than speaking the words and simply 'caring' within our minds. Compassion is most essentially practiced through action. Good spiritual practice should move individuals to act on their values to a greater degree – whether it is in their interactions with those around them in daily life, or whether this refers to doing good for others.

Many naturalists and their organizations have often focused on reason and rationality as the starting point or foundation. Reason is an important virtue and natural faculty, but it is primarily a tool. The ends for which that tool is used depend on our underlying motivations – and that is where the foundation of a philosophy is to be found. Reason is a means and, alone, cannot establish an ultimate goal or motivation. If compassion is not our motivation for which reason operates, then something else is our motivation, and we must examine this.

Rationality leads to a better understanding of our world, but regardless of what is true or false about reality – the simple fact of our coexistence here and now, and the benefits of compassion here and now, are true. The reason we promote rationality is precisely *because* of its ability to improve the lives of others and ourselves. This reveals that the true foundation of our philosophy is compassion.

But what is the real nature of compassion? Many ideas about what compassion is may include a kind of *pathos* – a deep suffering that disturbs our ability to have contentment in life. The aim of a non-attachment practice is to disassociate our sense of happiness from the ups and downs of our material circumstances. While empathy and compassion are central to development of a character that makes this possible, we will be no better off if we are likewise drug into deep despair by the ups and downs of the material circumstances of others. This kind of compassion, rather, is an association of others with ourselves, along with a wish to help others just as we act to help ourselves – but without unhealthy attachments, dependencies, clinging, and the suffering that accompanies them.

# PART II
# REASON & PERSPECTIVE

For naturalists, the science part is easy. We generally tend to look at the world in a rational, scientific way. But how do we get from science to spirituality? What role does science play in the spirituality of a naturalist? And, what roles does it *not* play? In this part, our authors take on the notion that science and spirituality are contradictory, or even merely 'non-overlapping'.

# Embracing A Natural Life

*DT Strain*

A friend told me last week that he recently, and suddenly, became an atheist—and wished he wasn't…

I had seen him move from conservative Christian, to a Christian with a more liberal belief about scripture, to something even more general over the past few years. He said he was thinking a few days ago and realized he didn't even really believe the last bit, and let it go.

What intrigued me most was his expression that he wished he wasn't an atheist. He said he'd like to believe, but just didn't really see any supporting logic that would make such a thing reasonable to believe. I asked him what exactly he'd like to believe. Turns out it wasn't so much about God, as it was the belief in immortality. God would be some guy hanging around on the side there, but the main point is that you'd be living forever, and that you'd get to see others who have died.

Admittedly, I think that would be pretty neat too.

We all have that desire, and it comes from the fact that we are organisms descended from others who have survived after countless generations where those who did not have a deep-seated instinctive wish to survive didn't try as hard and perished before contributing as many offspring to the following generation. In other words, everything alive today *really, really* struggles to live because those lineages that didn't have that desire died off—probably long before we even creepethed out of our ancestral oceans. Unfortunately, that explanation for our desire has completely zero relevance to anything that would affect the likelihood of an afterlife being true. Mix that desire with an intelligence capable of imagining what it *wants* to believe, and you've got a superstition cocktail.

My friend showed exceptional intellectual integrity and honesty in admitting his earlier beliefs had been based on things that aren't necessarily wise ways to establish them. Now he has before him the task of rebuilding a perspective, a sense of meaning, purpose, and value within his new worldview. It's a process not exactly the same, but similar to the one I went through years ago, and it can be an exciting process of wonder and discovery—one I am still hopefully on.

I told him that at some point, we can come to terms with our mortality. After all, death is no real mystery—I've been dead before. I was dead from about 13 billion years ago until 1971, and I don't recall it being all that bad.

There is yet another way to view the universe, or a perspective—no, it's something more. But it's one that a person can attain in which the question of death takes on a whole new light. Attaining that perspective is kind of like seeing the three-dimensional image in one of those scrambled pictures. It looks like nothing at first, but you stare at it until finally it all comes together. When it does you have an "ah ha" moment. In this case, when that happens it feels like a religious experience—what I call *profound experience*, or what psychologist Abraham Maslow called peak experience. I can describe it here, but those who have had it know what I'm talking about.

I first had that experience in the mid-90s. I was reading about complex systems theory. A person can read about the interdependence and interconnectedness of things, about how the universe is one big system of cause and effect. A person can look at time as a tapestry, but there is a difference between knowing something intellectually, and finally grokking it in a way that it is perceived directly. When that happened for me, it was like stepping outside and catching a view of an amazing sunset by surprise—I felt my heart beating. It sends chills down your spine. It sticks with you, and it shapes how you think from that point on. You seek it out time and time again, and you seek refuge in it. You try your damnedest not to forget it, and not to let the world distract you into thinking in those old ways again.

One can easily see how religious figures in the past have felt like they had a revelation from a higher being. One of the next sensations is a sense of great concern that you'll never be able to communicate the experience to anyone else. But that concern, too, is just a stage.

There have been some depictions in film which have tried to communicate the concept. In *Phenomenon* (1996), George Malley (John Travolta) attempts to explain to the children the place his death has in the world, with the example of an apple left on the ground, versus one that is eaten and becomes a part of us. In *V for Vendetta* (2005), Inspector Finch (Stephen Rea) has an experience where he sees all of the film's events, from the personal to the political and several seemingly-unrelated incidents, as all interconnected. This sense of interconnectedness is difficult to explain, but the film does a good job of communicating the emotional and conceptual content of such revelations. In the abstract film *The Fountain*, Hugh Jackman portrays three men in three different time periods (centuries in the past, the present, and centuries in the future), searching obsessively for immortality in some form, be it mystical or technological. Near the end, the three visions come together to reveal something disturbing and wondrous at the same time: disturbing because of what it means to our sense of ego and wondrous because of the larger vision it communicates. The nature of that larger vision is not fully communicable through the written word alone. It's not something you're going to read in a paper and get fully through language and conceptualization. While film is also no substitute for first person experience, the multimedia format, when it is presented well, goes much further in getting across the larger vision to which I refer. This is why I recommend viewing films like these if the reader hasn't.

In *The Watchmen*, Jon Osterman has become a being, Dr. Manhattan, that can experience his past, present, and future simultaneously. He naturally sees all events as one and interconnected, speaking of all of them in the present tense. This view affords him an extreme detachment from all things, even regarding life itself as irrelevant by the standards of value people typically use. But eventually, he perceives the beauty of life as an integral part of the intricate system we call the universe. He speaks of billions upon billions of tiny interactions that lead to specific forms, and his chest heaves as he struggles to describe the miracles under his nose. This sort of experience is required of "the One" in *The Matrix*. Neo is told that being the One is like being in love—no one can tell you when you are, you just know it. Eventually Neo has an experience that is portrayed visually, but which illustrates a non-visual event where what we have learned intellectually is perceived directly and fully internalized. Understanding becomes connecting and that "ah ha" moment ensues. Before Yoda told us we must "feel" the Force around us, Heraclitus felt it as he saw the intricate patterns of complexity woven in the natural world around him—the same perceptions that would inform Taoist philosophy, and that would be investigated more rigorously in complex systems theory and other interdisciplinary fields of study.

But complex systems theory is to this phenomenon what music theory is to the spiritual experience of music. You may have a Ph.D. in music, but nothing you learn intellectually can equate to the crescendo of a magical piece of music as it touches the soul and leaves one breathless. But not merely breathless, for the event is not merely an emotion one. It creates a perspective and a new way of evaluating the world, our place in it, and an appreciation of the beauty of all things. Concerning death, Chuang-Tsu said:

> *(to cry at one's death) is to evade the natural principles and increase human attachments… those who accept the natural course and sequence of things and live in obedience to it are beyond joy and sorrow.*

Notice that he doesn't say, "will be joyful," but are "beyond" both joy and sorrow. Here those two words refer to the ups and downs of our immediate circumstances. We have what could be called "big mind," and in that we understand intuitively that nothing we value, be it friends, family, even our own lives, is possible without that grand flux of ever-changing, interdependent causes and effects called Nature. The only way to curse death is to curse the very thing that makes our existence possible in the first place. After people have had that intuitive-level experience of seeing the world in this way, they don't need to convince themselves of this intellectually. They naturally tend to see it this way, or they can with some reminding perhaps. When they do, it becomes immediately obvious how silly it makes us to curse our mortality, and how sadly blind to some of the more beautiful aspects of the universe. This "beyond joy and sorrow" is what I experienced at my mother's passing. It was a sense of acceptance rather than sorrow, and an appreciation for the time had, but it wasn't joy. It washed over me like a profound and reverent moment, leaving me neither in despair nor in elation, but in the presence of some other sensation—something beautiful and awful.

Of course, death will always be dispreferred, and we will do what we can to avoid it and prevent it in others. To not do so would be improper and inhuman. This is not contradictory when one appreciates the distinction between setting our priorities and actions on one side, but understanding their limitations and roles within the grander scheme of things. This brings an appreciation and acceptance of what we can control and what we cannot. It doesn't mean we don't try to do what's right, try to survive and thrive, and so on. But it's about our *internal economy* – our sense of well being and a healthy outlook without attachment to particular results of efforts not fully within our control.

Ultimately one can develop a calm and appreciative acceptance of the workings of Nature and our finite place within it. Once I was flying on a plane, looking out the window. I was thinking about the plane crashing—not in a scared way, but just something I do from time to time. This is a Stoic practice of imagining negative things calmly, to keep the full spectrum of possible events in mind at all time, and keep myself accustomed to the transitory nature of life. As I imagined the situation, I thought to myself:

*This view I'm witnessing now, looking down on the clouds from above, is an experience that many throughout history would have given everything they own to have once. Plato wrote of Socrates speculating what it would be like, and he wasn't far off. So, I'm pretty fortunate. So much so, that of all the life forms that have lived on this planet over the billions of years of its life, I can't think of a life form I'd rather be. Not only do I enjoy my consciousness and intellect, but human beings have a better standard of living than most animals in the wild, living in the elements, fighting for survival, hunted by predators, and scrounging for their next meal.*

*Even among humans, I live in the best time yet experienced. In no past time would it be as easy to live than in the present. And even here in the present, I live in one of the most affluent nations on the planet, enjoying some of the best standards of living among human beings anywhere. And even within my nation, although I am not rich by American standards, I am by any reasonable global standard. Only a tiny, tiny fraction of life forms on the planet, throughout its history, have enjoyed the quality of life I have. Now in my 30s, I have lived to an age not far from the life expectancy experienced by most humans before the 20th Century. Given all this, how incredibly ridiculous it would be for me to think I'd have anything to complain about were I to die today.*

To live without fear. To live without attachment, without greed, without dependence. To live with an intellect capable of thought without bias, perception without delusion, including self delusion. As stated in the song "10,000 years" by Live, "If all of the ignorance in the world passed a second ago, what would you say?" None of us have achieved this, but at times it is possible for us to glimpse it, and that is something worth working toward. Many ancient philosophies that focused on Nature are good at providing a perspective that helps us see a larger reality beyond our egotistical concerns.

Returning to some of the wisdom of these ancient philosophies may be an important option for many Americans in the coming years. It seems that Christianity has been in decline in the U.S. According to religioustolerance.org, "the percentage of American adults who identify themselves as Christians dropped from 86% in 1990 to 77% in 2001... an unprecedented drop of almost 1 percentage point per year." Atheism and nonreligiousness are also on the rise. Many secularists are encouraged by this, but my encouragement is tempered by concern. As people leave one faith system it is important that they not simply be "lost souls" but that they have something of meaning, that is compatible with their new paradigm of seeing the world and their place in it.

On the Houston Church of Freethought's community forum, one concerned person wrote that he needed to find a therapist to help him because he'd been feeling down. He said:

> *I mean, if you believe that you're going to live in eternal peace and fluffy-cloudness in Heaven—then your shouldn't really have much need for motivational self help. Whereas, if you believe there's no God and, that you're just going to die and rot, and have as much significance as an ant... well then you might need a little psychological boost once in a while.*

This shook me, and related in my mind to what my friend had said about his concern. Consider in the above, again, how the point isn't really about God, but more about "just going to die and rot." There is also a second concern in this which has to do with "significance." We want to know that our lives will have meaning or purpose, and for that we look to an external objective source with which we can be compared. Further, within that objective framework, we want to be the *hero* of the story. But Chuang-Tsu noted on this:

> *But now that you have emerged from your narrow sphere and have seen the great ocean, you know your own insignificance, and I can speak to you of great principles.*

In other words, we cannot comprehend great principles until we know enough about the world to see that we are not the center of it. But when we realize we're not going to live forever, that we aren't the main character of the story, then we see our insignificance. While that insignificance may be frightening, it can be supplanted by something else—for only when compared to something tiny does something else seem huge, and there we see the magnificence of Nature and the beauty of living life for the sake of the experience of life itself. Each moment is not a means to some other end, but an end unto itself. Every moment has value in itself and it is in that amazing universe that we experience that moment. It will never come again, but it had value just for that reason. All beings share in that conscious experience of life, and that is the universal.

If you haven't had the kind of profound experience I'm talking about, then all this "everything is connected" talk is going to sound insufficient to make up for becoming worm food. Or, worse, it may sound to a secularist like new-agey nonsense. I'm not proposing some method by which we become like lemmings, completely unconcerned for our own lives. That would not be a very flourishing existence either. But there is a difference between acting according to rational goals, and being consumed by them or lost in obsession with them. Two people may outwardly be acting in the same manner, under the same conditions, yet one is miserable and the other content.

But merely having *profound experience* is not, alone, sufficient. Experiences of this sort can vary widely and convey a wide range of concepts. If not pursued further, they can be as fleeting as a wild drug-induced hallucination at a party and then discarded. They are generally far more effective when integrated with a philosophical framework and ongoing practices. How is it that these perspectives and practices lend themselves to an acceptance of our mortality? If these experiences are so wonderful and the universe so amazing, then wouldn't that engender an even deeper feeling of wanting to continue conscious experience within it?

This form of "spiritual gluttony" or "attachment to detachment" can happen to people as well. But generally, perceiving the universe as I've described engenders two things: first, an appreciation for the beauty of an ever-changing impermanent cosmos, and secondly a sense of ourselves as just a small part of that. It's one thing to begin with the mature realization that you can't change some things, and you're going to die, so you might as well learn to accept it. But when you add to that a deep, intuitive perception of the awe and beauty of the whole thing, it makes it easier to accept reality as it is, and even embrace it. We fall in love with the universe. That is the only way we will ever have a chance of living harmoniously within it. Living well is not a 'strategy' – it is a *relationship*. That includes all the so-called "bad" and so-called "good", for better or for worse. With each step, our pressing of foot to the ground is like taking the hand of our beloved. We begin to get a deep internal confidence that *the universe will unfold just as it should – the only way it could*. There is no "should have", no "what if"; no "if only". There is simply: *is*. And, in this, our own life path is wrapped up inseparably from the stream of the universe – both whole, perfect, and the same.

There is a process addressed in loving-kindness meditation and other techniques, and which was called *appropriation (oikeiosis)* in ancient Stoicism. It is a process where your sense of identity begins to migrate beyond yourself, to those around you and further out like concentric rings. As that sense of identity expands, we find that our biological survival becomes less of an issue. We look at things less temporally, and more in terms of quality over quantity. We come to fully internalize the notion that it is not living *long* that matters so much as living *well*. So, yes, these perspectives and practices lead to a greater joy for life — but it is a less self-centered joy, and that acceptance of our finite place within the universe is part of that increased capability.

This is not something readers can fully "get" by reading an article (or by reading all the volumes of human wisdom in existence for that matter). It's not a perspective you can fully take on deeply merely by choosing to. It's something that can only be appreciated fully by *doing it* — by engaging in the practices over time. But if you want to pursue it, I'd recommend keeping an opened mind, thinking not only analytically, but creatively, and then get out there: (1) read a lot of ancient philosophy, especially Taoism, Buddhism, and Stoicism, being tolerant of cases where something is stated that you might not fully agree with; (2) put it into practice, both applying specific practices, but also in everyday life; (3) have lots of conversations with others; and (4) experience new music, art, stargazing, and other awe-inspiring things.

Having engaged in this sort of process, I am convinced that there are many more aspects of a fully robust life practice waiting for us to explore. Aspects which are compatible with our naturalism and empiricism, but which tap into something we've yet to harness, and deal with issues and questions that have confronted all people throughout history. Naturalist thought must grow to encompass these aspects of what it means to be human— if it is to fulfill the needs of people and address the concerns of their personal life practices. But in order to do so, we naturalists and Humanists must be willing to go outside our traditional comfort zones and be willing to look boldly at all of the wisdom human history has to offer us, without flinching or turning away simply because, mixed into that, is a plethora of older ideas through which we may need to sift. Most importantly, we need to do more than discuss these perspectives *academically*. The key is to put the perspectives into practice in our lives and learn through experience which are effective and which are not.

# A New (old) Skepticism

*DT Strain*

Skeptics have often been accused of being cynical, negative, etc. They will (quite appropriately) correct us that skepticism is not the same as *cynicism* – always about denying or a denial that we can reasonably know anything. While skeptics might reject certain claims on the basis of lacking or contradictory evidence, skepticism also includes the *acceptance* of claims on that same basis. Skepticism can be a good thing because it is the opposite of gullibility and fuzzy thinking.

**So, that's skepticism as the skeptics know it. But this article is titled 'A New Skepticism' because I'm about to discuss how Spiritual Naturalists do skepticism...**

In the above there is some overlap with many of the ancient philosophies that might inspire various forms of spiritual naturalism. The Buddhist Kalama Sutra instructs us not to accept claims merely on the basis of authority, faith, tradition, or even our own musings – but rather because we have experimented and observed from that experience that it is true. In the West, the ancient Greek philosophers were creatures of reason. Although the modern scientific method would not be forged for several centuries to come, the elements of it comprised the way these thinkers approached knowledge. Through observation and reason they made their way – not by faith. Therefore, we spiritual naturalists have good cause to embrace a healthy skepticism.

But, unfortunately, some criticism of those who call themselves skeptics, and of skeptic communities, may be more difficult to shake. For those who are *merely* skeptics, or those who appear so due to their focus on this one value, an impression of being negative, inconsiderate, disrespectful, snobbish, or even brutish may arise. While the skeptic may be a perfectly fine person, this impression arises in the same way it might arise if we were to take any one value and emphasize it at the expense of other values which are meant to exist in balance. Further, much of this depends on the *style* in which skepticism is often promoted, and the motivation for doing so.

So, what is the spiritual naturalist approach to skepticism, and how does it differ from *mere* skepticism?

Naturalism is about more than just love of nature. It includes a reverent recognition of all things as a part of nature. And, it includes *an approach to knowledge* that cultivates the naturalist view. But, rather than talking about empiricism as some kind of key to perfect knowledge or as a superior possession to that of anyone else, the Spiritual Naturalist approach is different. Our aim is to envision and discuss this approach in terms of one of the many virtuous character traits we aim to cultivate in ourselves – namely, to see it through the lens of *humility.*

This is why I prefer to speak of "a humble approach to knowledge and claims". I don't talk about your beliefs – I don't know your experience. Rather, what I can say is that when *I* make a claim *my* personal practice is to limit what I take to be true to that for which I can provide or reference some kind of external evidence. Importantly, this also includes refraining from claiming the opposite – that x is false – without sufficient evidence. This path is one of recognizing and emphasizing *my own limitations* of experience and my own limitations in ability to know all things (certainly including the greater secrets of existence).

Thus, rather than using this approach as a weapon to scrutinize or dissect the beliefs of others, I say to myself that this is a practice *I have chosen* to undertake and look more often to the mirror, asking myself if I am living it well. Often, I have found it helpful to refer to this discipline by an ancient term, Epoché (eh-POK-ay), to help maintain an attitude about it as being a sacred practice. In the Supporting Member's section of our website, we have an article that discusses Epoché in more detail.

More generally, another big difference is that Spiritual Naturalists are concerned about many values beyond just epistemology. Here we try to show, by living example, that practice. Let us live in ways more centered on increasing compassion, mindfulness, kindness, helping others, forgiveness, mercy, self-discipline, and encouraging it more in the world. Let us proceed with a confidence that, when not being insulted or threatened, free human minds will tend toward reason in their own time and way.

When the impulse arises to criticize others' beliefs, let us turn that energy toward projecting love and understanding – and that includes refraining even from the passive aggressive kind of comparative phrasing. When a person leaves an encounter with a Spiritual Naturalist, the difference should be obvious and perhaps even striking. This is the noblest goal of a rational being that recognizes that the value of even reason itself rests on the primacy of compassion. And, it is this – not tedious argumentation – that will peak the interest of others to want to know what this rational spirituality is all about.

But this cannot merely be some PR (public relations) tactic. Remember that the focus of Spiritual Naturalist practice is greater happiness and flourishing, and only *personal transformation* can accomplish this. This is why our true inner motivation and mindset should be one of concern for others. That this approach also spreads both compassion *and reason* in the world (often more effectively) is a wonderful bonus.

Sometimes, of course, sharing information may be integral to compassion, especially if we think it can help others. But here we must check that this is the true motivation, and not egotism. When it comes to sharing beliefs with others, we remind ourselves that *Truth* is sacred to the rational being and a powerful thing (that is, importantly, *assuming* that what we possess is Truth). If so, then we also recognize: that which is sacred and powerful should not be thrown about carelessly or dispensed without consideration. Truth best flows where the landscape naturally cradles its rivers. One does not take the waters of truth and flood crops and villages, so to speak. Here, we combine rationality with the wise practice the Taoists refer to as Wu Wei.

We also realize that Truth, devoid of compassion, can be *abusive and vicious*. This is why we don't try to plant seeds in infertile soil. Instead, patience, reservation, love for those with whom we converse, and humility in our assumptions about our own knowledge are the hallmarks of a practicing Spiritual Naturalist.

# The New Copernican Shift: How Science is Revolutionizing Spirituality

*B. T. Newberg*

We are experiencing a new Copernican shift that is revolutionizing our spirituality. It is undermining our sense of humanity as something privileged in the universe, the sole possessor of "soul", standing above the beasts and apart from the inert dust of soil. It is questioning our free will, our magical power to move ourselves amidst the billiard-ball jumble that moves everything else in the universe. Our spirituality will have to change to embrace this new vision of humanity.

## The old Copernican shift

The heliocentric model of Copernicus showed us that the earth is not the center of the universe, that we are not special but a humble, integrated part of a larger whole called the solar system.

Suddenly, the earth had the same status as any of the other planets, and behaved just like them. This at once undermined both the specialness of the earth as the focal point of the universe, and the specialness of the other planets as exalted, transcendent entities. Both were of the same stuff, and that required a tumultuous shift in spiritual understanding.

## The new shift

In just the same way, we are now beginning to understand that the human mind, the psyche, the "soul" even, is not special either. Neuroscience, cognitive psychology, evolutionary biology, organic chemistry, and a host of other lines of research are converging on an inevitable conclusion: we operate according to the same physical laws as everything else in the universe.

Consciousness, thought, emotion, meaning, value – all these are emergent properties of a particular arrangement of organic chemistry.

Just as extreme hardness emerges when carbon atoms assemble in a certain manner to form a diamond, so consciousness emerges when carbon assembles in another manner to form life.

Suddenly our dreams, hopes, and aspirations – all that we hold dear – appear as if at the mercy of chance meetings of molecules. There is a beauty but also a horror to this.

Are we really nothing more than a random coagulation of stuff? Aren't we special?

## The special species?

Just as the earth is not the specially-privileged center of the universe, we are not the specially-privileged center of consciousness.

We may be unique on this planet – so far as we can tell, no other species has achieved our level of intelligence or aptitude for complex manipulation of symbols. But we are not special in how this came about. It's all due to the same fundamental process.

Meaning is not unique to us. Even amoebae detect the effluents of decaying bacteria, and know this *means* food is near. On an even simpler level, atoms are constantly seeking to acquire a complete set of electrons, and they bond with nearby atoms to acquire them.

There is no conscious intention to do so, but somehow the atom "knows" to do it. This "knowing" is no more than physical laws in operation, yet it is different from human knowing only in the level of complexity and nuance of response.

An atom knows to acquire electrons, an amoeba knows to move in the direction of food, and we know to breathe the precious air that gives us life. We know to circulate blood in our veins, we know to fire the neurons that bring up a certain memory, we know to respond to the caress of a lover with increased heartbeat and burning desire, and we know to pose one possible course of action against another and call up all the relevant social factors in order to decide what to do. We know to recognize patterns in previous experiences, and extrapolate what patterns are likely to continue in what we call the future. We know, finally, that this whole process of acquiring knowledge, ever incomplete, implies that there is and probably always will be more that we don't know.

In this litany of knowing, there is a clear progression from the simple to the complex, but it is all the same fundamental process. Consciousness creeps in gradually or all of a sudden, but it does not disrupt the essential process of knowing.

Our knowing, then, our thoughts, our dreams, our very experience of being, is not special. It is the knowing of animals, the knowing of plants, the knowing of amoebae, the knowing of carbon atoms, the knowing of all things that partake in this marvelous phenomenon called the universe.

We are not the center of the universe. We are not the center of consciousness. We are not the center of knowing.

Like people in the days of Copernicus, we may perceive this insight as a threat. We may react to it with fear and denial. But if, instead, we can learn to embrace it, we may discover something startling and new.

## Toward a new vision

Our spirituality must evolve itself to incorporate this new insight. We are essentially one with our universe. Every entity in the universe is unique and different – there's no denying that – but at the same time, on a fundamental level, they are the same.

I and my world are a single, seamless whole. Person and place are identical. The world "out there", and the experience "in here", are one.

Atoms are our brothers and sisters. All things in the universe behave exactly as we do, and we behave like them. We are at one with all things. We enjoy communion with each and every thing.

How could there be any deeper mystery than this?

# Beauty in the Equation

*Thomas Schenk*

> *"It is more important to have beauty in one's equations than to have them fit experiment."* –Paul Dirac.

There is a general notion that "beauty" is something that belongs to the arts and humanities and has more or less been banished from science. Yet, in the last hundred years, many prominent artists and humanists* have banished beauty from their consideration (e.g. the Dadist, Fluxus, and much of the Postmodern) and many prominent scientists and mathematicians have in their way proclaimed beauty as an inspiration and guide to scientific discovery.

The theory of beauty (aesthetics) proposed by twentieth century humanists tends to go from muddy to muddled. On the other hand, a scientist like Werner Heisenberg, in his essay "The Meaning of Beauty in the Exact Sciences," gives a straight forward definition of beauty as "the proper proportion of the parts to the whole, and to each other." Now the humanist might complain that this is overly simplistic, but from Aristotle to the present the notion of the integrity and proportionality of the parts to the whole has been a steady guide for artists, craftspeople, scientists and engineers.

In general, one will find a particular scientific theory more elegant than another by the greater diversity of phenomena that it can unify. The progress of science is always in this direction. Prior to Newton, one would not have suspected that the rising of a balloon and the falling of an apple were examples of the same phenomena: gravity. Prior to Maxwell and Faraday, the scientists exploring magnets and those exploring static electricity did not suspect that the phenomena they were exploring would turn out to be different aspects of the same thing. Among the other great unifications are Darwin's discovery of an underlying principle that unifies the diversity of living species and Einstein's unification of space and time, and matter and energy. In our own time, the goal of theoretical physics is guided by the belief in a final unifying theory, a theory of everything that will harmonize quantum mechanics and general relativity and gravity with the other fundamental forces.

In addition to the idea of unity in variety, Heisenberg's definition also speaks of proper proportion as being essential to beauty. Proportionality refers to ratios, and by extension to that which is rational. Thus the fundamental faith of science, that the world is ultimately rational, is an extension of this principle. The original of the idea that beauty has to do with proper proportion may have come from Pythagoras' discovery of the mathematical relationships of musical tones. Another prominent example is the ancient Greek ideal of the golden mean, a ratio that has had a great influence on art and architecture.

The humanist again might be quick to complain that such examples as music and the golden mean are exceptions, that in the real world there is little basis for the idea that beauty refers to correct proportions. As an example, most people would say that a butterfly is more beautiful than a human louse. But on what basis could one say that a butterfly is more properly proportioned than a human louse? We associate butterflies with summer days and flowers, we associate the louse with parasitism and an itchy head. Does not the beauty we attribute to the butterfly really come from these associations, which in the end are quite subjective? And, of course, there is also the butterfly's colorfulness. Pleasant associations and colorfulness are attributes of our common understanding of beauty – and one could argue that they are more central to it than the idea of proportionality. So can one justify the aesthetic ideal of proportionality?

As an undergraduate student, I took an entomology class from a professor who was a renowned authority on the human louse. He would get rhapsodic when showing slides of the louse's anatomy and would occasionally say how beautiful the louse was. My fellow students would roll their eyes at this, but the louse's internal organs are wonderfully proportioned to enhance its ability to survive its particular lifestyle. All living creatures are wonderfully proportioned in this sense – they are all beautiful in their own way. It takes a certain kind of detachment, however, to find beauty in a louse; indeed, it takes the kind of detachment required of a good scientist.

One of our most common uses of the word beauty is to refer to attributes that we find in other people, attributes that make others loveable to us. This connection of love and beauty is nearly opposite the kind of detachment that finds beauty in the form of a louse. One of the reasons, I suspect, that the idea of beauty is so muddled is that we have one word carrying many different meanings.

We might ask: When a physicist speaks of the beauty of an equation and when a young man speaks of the beauty of a Playboy centerfold, is there anything at all that these two uses of the world "beauty" have in common? At the emotional level, both are experiencing a kind of delight. But in terms of the object that is generating this delight, there is little or no similarity. The experience of beauty always has two poles: the pole of the experiencer and the pole of the object experienced. Different people take delight in vastly different objects. This fact has often been used as evidence that beauty is purely a matter of taste.

But is this not an oversimplification? Calling beauty purely a matter of taste does little to explain the complex phenomenon of the experience of beauty. I suggested earlier that a simple equation that explains a great deal is more beautiful than a complex equation that doesn't really explain much. An equation's explanatory power is not a matter of personal taste. Not everyone experiences beauty in the contemplation of mathematical equations, but those who do can often provide solid reasoning for their judgment of the difference between the more and less beautiful equation. If beauty were merely a matter of taste, any such reasoning would be fatuous.

Albert Einstein wrote "The most beautiful thing we can experience is the mysterious. It is the source of all true art and science." This would seem to be a very different idea of beauty than the one proposed by Heisenberg. I would suggest though, that it is a necessary addition. Not only every organism, but every workable machine fulfills the requirement of Heisenberg's definition of beauty – every good machine requires a proportionality of its parts and an integration of all the parts into a functioning whole. As with the case of living creatures, every successful machine also has its beauty.

But is there not something more to the beauty of a great work of art or to the works of nature, than this simple beauty of the machine? I would suggest that the difference is that a machine is not mysterious – there is always someone, hopefully the repairperson, who understands it fully. A great work of art is never fully understood, not even by the person who creates it. There have been thousands of articles written about Shakespeare's *Hamlet*, and thousands more will undoubtedly be written in the future. Hamlet the character and *Hamlet* the play are filled with ambiguities.

Ambiguity is the life blood of a work of art. It is what keeps us coming back. Compare a crossword puzzle to a good poem. A crossword puzzle can be incredibly engaging and enjoyable to work on, but the moment the last box is completed, the value of the puzzle plummets to nothing. When finished, a crossword puzzle is utterly without ambiguity. A good work of art, through its ambiguities, makes sure that we can never fill in the last box. One can gaze at the Mona Lisa's smile for ages, but you still cannot be completely sure what it conveys.

As ambiguity is to art, mystery is to Nature. For a few hundred years now, science has penetrated the layers of Nature's mystery, but as each layer is penetrated a new layer is discovered. And this is not likely to end. Even if physicists should complete the quest for a final theory of physics, it has become increasingly clear that the theory will not answer the question of why and how the universe came to have the properties described by that theory. Like the Mona Lisa's smile, Nature's mystery refuses final resolution.

From the point of view of mystery, we can see that Heisenberg's definition of beauty may be more a definition of value in general than a correct definition of beauty. Integrity and proportionality, wholeness and rationality, applies equally to the good, the true and the beautiful; the role of mystery, however, is quite different in each. A good machine or good legal system seeks to banish ambiguity; a true principle or theory acknowledges the presence of mystery, but seeks to penetrate it as far as possible. The beautiful object or idea celebrates the mysterious and invites contemplation of it.

The truth of science plays a dual role in relation to other values. On the one side, it is eminently practical and its discoveries are the stock-in-trade of the engineer, who turns these discoveries into a society's economic goods. But on the other side, its discoveries expand our sense of the world we live in, revealing its incredible diversity and the connections that hold this great diversity together — in short, revealing its beauty. Defined as Heisenberg defined it, it is not difficult to see how beauty can lead us to truth, and how truth can lead to beauty.

Connecting the world of ideas and the world of the senses, the physicist Murray Gell-Mann said at a Noble Prize banquet in his honor, "The beauty of the basic laws of natural science, as revealed in the study of particles and of the cosmos, is allied to the litheness of a merganser diving in a pure Swedish lake, or the grace of a dolphin leaving shining trails at night in the Gulf of California." To this, I'll say Amen! and leave it at that.

*Editor's note: Schenk here, has stated that he means 'humanist' in the sense of scholars in the humanities, and not referring to the modern secular humanist movement.*

# Real Religion?

*B. T. Newberg*

What makes for "real" religion? How do you know that what you're doing isn't just playing dress-up, a shallow parody of religion?

Well, maybe you "just know." But aren't there times when you doubt whether all your beliefs and practices mean anything? Don't you ever say to yourself, with Luke Skywalker on Dagobah, "Aw, what am I doing here?"

This question may be especially pertinent for those walking a naturalistic path. Who are we to strike off the well-trodden trail of traditional theism? How do we know we're not headed toward a muddy dead-end?

I struggled with this question. For a long time I was seeking something, I wasn't sure what. Something that would make this alien and hostile world feel like a home. So I passed through Christianity to Agnosticism to Buddhism to Paganism. Each gave me something special, but was I *really* practicing religion? Or was I just play-acting, trying on different costumes?

"Religion" may not be the best term for what I mean here, so replace it with "spirituality" if it makes more sense to you. But I don't want to debate semantics. I want to get to where the rubber meets the road.

How do you know whether your religious practice is genuine?

## A litmus test

One test I've found is whether you turn to your religion in times of trouble. When beset by hardship, does it give you strength, comfort, or solace?

Malinowski was the first to suggest that religion functions to manage anxiety. Burkert and Armstrong agree. But let's leave scholarship aside today and just look at personal experience.

If you find yourself riddled with stress, anxiety, or depression, and the farthest thing from your mind is your religion, it may not have really taken root yet.

On the other hand, if you find yourself going back to your rituals, meditations, walks in nature, or whatever it is that you do, and feeling buoyed up by them, there may be something deeper going on. When your ego is drowning, and then here comes the lifeguard to keep you afloat, that's real religion.

## My journey

As a young Christian, I never found myself praying to God when under stress, except when I was too little to know what I was doing. After high school, when I became agnostic, there was a certain confidence in myself that was of benefit, but ultimately agnosticism alone was too vague to provide real support. Eventually I found Buddhist meditation, and that got me through my college and post-college years. The ability to calmly and mindfully observe a situation was powerful. Yet Buddhism, with its notions of karma, rebirth, and enlightenment, just didn't work for me. It still felt alien. Not till I discovered Paganism did I find something that was truly my culture, something that felt like home.

Encountering the gods of myth through ritual and prayer proved surprisingly therapeutic. Something about reaching out to them, with words on your lips and a gift in your hands, activated something deep inside me. It may be what Martin Buber calls the *I-Thou* relationship. Or, it may be the human instinct for communication responding to the gods as supernormal stimuli, larger-than-life parental figures. In any case, it worked. I could talk to them, especially to the one with whom I'd become close, Isis. In times of stress, kneeling before her altar, I would pour my heart out. And then some insight would flash through my mind, or a feeling of release would come over me, and with it would be the strength to carry on.

Yet there was still something missing.

## Real naturalism, real religion

As much as Paganism relieved stress, it also produced it. The idea that there were gods "out there" with whom I could communicate went against everything I felt to be true about the universe. So, why was it working for me?

It wasn't until I realized where the power was coming from that I felt truly supported. The gods weren't "out there", they were *in here*. The therapy I was experiencing was coming from the mind's ability to project its inner reaches onto the images of the gods. In this way, I was able to make contact with that part of me that possessed the strength to carry on, the "big self." Meanwhile, the conscious ego, or "small self", the one that frets and worries, felt a part of something larger.

I still regularly kneel before my statue of Isis, ring the bell and offer her a cup of life-giving water. I chant a traditional hymn, then tell her what's bothering me. All the while I know I'm talking to myself, but it doesn't matter because, well, it *works*. By the end I feel release and a sense of strength.

That's how I know what I'm doing is *real* religion.

What about you? Is there something that convinces you that your spirituality is genuine?

# Big History: The Heart of Spiritual Naturalism

*B. T. Newberg*

As Spiritual Naturalists, we might have scriptures, sutras, myths, and so forth. These may be full of wisdom and inspiration, but we know they are not literal descriptions of the universe. For the real story, where do we look? What lies at the heart of Spiritual Naturalism?

Previously I argued that all forms of Spiritual Naturalism share the root metaphor of *nature*. If that's true, the real story can only be told through the epic of nature itself: Big History. I propose the narrative core of all forms of Spiritual Naturalism is Big History.

## What is a narrative core?

A *narrative core* is what unleashes the power of a root metaphor, like a combustion engine unleashing the power of fuel. The narrative unlocks the potential implicit in the metaphor. It turns it into a story comprehensible and moving to human minds.

It's not just any well-told yarn, though. A narrative core is a story by which we understand all other stories. It's an epic within which all other stories are embedded.

Loyal Rue describes it in *Religion Is Not About God*:

> *The narrative core provides members of a culture with vital information that gives them a general orientation in nature and in history. The narrative core is the most fundamental expression of wisdom in a cultural tradition – it tells us about the kind of world we live in, what sorts of things are real and unreal, where we came from, what our true nature is, and how we fit into the larger scheme of things. These are all cosmological ideas.... But the narrative core also contains ideas about morality, about*

*which things ultimately matter. It tells us what is good for us and how we are to fulfill our purpose. (Rue, 2005)*

In short, the narrative core elaborates the power of the root metaphor to "render the real sacred, and the sacred real." The narrative cores of Abrahamic traditions, for example, are told in the Torah, Bible, and Quran. Traditions without such explicit scriptures may relate their narrative cores implicitly through rituals, stories, histories, proverbs, and even daily interactions.

So, what is the narrative core of the many forms of Spiritual Naturalism?

## Big History

Also called the Epic of Evolution, the Great Story, or the Universe Story, *Big History* is the story of the cosmos gradually emerging from myriad lines of research across scientific disciplines. It is a product of the *consilience*, or agreement, among the sciences on our common origins and nature.

It begins with the Big Bang, proceeds through the formation of stars and galaxies, and narrates the emergence of increasing complexity. Physics gives rise to chemistry as atoms combine into molecules. Then, chemistry gives rise to biology, biology to psychology, and psychology to culture. We find ourselves at the latter end of that sequence (without implying any superiority), looking back at the great enormity of events that have led to this moment. As Loyal Rue says, "we are star-born and earth-formed."

The tale has been eloquently told by many. Ursula Goodenough comes to grips with it in her deeply reflective *The Sacred Depths of Nature*. Loyal Rue and E.O. Wilson play bard in their book *Everybody's Story*, as do Brian Swimme and Thomas Berry in *The Universe Story*. Michael Dowd and Connie Barlow have much to say on it, and Glenys Livingstone incorporates its themes into her PaGaian Cosmology. And don't miss David Christian's exciting TED talk, "The History of Our World in 18 Minutes".

# But… what does that have to do with *me?*

At a scale as large as the cosmos, it's easy to lose sight of the human. What do distant galaxies have to do with our everyday lives?

Although the universe dwarfs us, we are a part of it. Notice how each system is nested within those preceding it (physics > chemistry > biology > psychology > culture), and all are ultimately nested within nature itself. That means that we humans are a part of nature. By understanding nature, we understand ourselves.

We also understand something of how to live by grasping the story of the cosmos. All of nature's systems are interconnected. Any change can send reverberations throughout the whole. Locally, everything exists in a delicate balance; disrupting that balance may catalyze new relationships unpleasant or even hostile to us. So we ought to live in harmony with nature.

We learn, too, that nothing can be understood except by reference to everything else. Beginning our story not at our birth but at the Big Bang brings perspective, and reminds us who we are, where we come from, and where we're going.

Finally, if Big History still seems alien, maybe it's because the story needs to be told all the way down to the human level. After all, love, hate, and passion are no less natural than anything else. Why you lost your job, how your spouse still loves you, and what you're going to do with your life – all that is the cosmos in microcosm. Each of our lives is a chapter in the ongoing epic of the universe.

# One narrative or many?

At this point, some may be squirming at the thought of a single story informing all others – and rightly so, if that story were univocal.

Fortunately, Big History does not have one single form, like some kind of holy scripture. Rather, it is multiple and fluid by its very nature. As the sciences continue to debate and revise concepts based on new findings, Big History is always changing.

Furthermore, it can and must be told from different perspectives. Since we are human, it is usually told from a human perspective, but one could also tell the story from the perspective of a tree or galaxy.

Big History is thus truly *big*.

And it's what lies at the heart of Spiritual Naturalism.

### References

Rue, L. (2005). *Religion Is Not About God.* New Brunswick, NJ: Rutgers University Press.

# How Do You Understand Nature?

*B. T. Newberg*

I have previously made the claim that all naturalists share the root metaphor of *nature*. But that doesn't tell us all that much – not yet. What is nature exactly? And how can it suggest how we ought to live?

To recap quickly, a *root metaphor* is a metaphor by which virtually everything else is explained. According to Loyal Rue (2005), it fuses into one idea what's real and what matters, so that we understand both how the universe is and how we ought to live.

To address these questions, our metaphor needs to be more specific. So let's investigate a few alternatives.

## Nature-as-machine

The predominant paradigm bequeathed to us by scientific materialism is *nature-as-machine*. We have grown used to thinking of matter as inert, dead, stupid stuff that gets knocked around by other matter, like balls on a billiard table. Modern physics has not improved on this metaphor (witness "quantum *mechanics*").

One problem with this metaphor is that machines are tools for our whims. They do not transcend us, we transcend them.

Another problem is that traditionally matter was complemented by the intelligence of soul as well as by its designer, God. If you no longer believe in soul or God, then there is nothing but stupid, meaningless stuff all around. This lays the foundation for the famous quote by physicist Steven Weinberg: "The more the universe seems comprehensible, the more it seems pointless" (Weinberg, 1993).

The metaphor of machine cannot help us understand who we are or how we ought to live. At most, it says it is up to us to answer these questions for ourselves. While that may be true, I think we can do better.

## Nature-as-person(s)

Another metaphor in play today is *nature-as-person(s)*. This is like the God-as-person metaphor of traditional theism, but swap nature for God. Nature acquires some or all of the human-like traits of God, such as will, intention, personality, wrath, compassion, and so on. This metaphor shows up in some forms of animism and some Gaian paths (note that the Gaia Hypothesis of James Lovelock and Lynn Margulis does *not* use this metaphor, but posits the planet earth is a self-regulating organism; Lovelock, 1995).

It's certainly a powerful metaphor, allowing for a high degree of what Robert McCauley calls *inferential potential:* the capacity to permit one to "utilize a huge range of *default inferences* that accompany our maturationally natural ontological knowledge" (McCauley, 2011; italics his). In plain language, he means it lets us quickly draw a number of conclusions with little but the brain's natural intuition. Specifically, it draws on our species' highly developed social intelligence.

An example will make that a little less arcane-sounding. The *God-as-person* metaphor allows one to take an event such as a failure of crops and activate the brain's module for dealing with persons, leading to a whole suite of new inferences: If all happens by divine will, then a god willed the crops to fail, and it must be because he is angry, so we should offer a gift to appease that anger, and hereafter live in ways conducive to a better relationship with the god. In this train of thought, the idea of how things happen (cosmology) leads directly to what to do (morality).

The *nature-as-person(s)* metaphor would seem to allow similar inferences (though without necessarily reaching the same conclusions). However, the main problem with this metaphor is the same as that of *God-as-person*: credibility. It just doesn't seem plausible for many naturalists today (with the possible exception of certain proposed solutions to the 'hard problem of consciousness'). Anthropomorphism is not necessarily a bad thing if used consciously and for specific purposes. However, used as a root metaphor, which usually operates unconsciously and at the highest level of generality, it seems inappropriate for naturalists.

## Nature-as-Creativity

A third metaphor is *nature-as-Creativity*. Representatives in this line of thought include Stuart Kauffman, Gordon D. Kaufman, Thomas Berry, Brian Swimme, Michael Dowd, Connie Barlow, and PaGaian's Glenys Livingstone. It may also hark back to Spinoza's *natura naturans.*

The idea is that nature is inherently creative, producing marvelous patterns and complexity out of its own self-organizing propensities. It is not inert stuff, nor is it the tool of some other thing that transcends it. This grants nature inherent value. It also gives nature and humans something in common, namely creativity, without going so far as to turn nature into a personality. Finally, it tells us who we are: part of the great story of unfolding cosmic creativity.

"Creativity" is quite abstract, though, and it's not very clear how we ought to live as part of this Creativity. It seems short on inferential potential. If a crop failure happens due to natural Creativity, then it must have a meaningful place in some emerging pattern. There is something inspiring in that idea, but it doesn't seem to suggest much of a role for us in the matter other than perhaps to marvel in tragic awe at the new pattern (or am I missing something?).

## Nature-as-Big Self

Here's the idea: Nature is so much greater than us, yet we are an integral part of it. Our tiny conscious ego (small self) is dwarfed by, yet interdependent with, the greater world of being (Big Self).

Alan Watts eloquently expresses the notion:

> *We do not "come into" this world; we come* out *of it, as leaves from a tree. As the ocean "waves," the universe "peoples." Every individual is an expression of the whole realm of nature, a unique action of the total universe.* (Watts, 1989)

As does Albert Einstein:

> *A human being is a part of a whole, called by us 'universe', a part limited in time and space. He experiences himself, his thoughts and feelings as something separated from the rest... a kind of optical delusion of his consciousness. This delusion is a kind of prison for us, restricting us to our personal desires and to affection for a few persons nearest to us. Our task must be to free ourselves from this prison by widening our circle of compassion to embrace all living creatures and the whole of nature in its beauty.*

There is inferential potential here: If I am an integral part of nature, however small, then how I live must have an effect. Since we *are* nature, we ought to value it as we value ourselves, treat it with care and respect, and live in ever more sustainable ways. The crop failure would be met by questioning how our own actions have contributed to this (trans)personal crisis, what we might do to heal the wound, and how we might live healthier in the future.

One problem with this metaphor is that it seems to obscure the radical otherness of nature. But I don't think it's a big problem, because contemplation of it leads right into the experience of otherness. Confronted by the proposition that nature is us, we immediately ask "How can this be? I'm nothing before the vast depths of nature." Nature appears as an Immensity (to use Brendan Myers' term). This plunges us into what Rudolf Otto (1958) calls "creature feeling": the emotion of being overwhelmed with awe before what transcends our own smallness. Finally, integration comes when we realize it is not the tiny ego but rather its participation in the greater whole which is meaningful.

An alternative version of this metaphor might be *nature-as-body*. If "self" is too psychological of a term, "body" might achieve the same extension of personal identity without suggesting any kind of cosmic consciousness or intelligence. Those living with the *nature-as-body* metaphor may see trees as their lungs, and rivers as their blood.

## Nature-as-kin

Last but not least, the metaphor of *nature-as-kin* may have something to say today. By this metaphor, Earth becomes our mother, sky our father, and all creatures our brothers and sisters.

This metaphor has recurred again and again across history in many times and places. It's probably not by accident, either: sociobiology suggests we are genetically predisposed to aid our close kin first, since they likely carry identical copies of our genes (this is called *inclusive fitness* or *kin selection*; Dawkins, 1989). If this is so, then viewing nature as kin may activate deep-rooted motivations to treat nature with respect, care, and devotion.

This reverses the original function of the predisposition (widening rather than narrowing the field of aid), but that doesn't matter – evolution re-purposes things all the time if it makes for greater fitness. In our age of ecological crisis, whatever best motivates eco-centric behavior will exhibit the greatest fitness.

Another advantage of this metaphor is that it has the virtue of being *modestly counterintuitive*. Pascal Boyer (2001) counts as counterintuitive something that violates our most basic, inborn intuitions about classes of objects. Children know from a very early age that an owl can't give birth to a lizard (McCauley, 2011). So, saying that the earth is our mother is counterintuitive. This makes it an interesting meme, and therefore more likely to be passed on. Yet it is not radically counterintuitive – it doesn't take years of training to grasp, as do science and theology. Boyer finds the best balance or *cognitive optimum* is a modestly counterintuitive idea with just one or two violations. In other words, *nature-as-kin* is a highly fit meme in the game of cultural selection.

A difficulty, though, might be that it seems all too ready to merge with the *nature-as-person* metaphor. Since our kin are normally human, calling the Earth "mother" seems to invite anthropomorphism. The metaphor would then suffer from the same credibility problem that plagues *nature-as-person.*

## Other metaphors

There are, of course, many other possible nature metaphors. Michael Cavanaugh suggests Big History as a possible metaphor (Cavanaugh, personal communication). I'm sure the reader will come up with plenty as well.

You may be interested in the results of a poll taken of the root metaphors preferred by the Humanistic Pagan community.

## Can we really choose our metaphor?

Ultimately we may not be able to choose our root metaphor; we may just find ourselves using it. But however we identify it, it will determine how we think, act, and forge symbols as we embark on our naturalistic paths.

## References

Boyer, P. (2001). *Religion Explained.* New York: Basic Books.

Burkert, W. (1989). *Greek Religion.* Cambridge, MA: Harvard University Press.

Dawkins, R. (1989). *The Selfish Gene.* New York: Oxford University Press.

Lovelock, J. (1995). *Gaia: A New Look at Life on Earth.* New York: Oxford University Press.

McCauley, R. (2011). *Why Religion Is Natural and Science Is Not.* New York: Oxford University Press.

Myers, B. (2008). *The Other Side of Virtue.* Hants, UK: O Books.

Otto, R. (1958). *The Idea of the Holy*. New York: Oxford University Press.

Rue, L. (1989). *Amythia.* Tuscaloosa, AL: University of Alabama Press.

Rue, L. (2005). *Religion Is Not About God.* New Brunswick, NJ: Rutgers University Press.

Watts, A. (1989). *The Book: On the Taboo Against Knowing Who You Are (Vintage Books Edition).* New York: Random House.

Weinberg, S. (1993). *The First Three Minutes*. New York: Basic Books.

# Saving the Marriage of Science and Myth

*B. T. Newberg*

Marriage is hard. Zeus and Hera were constantly bickering. Inanna banished her husband Dumuzi to the underworld. Skadi and Njord couldn't live together no matter how they tried. Are all marriages doomed to failure?

Humanistic Paganism bills itself as a naturalistic "marriage" of science and myth. It would be nice if it were a neat, sweet, picket-fence relationship. But that's not how most marriages go, is it? Marriage is hard work, but it's worth it.

This metaphor is particularly poignant to me since I'm two and a half months into a marriage of my own. The honeymoon phase is over. No one said marriage would be easy, whether it's between two people or two cultural phenomena like science and myth.

By *science* I mean that modern method of empirical investigation which has given us everything from toasters to quantum physics, and which takes naturalism as a working principle. By *myth* I mean the ancient stories that have given us the likes of Zeus, Thor, and the Morrígan, as well as the rituals, meditations, and other practices that go along with a living tradition of mythology.

Now that we know what we mean by science and myth, what does it take to make their marriage work?

## Couples counseling

No marriage has much hope if the couple can't learn to listen to each other.

It takes courage to hear hard criticism. Science and myth have plenty of grievances, so they'd better find a way to air them in a safe space. HP aspires to be just such a safe space.

It also takes patience. We aren't necessarily able to express our feelings coherently or all at once. Each person must discover themselves in the process, while the other waits patiently for them to work out their issues. On HP, we have folks more science-oriented and folks more myth-oriented, and both need the patience to let the other speak their truth.

Finally, it takes responsiveness. It's not enough just to listen, you also have to be willing to be persuaded. On HP, we've been challenged by critical voices, and we have to recognize the value of that process. Likewise, critics need to be open to having their challenges met.

As with couples counseling, we must find the courage and patience to talk through the tough issues, and the willingness to let the process change us.

## The parent trap

It also takes creativity to make a marriage work.

Remember that old movie *The Parent Trap*? Two teenage twins conspire to get their divorced parents back together. Their cutesy antics may make you laugh or vomit, depending on your taste, but the point is they use creativity to re-ignite love.

Theology is a lot like that. A recent term in religious studies is *creative misunderstanding*, whereby a tradition changes by re-interpreting the old in a new way. This enables a community to meet the needs of the present while maintaining continuity with the past.

It may take some creative misunderstanding to keep science and myth together. Like the twins in The Parent Trap, we may need ingenuity to rekindle their flame.

## The languages of love

Gary Chapman has a book for couples called *The Five Love Languages*, which proposes you have to learn how the other expresses love, and learn to speak that language yourself. Science and myth speak different languages, and they may need to learn the other's in order to communicate.

HP is about learning to speak the languages of both science and myth. Michael Dowd frames these in terms of *day language* and *night language*, respectively. Science speaks of reality in the clear light of day. Myth also speaks of reality, but in the strange imagery of dreams in the night. Both have important things to say, and it takes learning the other's language to achieve understanding.

## Awesome make-up sex

Often the best love-making is after a fight. When couples kiss and make up, they re-affirm they'd rather be together than apart, despite their differences.

Science and myth have had a rocky relationship, and currently stand facing away from each other with crossed arms. Can HP turn them toward each other again?

If so, we're looking forward to an awesome make-up.

It'll be like Psyche and Eros, or Isis after finally recovering her lost husband Osiris.

# Three Transcendents

*B. T. Newberg*

As my wife and I slogged along on our bicycles, generally irritated at each other, suddenly there was a pop. Her back tire went flat, and we were in the middle of nowhere on a Korean highway. We had to find a repair shop, communicate our problem, and somehow make it home.

As we pulled through this minor crisis, a peculiar thing happened: we were no longer irritated at each other. Through working together as a couple, each of us had moved from *me* to *we*. In some small way, we'd experienced a tiny moment of transcendence.

## The urge to transcendence

> *"Birds gotta fly, fish gotta swim, and humans gotta be part of something greater than themselves."*

These are the words of social scientist Jonathan Haidt in a recent *Point of Inquiry* podcast. He expands on this insight in a video interview:

> *"Happiness comes from between. Happiness comes from being merged in, bound in, connected in the right ways to other people, to your work, and to something larger than yourself."*

In both of these quotes, Haidt links human nature to transcendence, feeling part of something greater or larger than yourself. The first suggests a brute need for it, the second that happiness itself is the result.

This squares with evolution. Multilevel selection theory observes that humans have a remarkable capacity to organize into groups, and well-organized groups out-compete others, leading to enhanced reproductive fitness for members. Thus, it does not seem a stretch to speculate that our evolved capacity to form into groups may derive from a general urge to be part of something greater than ourselves.

## Naturalistic transcendence

When I speak of naturalistic transcendence*, I mean an experience of something greater than you not only in degree but also in kind, yet in which you nevertheless participate. In experiencing your participation in this something greater, you encounter something which challenges and transforms your whole sense of who and what you are, your way of being-in-the-world.

For example, stand at the foot of a mountain and you may be impressed by how much greater it is than you in degree, how alien it is from you in kind. Climb that mountain and confront limits of endurance beyond which you thought yourself incapable, feel the relation between yourself and the mountain's flora and fauna as part of one interdependent ecosystem, and discover how the experience of the mountain becomes part of you and changes who you are – then you may draw close to something like transcendence.

*I have not always been entirely friendly to the language of transcendence. In fact, I have argued for non-transcendence as a key value. What I meant, though, was non-transcendence of the physical universe, of this earth, this body, or this life. Nowadays, I recognize that naturalism better sums up what I meant then.

## Symbols of transcendence

One of our recent polls asked what symbols of transcendence most appeal to our readers. From these, I'd like to distill a set of symbols that may stand at the heart of a naturalistic path and embody its vision of transcendence.

Your personal symbol set may vary, but I'm going to pick out a triad that groups the most popular and vital together. The three are:

- *nature*

- *community*

- *mind*

The triad lends itself well to any kind of triple representation, like the triple spiral for example, but I prefer a series of concentric circles, like this:

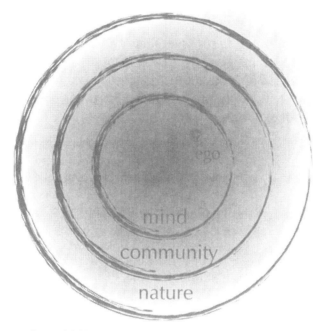

Near the middle is a dot, representing the individual vantage point which makes up our conscious experience. It is off-center to underscore that *you are not the center of the universe.*

The individual ego is transcended by the whole mind, conscious and unconscious (inner circle), each mind is transcended by its communities (middle circle), and all communities are transcended by nature (outer circle).

Concentric circles are also the pattern of ripples, which one can imagine radiating from any point in the mandala to interact with the other circles.

The three bear some similarity to John Halstead's "*kindreds*" (the physical world, ancestors, and the deep self), ADF's *Three Kindreds* (Nature Spirits, Ancestors, and Gods and Goddesses), and the first two of three of Brendan Myers' *Immensities* (the Earth, other people, death, and solitude).

Since these are intended as symbols and not analytical constructs, they may be interpreted broadly. Various alternative or elaborative terms may stand in, if they speak to you (e.g. cosmos for nature, ancestors for community, psyche for mind, etc.).

Also in keeping with symbols, these invite one's own experiences to be reflected in them. Insofar all are included in nature, and nature includes all that is, every experience and every thing can be found somewhere within this triad. It thus forms a mandala for all experience.

The Three Transcendents share a few characteristics:

- they are greater than us in both degree and kind

- we participate in them even as they transcend us

- when they manifest as challenges, they do so not as problems that can be solved but as predicaments that can only be confronted and integrated

- there is no avoiding or escaping them for any human being; they are part of the human condition

- they demand to be handled with care, so as to affirm rather than negate the individual

- they are "Immensities" in Brendan Myers' sense, a term he borrowed from Yeats:

*When we have drunk the cold cup of the moon's intoxication, we thirst for something beyond ourselves, and the mind flows outward to a natural immensity*

## Why symbols of transcendence?

> *"Ritual is the* engine *of shamanic ecstasy and symbol is the pilot."* (Laughlin, McManus, & D'Aquili, *Brain, Symbol, and Experience*)

In my experience, what's missing from Humanist, Atheist, Agnostic, and other such movements is a consciously-recognized, explicitly-articulated valuation of transcendence. John Halstead has made a similar observation of Unitarian Universalism, identifying the missing element as the *enthusiasmos* of transformative experience. The imagination must be captivated and transformed by a vision, not of what one is *not*, but of what one *is* or *could be*.

This missing element may be embodied in symbols that remind, invite, and inspire. The individual must be able to interact imaginatively with the symbols in ritual or meditation, and fill them up as it were with experience and affect. At that point, when they are charged with personal meaning and emotion, they may become powerful motivators of thought and behavior.

They radiate the power to transform.

## Nature

In our modern parlance, nature connotes that part of the environment which is beyond the domesticated human sphere. In its broader and more original sense, though, nature is quite simply *all that is*.

Those are two different meanings, and their tension is instructive. The former is an "other", the latter a oneness that transcends self and other. This is a dynamic that proves characteristic of transcendence.

In encountering wild nature, that which is quite other than our usual domestic, artificial, controlled habitat, we may become aware of an acute alienation, a sense of distance. In perceiving the vastness of nature, its scale and ancientness, we feel small by comparison. "Creature feeling" may overwhelm us, to use the term of Rudolf Otto. An experience of the *numinous\** may arise as we behold the *mysterium tremendum et fascinans.*

Then, in contemplating how we too are a part of that vastness, how we have come out of it, belong to it, and contribute to it with every thought and action, the natural/artificial duality erodes. An experience of the *mystical\** may arise as individual identity dissolves and a sense of participation pervades nature.

Finally, as we attempt to integrate this insight into our identity, an experience of the *visionary\** may arise as inspiration flashes before us our true place in nature and how we ought to live our lives in consequence. Integration affirms the worth of the individual even as it appropriately subordinates it to the whole.

This kind of experience can happen whether looking into the eyes of a wolf, as in Aldo Leopold's hunting experience, or gazing at the farthest reaches of the galaxy, as in Neil deGrasse Tyson's "most astounding fact."

*\* numinous, mystical, visionary: Religious experiences as defined in Loyal Rue's Religion Is Not About God: In numinous experiences the subject-object distinction is preserved, even amplified, as the subject is filled with intense love and peace that comes with a sense of the presence of a holy and awesome transcendent power... Mystical experiences are characterized by the annihilation of conscious distinction between subject and object, self and world. The mystic enters an altered state of pure unified consciousness wherein all reality, the self included, is immediately and blissfully apprehended as essential oneness... Visionary, or prophetic, experiences are often characterized by a trance-like state in which the seer receives a concrete message or vision communicated directly from an irresistible transcendent source.*

## Life and evolution

Insight into our relationship with nature can be aided by examining the concept itself. When we delve into its history, we find nature is not so much a thing as a process.

Our word "nature" comes from the Latin *natura*, which translates the Greek *physis* (whence we get "physics"). Gerard Naddaf explains in *The Greek Concept of Nature* that this word first appears in Homer as the intrinsic way of growth of a particular species of plant. As the term is picked up by philosophy, it continues to refer to how a thing comes to be of its own accord.

This emphasis on growth, on the dynamic self-unfolding of a thing, captures the process of life. It remains more or less intact in our concept of nature today, and is nowhere better embodied than the theory of evolution.

Thus, when we speak of participation in nature, we speak of taking part in the evolving process of life itself. We join in what Karl E. Peters calls "dancing with the sacred."

## Cosmos

With the beholding of our place in the marvelous unfolding of existence, nature becomes *cosmos*. This is a term most employed at the universal scale these days, but its actual meaning is an ordered, beautiful world:

> **cosmos.** from Gk. *kosmos* "order, good order, orderly arrangement," a word with several main senses rooted in those notions: The verb *kosmein* meant generally "to dispose, prepare," but especially "to order and arrange (troops for battle), to set (an army) in array;" also "to establish (a government or regime);" "to deck, adorn, equip, dress" (especially of women). Thus *kosmos* had an important secondary sense of "ornaments of a woman's dress, decoration" (cf. *kosmokomes* "dressing the hair") as well as "the universe, the world." (Online Etymology Dictionary)

When we speak of cosmos, then, we speak of "good order" and, anthropomorphically, the ornamented "dress, decoration" and beautiful "hair" of our mother, nature.

We are participants in that beautiful order, one of the flecks in one of the diamonds in one of the barrettes in her flowing hair.

On August 28th, 1963, over 200,000 men and women descended upon Washington, D.C. Had an alien observer looked down on this from orbit, it would surely have been a curious site: *What a remarkable capacity this species has to form groups!*

Such a distant observer might have compared it to other earthly sights, such as the buzzing of a beehive or the march of an ant colony. Certainly they shared something in common. Yet this would have missed that this collective unit was also a gathering of individuals. Hundreds of thousands of unique personalities joined to demonstrate commitment to something greater than themselves: the ideal of justice.

It might not have been obvious to our alien anthropologist that the gathering expressed deep rifts in the community, frustration at the systematic disenfranchisement of an entire race. It might not have been clear that the footfalls of each individual rang with suffering, and hope against all odds for something better.

We know better. Our species has a deplorable capacity for cruelty, especially toward outgroups and deviants within-group. At the same time, we also have the power to cooperate and achieve great things when we come together.

## Society and culture

To belong to a group, to embody its goals, is to transcend oneself.

A society is more than the sum of its constituents; a group will emerges that moves in ways no single member may direct or predict. It transcends the individual in both degree and kind. At the same time, individuals participate in that greater movement, part and parcel of it, and may dissent as part of the greater process.

We are social animals, said Aristotle. Nearly two and a half millennia later, it still rings true. Our urge to form associations is bred into us by evolution. Groups able to organize around common goals out-competed those who could not, and we are the genetic results of the more successful groups.

This is not always a rosy situation: groupishness is good for in-group cooperation, but also fosters nastiness toward other groups as well as deviants within the group.

Yet, for better or worse, we cannot deny ourselves. We are tribal by nature. And in taking part in groups, we reach toward something larger than ourselves.

Nor could we ever truly get outside the social, even if we tried. Even a hermit in solitude, gazing across untouched wilderness, *sees* that wilderness through the eyes of a culture. One continues to think in the language and categories of one's society. It is no more possible for a human to exist without culture than to exist without a physical body. Culture is part of our very being.

This is not to suggest there is no such thing as freedom or individuality. Each of us integrates diverse cultural streams in unique ways, and we can produce creative new expressions. Yet there is no denying the fact that each free and unique individual is part of society, just as each wave is part of the sea. Society is part of the human condition.

Thus far I've been using *community, society,* and *culture* more or less interchangeably. Now, I want to draw attention to some more specific concepts.

## Community vs. collective

I chose the example of the March on Washington for several reasons.

First, it's not overly optimistic. The march protested problems that still persist today, problems endemic to the tribal nature of our species.

Second, it's not overly pessimistic. The march is widely credited with helping to pass the Civil Rights Act and Voting Rights Act.

Finally, it shows the care demanded by this form of transcendence (and indeed all forms) to affirm rather than negate the individual. Communities involve individual sacrifices for the good of the whole, but must at the same time promote the individual interests of all members.

In this vein, Martin Buber distinguished between *community* and *collective*. The former promotes the group *for* the individual, while the latter promotes the group at the *expense* of the individual. There is always a tension between these two in any group. Community is of course the ideal, which requires vigilance against collective.

## The ancestors

Through community we can reach not only outward to other people, but also backward to our ancestors.

By identifying with our predecessors, be they ancestors of blood, culture, or inspiration, we become aware of the shoulders on which we stand. Those who came before can teach us about ourselves. By appreciating their contributions, we can learn humility and gratitude. By studying history, we can also learn their hard-earned lessons, including patterns we should not repeat.

Ancient ways, by virtue of having evolved over great spans of time, frequently embody knowledge we hardly suspect. This is one reason why I advocate strongly for working with ancient myths rather than creating new ones. Ancient myths evolved their forms by cultural selection over time. They survived because they spoke to people across many generations, made sense of diverse challenges and calamities, and empowered multiple ways of life. There is no reason not to try out new myths as well, but neither should we ditch old ones in our haste. Ancestral traditions deserve our continuing reverence.

Through contemplating our ancestors, we come to know ourselves as beings in time. We feel ourselves glints on a wave pushing across an ocean.

## Beyond the human: A community of all beings?

The question of revering ancestors leads to another: how far back shall we trace them? To the golden age of our favorite culture? To the emergence of *homo sapiens?* To the first life? Or all the way back to the Big Bang?

Contemplating these questions, ancestry expands to include all of Big History. Nature then appears in its aspect as community, a cosmic family. Earth may become mother, sky father, and creatures cousins.

This reveals a characteristic typical of symbols: the deeper you follow them, the more they appear everywhere. They blend one into the other in an endless web of meaning.

## Community and compassion

Finally, a word may be said about the moral potential of transcendence through community. This can hardly be better expressed than in the *Charter for Compassion*, proposed by Karen Armstrong to serve like a Magna Carta for the world's major religions:

> *The principle of compassion lies at the heart of all religious, ethical and spiritual traditions, calling us always to treat all others as we wish to be treated ourselves. Compassion impels us to work tirelessly to alleviate the suffering of our fellow creatures, to dethrone ourselves from the centre of our world and put another there, and to honour the inviolable sanctity of every single human being, treating everybody, without exception, with absolute justice, equity and respect.*

I would only add that this principle goes beyond religion to include most secular societies as well. Despite atrocities committed by both religious and secular groups, most all communities have compassion at their core. Sometimes it is only a seed, and our job is to constantly water it in anticipation of its bloom.

The power to transcend ourselves through compassion, "to dethrone ourselves from the centre of our world and put another there", is a basic human capacity.

In our recent poll on symbols of transcendence, *nature* proved the most popular, with *cosmos* a close second. One that didn't rate highly was *mind*. Perhaps it should come as no surprise. On the face of it, the very idea of it seems absurd: how could you possibly find something greater than yourself in, well… yourself?

But that's exactly the misconception I seek to challenge: mind is *not* ourselves, or at least not what we routinely think of as such.

## We are not our minds

What most of us, most of the time, think of as ourselves is more or less our conscious ego, especially the part where we feel like we're thinking, willing, imagining, feeling, remembering, deliberating, and so on. It's our most immediate experience, and it's what we may fear ceasing to exist after death. However, this represents only a tiny fraction of the total process of an individual's mind.

The unconscious is far more vast. To give a taste: cognitive psychologist Timothy D. Wilson estimates in *Strangers to Ourselves* that our minds assimilate some 11,000,000 pieces of information per second from our sense organs, but only about 40 can be processed consciously. The rest, according to Wilson, are handled by the unconscious.

There may even be parts of the mental process external to the individual body. The field of embodied cognition studies the mind in its holistic interaction with body and environment. Clark and Chalmers even go so far as to ask whether there is any difference between storing information in memory or in a notebook. Such mental prostheses, they argue, free up mental processing space by offloading some of it into the environment. This is a controversial claim, but one worth a moment's pondering.

By *mind* I mean the whole mind of the individual, conscious and unconscious. You could also say *psyche*, a term more popular in Jungian psychology. It is the root of *psych*ology, and originally meant "soul." *Psyche* is one of many words that have been thoroughly naturalized, just as "god" and "spirit" may one day come to be.

## Deep and vast

So, the other parts of the mind do a lot, but do they do anything interesting, or just take care of the tedious stuff?

Consider this: Where do your words come from when you speak? You may have a vague plan of the idea you want to convey, but do you consciously decide the words or even the nuances of the ideas? Or do you discover these things in the process of speaking?

Ancient poets like Homer and Hesiod claimed to receive their lines from a muse. Perhaps, in some sense, they were right. The "muse" lies in the unconscious. In a similar vein, Carl Jung said we are not the authors of our thoughts; they are handed to us. I tend to agree.

Jung also felt that messages from the unconscious await us in our dreams, and such content somehow "compensates" or balances the conscious mind. I'm not sure how to test that claim, so I remain skeptical. It may be a case of seeking pattern where there is none. But there is one thing that experience has proven to me time and again: my unconscious mind can do certain things that "I" can't.

## A power beyond "me"

When I sit down at my Isis altar with an emotional knot that I've been working on for days without resolution, and that knot looses within minutes of chanting and talking to Isis, it's hard to argue with that.

Somehow, an unconscious process is facilitated by the images and actions involved in devotion. Perhaps the image of a supernormal mother figure like Isis and the bodily actions of rhythmic chanting, gift offering, and intimate confession are mental prostheses in the manner proposed by Clark and Chalmers. Ritual devotion may not be unique in its ability to facilitate this, but it appears to be one way to do it, and an effective one in my experience.

I'm sure other people's experiences with ritual may be quite different. Regardless, this example demonstrates, like a pebble cast into a well, just how far down the unconscious mind goes. It is not "me"; it is radically "other." It is greater in both degree and kind. To sound its depths is indeed to discover something greater than oneself.

So, although *mind* did not rate highly on our poll, I'd like to suggest reconsidering it, not only because it is perhaps the most well-established among naturalists (via Jungian Paganism), but also because it helps us to discover transcendence "closer than your own jugular."

# PART III
# PRACTICE & RITUAL

Thinking rationally about science and its role in human spirituality is one thing; but Spiritual Naturalists aren't merely intellectuals interested in examining spirituality from the outside. They are *practitioners* – they apply rituals and practices to their daily activities, for the real and practical purpose of cultivating qualities in themselves that will make for a better life. In this part, we address the specific ways Spiritual Naturalists go beyond the academic, to *walk* such a path.

# Naturalist Practice: The Big Picture

*DT Strain*

We are at the beginning of an important movement to gather again, a spirituality that is fully natural and rational, yet not shallow or merely technical and descriptive – one that engages all of what it means to be a full and complete human being, not merely an intellectual exercise. Within Spiritual Naturalism, or Religious Naturalism, there are numerous emerging books and articles from a variety of backgrounds.

In these, we often speak of things like: ritual, meditation, awe and wonder, ethics, philosophy, practice, ego, non-attachment, science, virtue, religious experience, compassion, and more. While many of these may seem beneficial or important, it may be difficult to know how they all relate to one another. How do these pieces fit together into a whole system or practice? This big picture is what I'd like to outline, very briefly, in this article. Of course, each part of this can (and should) be expanded upon greatly. In fact, we are developing a course in Spiritual Naturalism that will go into this detail, but for now, let me try to give an outline of a possible system of practice for the naturalist…

We begin, first, with the entire goal of our effort: happiness. Or, the answer to the question as the ancient Greeks put it, "What is the best way to live?" The human being is a natural entity – a part of Nature and with its own objective nature, living in an objective environment. This is a world of consequences. Therefore, *how best to live* is a matter of *engineering*. That is, the engineering of our subjective experience, our habits, our character, and our life so as to yield happiness.

By *happiness* we mean, not mere pleasure or circumstantial delight. This has proven to be a poor predictor of well being or happiness. Rather, we mean a deep sense of inner peace and joy –

a happiness that is not contingent upon the vicissitudes of external conditions but also inspires an engaged good life, in both senses of the word. We might call this *True Happiness* to delineate between it and the shallow forms of fleeting happiness with which many confuse it.

This kind of happiness is difficult if not impossible with the 'default character' that tends to emerge without a focused spiritual practice, or some de facto approximation of one. Normally, we are plagued with fear, greed, regret, anger, jealousy, concerns about what others think of us, and so on. These not only infringe on our happiness directly, but they encourage further behaviors and habits that are contrary to it. Such beings, unable to approach True Happiness, cling to the closest thing they can approach – pleasure derived from possessions, relationships, status, reputation, money, and so on. Yet, these are impermanent and shaky things on which to base one's happiness. Disappointment and suffering are inevitable.

So, for a naturalist, a sensible spiritual practice will be a system by which we achieve character transformation. Perfection in this is unlikely, but the degree to which we can transform ourselves will yield a similar degree of freedom from that egotistical outlook and corresponding levels of True Happiness in life. Further, the practitioner may find that the degree of transformation possible in the human character can be astonishing.

How is such character transformation achieved? Experience will tell us that a few things are certain: *reading* is not enough, *knowledge* is not enough, *intellectual assent (agreement)* to even the best wisdom is not enough. You have read many wise things, and dutifully shared them (along with pretty pictures of sunsets) on social media, email, or in conversations with your friends. Yet you have found yourself acting in discord with them time and again when the rubber meets the road. You "know better" but knowing better is not enough. If you were truly enlightened, your character would be such that it would *automatically* and *naturally* react to real life situations in accord with the best wisdom you have read. There is no number of internet posts you can share or 'like' that will get you to this place. But *this* is what our spiritual practice should be designed to achieve.

The bottom line is that spirituality must include *practice*. By *practice* we mean your daily activities and your ways of thinking will need to change. And these activities cannot be merely the end products of 'how a wise person behaves'. In other words, you can't become more compassionate by beating yourself over the head yelling to yourself "be more compassionate!"

Rather, *practice* means engaging in practices and rituals designed to reformat your thought and judgment process, altering your *inner value system*. The key to understanding how and why these practices and rituals work, is getting over your dismissal of the subjective. Society has told you the subjective is 'less real' or 'matters less' than the objective. Yet, our very goal – happiness – is a subjective state. Therefore *subjective things matter*; things like: the language we use to describe and frame things, the categories we use, our perspectives on Nature and our place in it, simple outward movements and poses of reverence, how we feel about things, our speech and mannerism. For many, this may seem obvious, but for many naturalists, we are used to looking at the world scientifically and therefore tend to find comfort and refuge in highly technical and impersonal descriptions. Yet, one of the core aspects of Spiritual Naturalism is that we can have a role for good, solid, science – and – inner beauty with a sense of the sacred. One need not contradict or betray the other.

In these practices and rituals, we open both our thoughts and our feelings. We use metaphor, poetry, art, iconography, music, dance and other movement, and more. We use these because our minds have multiple ways of approaching the world. It is by a distributed connection to the deeper truths of wise teachings that all of these aspects of our natural soul are touched. And, in that multi-sensory and emotional/intellectual mixture, they become an increasingly deeper part of our way of looking at the world. Here, intellectual knowledge becomes *intuitive*. Character is transformed such that 'ways of living' becomes 'ways of being'.

This is a path of continuous epiphany, profound experience, and deeper understanding. But to engage in such a practice requires a few things. For one, it requires the naturalist to give up any deep seated animosity and resistance to anything with the tinge of sounding too religious. This means not caring if others might misunderstand and think we have given up reason. It also means having the confidence that it is possible to set aside the 'culture war' against religion in our hearts but still be able to act in the world against ignorance, intolerance, and improper religious political actions.

Another thing this path requires is the willingness to change our life – you know, that thing that goes on when you finish reading this article and get up from the computer. It means doing something different when you wake up in the morning than you did before; and sticking with it. It means actually driving to new places, possibly bowing, ringing bells, lighting candles, vocalizing ritually, and so on. Many will read this and agree with it, but then their minds will resist change and quickly convince them that the answer is to click onward to read more things – as if that's the next step. But *you will never reach a point where you have read enough*, fully understand, and then are ready to engage in practice. If that is your process, you will die having only read.

## Practice as a System

So, as a system, this begins with the basic facts provided to us by reason. And, by reason, I mean that we believe knowledge comes to us through observation and what we can infer rationally from those observations. We are limited in our ability to know all things. This process includes science, but also the use of reason in our own lives, and most importantly – *humility*. That is, a humble approach to knowledge and the claims we make. In addition, humility in the sense that I focus on what *I* believe rather than worrying so much about telling others what they ought to believe.

But these facts about the world and ourselves are just the beginning of wisdom, not the end. From here, what is important is our *perspective* on those facts. Often, people point out that something is a 'value judgment' as a way of dismissing it. But value judgments are what we must make. They are critical. And, getting them *right* is critical to our happiness.

Yes, there are *correct* and *incorrect* value judgments; at least within such a system. We can say they are correct if they fulfill the purpose of humans making value judgments. In other words, if these judgments guide us toward positive thoughts and actions which are really conducive to a good life, then they are correct because they are consistent with their purpose.

For example, science will tell us there is a glass, and half of its inner volume is occupied by dihydrogen monoxide. We can look at that glass of water and we can judge that it is *half empty* or *half full*. This is the difference between a *claim* and a *perspective*.

One of the 'advances' of naturalistic spirituality is that we do not use our spirituality to make claims or rest parts of our spirituality upon those claims. Unlike some belief systems which get their facts from faith or revelation or scripture, we leave fact finding to those who are putting in the hard work of observing and recording them. But perspectives on those facts is where philosophy and our spirituality pick up. In this way, our spirituality is not opposed to science. Nor are the two "non-overlapping magisteria". Instead, science has become a respected and functional department within our spirituality, with no need to put words in its mouth or corrupt the purity of its method.

Now, to the strict intellectual/skeptical naturalist, the question of whether the glass is half full or half empty is just a silly little word game and the terms are interchangeable and of little consequence. But another of the crucial realizations of Spiritual Naturalism is this: the difference is *monumental*. This principle, extrapolated to the rest of our life, can be the distinction between two people in the same external circumstances – one with a full and happy life, and the other ending it in suicide. When we come to terms with the significance of our conceptualizations and judgments, the rest of spiritual practice begins to make functional sense – from meditation, to ritual, to all of the other many practices, sacred language, and more.

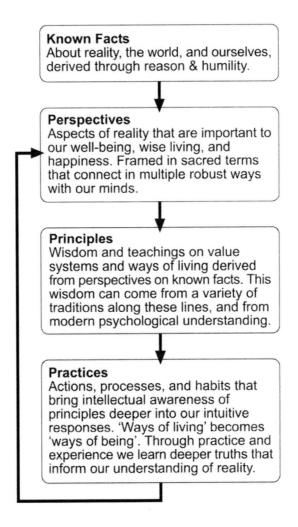

As we build habits of value judgment through various practices, and find new perceptions of wise teachings through rituals designed to elicit epiphany and peak experience, our baseline responses will begin to shift. That deep perspective shift includes the little often subconscious judgments we make and the emotional responses that kick in following those judgments. There has been a wealth of wisdom developed along these lines, going back to Taoism and Buddhism in the East, and Stoicism and Epicureanism in the West, and many others. But, again, putting that wisdom into *practice* is when the process begins. Now that you've reached the end of this article, what you *do* in your life is what will make the difference.

# Meditation 101

*DT Strain*

Breathing meditation is the most general kind of attention practice, and necessary in order to perform other kinds of attention practice. It will therefore tend to be the most commonly practiced and introductory of forms. However, foundational though it may be, mastering meditation requires just as much discipline and skill as mastering any other practice, so it would be a mistake to consider it necessarily easier or less advanced than other practices.

While meditators may appear to the outside observer to simply be relaxing, very specific mental exercise is taking place within. A person may seem exactly the same in two sessions but may have had a wonderful success in one session, and performed poorly in another. It is normal for beginning meditators to find meditation trying and difficult. At first, they may even wonder what the big deal is. But over time, noticeable improvement is made, and you will know it in your session as you attain deeper levels. The improvement will also manifest outside your session in the form of greater attention span, depth of attention, focus, and peace of mind. The ability to focus attention and increase awareness is what allows for greater inner and outer *mindfulness* – and these abilities are foundational to many other practices, as well as the overall endeavor to internalize many philosophic teachings from mere knowledge to a more intuitive level.

## Purpose

The basic premise is simple: our untrained minds generally tend to bounce from topic to topic, state to state. This sort of associative jumping about is called 'monkey mind' by the Buddhists. It is very noticeable in children, but adults usually suffer from it as well. Even very intelligent people (sometimes *especially* intelligent people) will tend to ruminate over all kinds of things endlessly. This is seldom a matter of efficient 'multitasking'. Rather, it is a sort of daydreaming that, at best, results in a lack of focus and being 'someplace else' than the present. At worst, ruminations can be a source of great frustration and stress. In either case, mindfulness is not possible in such a state because mindfulness involves constant awareness of one's self, one's thoughts and feelings, one's environment, and one's situation in the present, both internal and external.

Meditation allows us to improve our ability to consciously direct our attention where *we decide* it will go, and for how long. This is done much like working out a muscle. In meditation, we select something constant upon which to focus. One of the best and oldest things to select is the breath – because no matter your circumstances, your breath is always with you as long as you are alive.

## Position

First, it is important to consider your body position. Most people have seen meditators seated with legs crossed, hands either folded in the lap or upturned and resting upon the knees, and a straight posture. These traditional positions may work for many people but we are not so concerned with any one specific position. The key concern, rather, is this: you should sit in a manner that (a) allows you to breathe easily, (b) allows your body enough comfort that you can remain in that position throughout your meditation without your body becoming a distraction, and (c) is not so comfortable that it encourages you to fall asleep.

It is therefore not recommended that you meditate while lying down. Some may choose to sit in a chair, but the chair should allow your posture to be straight enough to breathe well – not slouched. Sitting up straight is one area where initial muscle discomfort will be worth the practice of learning to maintain the posture. As for legs, conditioning over time may enable you to become capable of sitting on the floor with them crossed if that is currently uncomfortable. However, that is a separate *physical* practice and endeavor – distinct in many ways from the practice of meditation per se. Thus, a seated meditator can become as proficient at meditation as a cross-legged meditator. Again, regardless of the position, the essential matters are that it allows good breathing, is not distracting, and will not make you fall asleep. Essentially, you should use a posture that will allow you to 'forget about your body' during the duration of your meditation.

People meditate with eyes open or shut, but shut is generally the preferred. Further, when shutting your eyes, it will be important to learn not to visualize various imagery (something that can be challenging at first for visual thinkers). Instead, the vision should simply be 'switched off', even including internal 'mental visions'.

The mouth can be slightly open with the jaw hanging loose. A good position for the tongue can be let loose, but touching the back of the two front teeth and roof of the mouth, but this may vary for individuals. Again, the key should be relaxation and no distraction.

## Meditation Aids

You will also need to think about how long you're going to meditate. 15 minutes may be a good amount of time for beginners; for some 20 minutes may be ideal. You can eventually work up to 30 minutes. Some meditate longer, but if you want to establish a daily routine it is important to select something reasonable and sustainable within your schedule. You'll need to establish a way to alert yourself when the time is up. This can be done simply with a stop watch, a kitchen timer, etc. If you are in a guided meditation the guide will alert you. There are smartphone meditation applications that allow you to set a time and have nice relaxing chime sounds to choose from. There are also online videos available with guided meditations featuring voices, music, etc. However it is achieved, a simple chime after a designated time is probably best for beginners.

Some people light incense when meditating or performing other rituals. The olfactory sense (smell) is one of the most intimately connected senses with our memory centers. Therefore, having a special scent is a good way to *shift* our state of mind into one that is conducive to the focus of the ritual or practice. Various cushions and furniture may be desired by some depending on the setting and position you choose, but beware of being persuaded into spending a great deal of money on superfluous things. Some people may like to have small sculptures or pictures of people or subjects which inspire them or remind them of various values or principles, or simply create a pleasant environment, but these too are not strictly necessary for meditation. It's up to you!

With your surroundings established and your physical position selected, you are now ready to begin.

## Body Scan

The first part of the process should be a mental review of your body to ensure you are actually relaxing it. Often we hold muscles tightly clenched without even realizing it. Therefore, you should take a deep long breath and let it out through your nose. Now imagine the top of your head being scanned. As the line around your head moves down over your face, your muscles in that area should relax: first the temples, forehead, brow; next your cheeks, jaw muscles, ears, neck, etc. Move the encircling line down over your neck, shoulders, down your arms to your fingers, down your back, stomach, legs, feet, and toes – relaxing each group as you go. Do not go too quickly so you may consider all areas. If you feel you need to, you can slowly return to the top of your head.

Now take one more deep breath and release your attention from your body. From here after, your breathing should not be controlled – just let yourself breath in and out automatically without trying to direct it, regardless of how fast, slow, deep, shallow, regular, or irregular that is.

# Focusing

Now, keeping your eyes closed, focus your attention on your breath. There will be a temptation to control your breath or try to make it regular or deeper, but you should avoid that temptation. Simply *watch* your breath without directing it. The portion you should zero in on is the air moving just past the edge of your nostrils, as it moves in and out. You will hear it and feel it moving past the nostrils like a tide coming in and out. Try to focus exclusively on that experience without thinking about it in 'words'. Also ignore any visualizations, sensations from your body, or other thoughts.

At this point, you may find it helpful to count your breaths. If you do so, as you inhale do not think anything – just focus on the inhalation. Then, as you exhale, think, "one…" You can think this word as lasting as long as the exhale, still focusing attention on the air moving out of your nostrils. As you breathe in, try to think nothing in between other than simply observing the inward breath. Breathing out, think, "two…" Go up to five and then return to one. Remember, while you are watching your breaths and counting along, you are not controlling them in any way – simply letting them happen as your body naturally reflexes to breathe.

After you exhale and count a number, if you are rested, there will probably be a few seconds before your body naturally induces the next inhalation. Because you are focused on the inhalation during it's time, and you are counting during the exhalations, this short period may be the most tempting for your attention to wander. As you complete a counting, such as, "twooooo…", try to let your mind simply drift off of the end of the word and remain still, thinking of nothing at all until the next inhalation arises to focus upon.

By the way, returning to 1 in the counting in a cycle is important. If you do not return in this cycle from 5 back to 1 and instead continue on to higher numbers, it will be easy for the counting to end up on 'autopilot' as your mind wanders off to other things. The return is the indication that you really are paying close attention to the counting. Furthermore, if you fail to remain focused on your breath, you can attempt to simply get through one whole cycle 1-5, thus making the challenge one of bite-sized chunks. Then, you can attempt another cycle – always remaining in the present.

## Wandering & Correction

As you attempt meditation, your mind will inevitably wander. Things will pop into your head such as the day's to-do items, what others around you might be doing or thinking, what the random little sounds you're hearing might be, physical discomfort, interesting or random memories, or perhaps more concerning ruminations about various life problems. As this happens, it is important to catch yourself and return your focus exclusively to your breath. If you did not, then meditation would not be unlike daydreaming or lucid dreaming. Perhaps a nice endeavor in its own ways, but not meditation. As these things arise in your mind, simply see them as objects and set them aside, moving your focus gently back to the breath.

Despite your best efforts, your mind will do this many times, and will need to be brought back to the breath many times. Just as important as catching and directing yourself back, it is also essential that you not let this frustrate you. Remember, thinking about the fact that you're not thinking about your breath is *also* 'thinking about something other than your breath'. Instead, simply bring your attention back to your breath as though it were a solitary task – without frustration because of past needs to do so, and without aggravation because of a fear of needing to do it again in the future. As you meditate there is only the present, and in that present only the breath. Do not think of this wandering as a 'failure to meditate' or as an exception to meditation. The wandering, and the following corrections in focus, are all *part* of meditation – all is just as it should be.

## Going Deeper

Even though a wandering mind and the need to correct its focus back to breathing is to be expected, it is a fact that over time you will become better able to keep your attention on your breath without any other thoughts arising and for longer periods of time between mental wanderings. This increase in ability is noticeable within sessions, but also continues from session to session if you practice meditation regularly.

With that increased ability to maintain attention, comes other effects during the time you are in a meditation session. These include: greater environmental awareness, loss of body, and consciousness detachment.

The first, and easiest to see, is greater environmental awareness. During a meditation you come to notice all of the little and subtle sounds and sensations around you – the clock ticking, birds, cars driving by, the wind, people talking in the distance, and so on. The fact of this awareness as you progress may seem contradictory since these things can be distractions which cause you to have to reset your focus back on your breath. While that is true, it is also true that before you were meditating many of these things would have gone completely unnoticed by you. The reason you notice them during your session is a sign that your mind is becoming *still*. Throw a pebble into a stormy ocean and its effects are lost, but in a still pond its ripple effects are significant. While the perception of these previously unnoticed things is indeed another set of thoughts to be set aside so focus can be returned to the breath, they are also a sign of progress because a *still mind* is one of the aims of meditation.

The second effect you may experience during a session may take some practice, perhaps over several sessions, before you start to get glimpses of it. *Loss of body* is, of course, a figurative description. But the general sensation will be a lack of perception of the body; its little aches, itches, tiny movements, etc. This will bring about a feeling of detachment from the body, but is simply the result of an extreme focus. Nevertheless, this feeling – when it happens – is a sign of improvement in your technique.

The tricky thing about loss of body, is that it is not only rare at first, but tends to be very brief. If one is consciously focused on trying to have a loss of body experience, then it is impossible, as the experience results from a lack of conceptual thinking. Once the experience happens, it often ends quickly. Usually, as soon as a person begins to notice that they are experiencing a loss of body sensation, the noticing of it causes the mind to put a label on it, and turn the experience into a mental object. The moment you think, "I'm having a loss of body experience!" you have now lost your focus. Before, you had begun to enter a state of experience without language and labels and without distinctions between things. But calling your mind to think of the loss of body experience creates a distinction between it and other experiences, and between you and your environment. Inevitably, all of the usual concepts flood back into your consciousness. The mind looks to see if the body is there and, of course, it is. Your mind begins 'checking the mailbox' to see if any messages (sensations) from the body have arrived – which, of course, they have.

But like everything else, the mind improves over time. With continuous practice, these experiences become more frequent, easier to enter, and last longer.

Another experience you may have during mediation might be called consciousness detachment. We, as persons, are made up of many functions and properties (aggregates) which, working together in complex relationships, yield an overall impression of 'self' which we think of as 'us'. These include memory, emotions, logical ability, selection capabilities, perceptions, and more. But if we were to slowly imagine these properties peeling away, and if we were to look at them individually, there is no one property we could convincingly identify as 'us'. We are, rather, a function of all of these activities. Another one of these aggregates is *consciousness*. This is not so much awareness of certain information (such as awareness of our surroundings or of the contents of our thoughts). Rather, this is the actual first-person experience of 'likeness' – i.e., what it is 'like' to be an experiencing being. One might imagine simpler animals or insects having this feeling of what it is like to be them, without the sophistication of integrated memories of any complexity. Some consciousness philosophers and neurologists call this sensation *qualia*.

After a person leaves behind all other sensations of body, their surroundings, and other tangible thoughts, their minds enter another state. Here they experience that consciousness in a completely detached form, without the usual accompanying thoughts, feelings, opinions, judgments, memories, labels, sensations, concerns, and other impressions. They simply 'exist'. Here it is said one can experience the universe 'as it really is' bereft of our usual framing of it.

## Immediate After Effects

What short-term after effects can one expect from a quality meditation session? The most basic effect is a relaxed and low-stress state, usually accompanied by a sense of patience, contentment, and pleasantness. In addition to these, the mind will be much more focused, controllable, and deliberative. If one were to watch a speaker just after, for example, it would be easier to focus on the speaker for an extended period, while all other distractions would be easily set aside. If one were to engage in some kind of mental task, they would likely be more effective at it, in a heightened state of concentration.

This 'laser focus' usually disperses over time. As the day's activities carry on, the mind has to handle more things simultaneously and attention can become diffused. Certain things have a great tendency to diffuse attention quickly. One of the best examples of things that diffuse attention is listening to or watching media, such as music or television.

Importantly, you have a degree of choice in how quickly or slowly your attention becomes diffused, based on your intent. If you purposely begin filling your mind with a number of ruminations and concerns, you can diffuse your attention more quickly than if you try to remain mindful and in a semi-meditative-like calm after your session.

## Long-Term Effects

Longer-term effects are usually enhanced when meditation is combined with a solid philosophic foundation. Most of the skills developed in meditation relate to specific philosophic principles and can be used to live these principles more skillfully in life. If meditation were only about the experience during a session, and only about greater focus and stress relief, then it would not have the profound place in spiritual practice that it has had for thousands of years. The general concept of meditation is that, while it may begin as specific sessions, we eventually learn to expand meditative mindfulness into the rest of our lives, thoughts, and actions.

For instance, the first of the deeper effects mentioned earlier, *still mind*, is something that can be taken into our lives as we live out our day. Beyond that, the ability to notice subtle things that comes from a still mind, can alert us to disruptions and the like arising in our minds before they have the ability to consume us. It may also make us more aware of subtleties in the behavior of others, enhancing our ability to act toward them with empathy.

Having experiences of separation from our bodies and consciousness detachment can create a sensation of oneness with the universe. The ability to enter into such states can create a greater tendency to see things from more of a universal viewpoint than from the viewpoint of our shallow self centered perspective. Some neuroscientists study the physiological effects of meditation on the brain, and these studies have so far lent credence to the notion these changes are more than mere placebo effect. In meditation, we have an integrated practice-philosophy which involves active alteration of our neural architecture, along with mental habits and abilities which facilitate greater application of wisdom teachings, and greater integration of them into our natural responses.

It is in this manner that mindfulness is increased, which can then interject into our normal judgment centers, and better monitor our own thoughts and feelings about things, rather than allow them to consume us mindlessly.

## Other Forms

The mindfulness developed through this kind of meditation can form the basis for other kinds of attention practice, such as contemplation or introspection, each with their own techniques and purposes (these two forms are discussed in the educational archives for members). There are also other forms, such as loving-kindness meditation. SNS Advisory Board member Rick Heller of the Humanist Community at Harvard, has a wonderful step by step guide to loving-kindness meditation on his site, *Seeing the Roses*.

# Bicycle Meditation

*Thomas Schenk*

*"What better place is there to ride a bike than right here, right now?"*

I love to wake early on a Sunday morning and go for a bike ride. Unlike the many people who pass me as I plod along, I do not ride for exercise or any other discernible purpose. I have no particular destination, and no time table. I ride just to explore and look at the world, for though I have been exploring and looking for nearly five decades, I still find the world incredibly interesting and beautiful.

I live in a city, and sometimes I ride through industrial areas or train yards, sometimes I ride through residential areas, and sometime I ride in parks or out to the countryside. The distinction between natural and man-made is not of much use to me as I ride along; what's there is there, and what's there is what I am interested in seeing.

Occasionally on these bike rides I become utterly unaware of time and unconcerned with distance as I ride. Hours and miles pass by, but absorbed in the sheer joy of exploring the world I lose track. Yet inevitably, at some point, this changes; my legs start to tire, the thought of returning home settles in my head, and then I grow impatient.

In that duration when I am unaware of time and unconcerned with distance, I am exactly where I want to be. The moment that I want to be somewhere else, I become acutely aware of time and distance. Up to this moment the miles passed effortlessly; after this moment the miles are an obstacle, and I am keenly aware of the amount of effort required to overcome them. Whereas I had been completely content with where I was, now I'm discontent.

The 6th Century Zen poet Seng-ts'an wrote "Do not like, do not dislike, all will then be clear. Make a hairs-breath difference, and heaven and earth are set apart." Perhaps, on these terms, heaven is just to be fully at home wherever you happen to be peddling; earth, what the Buddhist calls "samsara," is the desire to be a little further along.

# Love Naturally

*Rick Heller*

"Love they neighbor as thyself" is one of the finer sentiments contained in the Bible. But it's not commonly practiced. One reason may be that the Bible doesn't provide any good tips on how to actually love someone you don't really like.

The Buddhist practice of loving-kindness or metta meditation provides a mean to do exactly that. Although some religious Buddhists may believe that loving-kindness practice works through metaphysical means, there is good reason to believe that it has a natural basis that exploits a quirk of the brain.

In loving-kindness practice, one first brings to mind people one does love—friends, family, and benefactors, and yourself. One rouses oneself to a state of positive emotion. So far, this is not much different from a gratitude practice. The trick, then, is that you redirect your positive feelings toward people you do not love—first, people whom you neither love nor hate, and then eventually toward people you actually dislike.

The reason this works—although it can take several meditations for it to work with people you really don't care for – is that emotional arousal is non-specific and doesn't have a quick on/off switch. Just as anger can bleed over toward others who did not arouse a person's rage, so can affection.

We have been practicing metta meditation for some time at the Harvard Humanist Community. We've now created a Web site called *Seeing the Roses* with instructional videos that show how to do loving-kindness and mindfulness meditations. If you dig into the site, you can also find some more details on the neuroscience that explains how it works.

The cultivation of love is something that could be called a spiritual practice. As secularists, though, we locate this not in the ethereal world but in the natural world and in the human body, and to be a little bit picky, not so much in the heart as in the brain.

# What is Spiritual Transformation?

*DT Strain*

Coming from a middle-American Christian background, one of the things that struck me as I learned more about ancient philosophy and Eastern schools of thought was the notion of one's religion or philosophy being about a *practice* rather than merely a *set of beliefs*. In Christianity, as it is more commonly promoted, the emphasis is on what you *believe*. This, not 'works' is what will determine your damnation or salvation. Even my later conversion to secular humanism would not get me out of this belief-based mentality. The Humanist Manifesto describes humanism as a worldview and a "lifestance" while listing a group of (excellent) principles, the assent to which is sufficient to count one's self as a Humanist; absent any glaring obvious misbehaviors. Today it seems almost the entirety of humanity assumes that being a member of any particular religious or similar group is merely a matter of opening one's trap at a cocktail party and proclaiming the right combination of talking points.

Yet philosophy, as practiced in ancient Greece for example, was more than a mere academic pursuit. It was more than a set of positions on various issues or a set of beliefs. The philosopher of ancient Greece and Rome engaged in a set of practices designed to cultivate the flourishing life – and that was almost entirely centered on the development of *inner character* in specific, guided ways. Thus, they tended to live and fulfill a role more akin to a Buddhist monk than the professorial types called philosopher today.

This is the avenue (via the ancient Western philosophers) by which I came to begin investigating Buddhism and was similarly struck by its nature. Buddhism is not so much about what you *believe* as it is about what you *do*. It too is a practice by which we cultivate ourselves and in so doing, achieve enlightenment and release from suffering. Having come to Buddhism through the practice-oriented Greek philosophers, I had fortunately been prepared to receive this approach without prematurely dismissing it simplistically as some Eastern parallel to Christian supernatural salvation. There are many other examples of practice-centered traditions beyond Buddhism.

## Enlightenment is a Process

The original title for this article was going to be "What is Enlightenment?" But for the naturalist, enlightenment is not a single moment of omniscience. Rather, it is a spectrum on which we all move in a continual process of development and transformation. So, the more appropriate question is to ask, "What is spiritual transformation?"

Simply put, spiritual transformation is the result of a successful *spiritual practice*. Remember, here we use the term 'spiritual' in the sense that is applicable to a naturalist – as that which is *essential* (as in "spirit of the law"); that which relates to the deeper, foundational principles pertinent to the good life. A 'practice', as opposed to a 'faith', 'belief', or a 'lifestance' – is a *way of living* whereby we engage in various regular activities and thinking habits designed to change ourselves in specific helpful directions. That is, to be more capable of experiencing True Happiness (a deeper happiness and contentment not dependent upon mere external circumstance). This is a long-term *project* in which we expect to see progress over time. For this reason, it is referred to as a 'path' or a 'walk'.

Many naturalists and secular people have come back from events where ritual or other practices took place, and reported the experience as empty, or as merely *going through the motions*. This may happen when an atheist attends a Unitarian Universalist service, or when a Humanist tries out meditation, or when a group of Freethinkers feel uncomfortable singing odes to reason at a group celebration – even if they agree with the lyrics and were just jumping up and down at a rock concert a few nights prior.

This disconnect happens when we lack awareness of the philosophical foundations of practice. We don't fully understand what we are doing, and why we are doing it. In fact, even many people who enthusiastically embrace various practices do not have a full grasp on how all of these 'spiritual things' fit together in a whole system. How does meditation relate to our value system? What role does *religious/peak/profound experience* play in a spiritual practice and why? How does awe/wonder fit in to our knowledge of nature? And how does all of that relate to ritual? Without some kind of general picture of one's practice as a complete system of self-development, all rituals and practices may continue to feel like empty theater.

This difficulty is not the fault of these folks, because our culture has yet to fully realize well-established naturalistic spiritual practices. Therefore those of us (who even see the value in such a journey to begin with) end up fending for ourselves and grabbing things a la carte from various traditions in the hope it all works together. Indeed, addressing this issue and building informed spiritual foundations to naturalist practice is what the Spiritual Naturalist Society is all about. With that in mind, I'd like to share some of what I've come to after about eight years of carefully studying Eastern and Western comparative philosophy.

## Engineering the Subjective

The endeavor of spiritual practice is predicated on the observation that different people in the same material circumstances can have vastly different *subjective experiences*. These affect their happiness, contentment, equanimity, fortitude, and overall quality of life. The rational/empirically minded among us have the habit of looking at things scientifically, which means *from a third-person external perspective*. This can encourage many of us to dismiss the subjective as 'not real' or even 'not important'. Yet, if happiness is our aim, and we know that both happiness and suffering exist in all external circumstances, then we must begin by acknowledging that our aim is a subjective one. Of course, for ourselves and others, we will continue to harness our energies toward less poverty, war, and illness; greater works; better technologies; and so on. But when even the wealthiest among us can be found committing suicide or lingering in bitterness or despair, then something more *essential* must be addressed. The endeavor of crafting a spiritual practice, therefore, is a matter of *engineering the subjective*. In other words, *the subjective matters*. Admitting that will have profound implications as we proceed to understand naturalistic spirituality.

The next obvious question is, what is the difference between someone who can retain equanimity under harsh conditions and one who becomes crushed? What is the difference between one who remains balanced amidst plenty and one who yet continues to suffer, perhaps more? What is the difference between a happy and an unhappy person, both in moderately reasonable conditions? Philosophers have pondered these questions and it turns out that we've had some pretty good thoughts on all of this well before the Common Era. I'm going to jump ahead a bit and simply list some character traits that many traditions have seemed to zero in on. Since none of us are perfectly enlightened, it is always easier to recognize the absence of enlightenment. So, I will begin with a list of what I call "the default person". That is, the person as typically develops in the absence of any notable degree of wisdom...

# The Default Person

## Drives

### Self Preservation

Preservation of the biological aggregate (delusional) self is the primary drive.

### Ego Driven

Imprisoned within the first-person. Minimal self-awareness / mindfulness.

### Fear & Desire

Enslaved by passions and manipulated by fears and desires.

## Perspectives

### Small Mind

Perspective limited in time span and scale of anecdotal events and happenstance.

### Change Resistant

Expects, seeks out, and harbors illusions of constancy and predictability. Aversion to thoughts of loss.

### Dualistic

Trapped in me/you, us/them, body/mind, individual/society dichotomies.

## Values & Limitations

### Opinion Reliant

Concerned with, and influenced by, the praise, blame, and approval of others.

### Monkey Mind

Attention scattered and mind clouded with ruminations. Inability to focus or still mind.

### Circumstantial Dependency

Prerequisite of external conditions for happiness.

### Loves Possessively

Practices and understands love in terms of possession, based on desire for the object of love.

 www.SpiritualNaturalistSociety.org

Of course, we could go into detail about each of these areas, from what truths they arise, and how they pertain to happiness. But this brief listing should give a sufficient indication of the relevant qualities for purposes of this article.

Nearly all practice-based traditions have some kind of representation of the 'perfect practitioner'. For some of them it is a specific character or person, for others it is more of a title, and still others it is a general type of being. This entity or entities may be thought to be literal or hypothetical. The Buddhists have the concept of 'buddhahood' and the Stoics had the 'sage'. But in all of these cases, the enlightened being served as an ideal example or a model to help guide practice and establish goals. In our case, we can inverse the above qualities to get a picture of what we are aiming for in our practice. I call this, the "transformed person"…

# The Transformed Person

## Drives

### Rational-Moral Preservation

Acting in accord with the nature of a rational-moral being is the primary drive.

### All-Being Driven

Full mindfulness of Reality, internal and external, including delusion of ego. Third-person perspective.

### Fearless & Content

Content. Without fear and distress. Not controlled by attachments.

## Perspectives

### Big Mind

'God's-eye view' not bound by arbitrary time spans or scales. Primacy of pattern over incident.

### Flowing

At one with change, perceiving impermanence intuitively and harmonious with it.

### Holistic

Intuitively perceives all things as interconnected and One; systemic rather than competitive outlook.

## Values & Abilities

### Free from Opinion

Not motivated or moved by the praise or blame of others.

### Still Mind

Mastery of attention. Can direct attention and still mind at will.

### Free from Circumstance

True Happiness, equanimity, flourishing not dependent on external conditions.

### Loves Universally

True Love and compassion flowing naturally from expanded sense of self encompassing all beings.

Most naturalists would likely agree that perfection is not possible or reasonably expected. And while these two lists paint a picture of a person as either 'default' or 'transformed' what this more aptly suggests is a scale between two extremes. As we engage in our practice, the purpose is to continually shift our character such that we become less like the former and more like the latter. And, more importantly, we will experience greater happiness and less suffering to the degree to which we achieve this.

## Reasonable Goals vs. The Ideal Model

Since the Transformed Person described above is taken to be a perfect ideal, there are some cautions we should heed. First is the reminder that the ideal is an abstraction and not expected to be achieved, as no human being is perfect. Anyone claiming to have achieved this state should expect a high degree of skepticism from others and should be skeptical of themselves. Further, we should also not blame ourselves if we fall short of the ideal, as this is inevitable. Should an ideal model become a source of self-blame, that would be contrary to the flourishing life that is our aim, and not a rational or accurate perspective. Yet ideal models, if used properly, are important because they point to the horizon and give us a pure way of discussing basic principles without particulars and the pragmatic realities getting in the way of understanding.

But then, of course, we must deal with pragmatic realities in a realistic practice. For this reason, it may also be important to have other models to guide us. These models may not represent the perfect or ideal practitioner, but may outline achievable mile markers along the path. They would represent a practitioner that is *making progress*. In conversations on this topic with B.T. Newberg, he has written an excellent description of such a person as follows:

> *"Thus, the [practitioner making progress] should cultivate humility, defined as an awareness of personal bias leading to an eagerness to overcome it through the*

*process of peer critique (this necessitates community).
Rather than seeking to be unmoved by praise or blame,
the practitioner should seek to receive both praise and
blame with grace and gratitude, while filtering it through
critical analysis and peer advice. The ideal practitioner
should also cultivate right relationship with external
conditions, striving to receive circumstances with the
same grace and gratitude as praise or blame, while fully
accepting his or her power to change those circumstances
that can be changed and accept/integrate those that can't.
The ideal practitioner should also cultivate courage,
defined as right action in spite of fear, as well as a kind of
virtuous desire, defined as eagerness for that which is
most likely to yield long-term flourishing. To these ends,
the practitioner will have to achieve an awareness of and
facility with the many intuitive impulses that lead in other
directions, and integrate them in right relationship with
the reasoning process as well as social propriety. Mastery
of attention, big mind, and most of the other bullet points
of the transformed person may be invaluable tools in this
endeavor. In the end, the practitioner should focus on
becoming not a sage but a better member of a community
of sagehood." –B.T. Newberg*

## Is Extraordinary Transformation Possible?

Granted, a more modest model of progress is essential, and
perfection is most likely impossible. However, my experience in
practice leads me to believe that, once one achieves a state
similar to even an ambitious realistic model, one will tend to find
that further improvement remains possible. This results in the
limits of human transformative potential being surprisingly
further than we may be willing to believe at the start of our
practice, if we are disciplined and patient. We might call this
extraordinary transformation; a kind that truly shifts our 'root
operating impulses'.

It is reasonable to ask whether this kind of transformation is
possible. We may notice that spiritual leaders, who are supposed

to be the exemplars of a practice, may often seem to have many of the same faults as anyone else. But I think it is a mistake to look toward leaders in evaluating the transformative potential of spiritual practice. The chief reason for this is that there is a distinction between the *organizations* of spirituality and spiritual practice. Spiritual practice is a deeply person thing which is about working on the person in the mirror. Only you have the ability to know if this is your true intent, and more importantly, only you have the ability to measure its results and progress. By contrast an organization, even the best of them, is a project of human inter-activity that focuses on external conditions by its nature. It is about actions in the world and seeking certain results (even if those desired results are more people engaged in personal practice). As someone who works in the Spiritual Naturalist Society for example, I must always be aware that my activity for the Society is not the same as my personal practice, or a substitute for it.

This distinction has real consequences when it comes to the distinction between people who become leaders in an organization and those who employ the practices for which those organizations stand. Very often, we will find that leaders of an organization do not practice its tradition as well as some. In fact, they can often be extremely poor examples; especially if they confuse their success as an organizational leader with success in their own walk. At the same time, many of the most successful and advanced practitioners may be on the outside of organized activity, as they may have chosen to focus their time and attention on their practice rather than on publications, promotions, events, giving talks, etc. So, this lack of correlation between leaders in organized traditions and differences in character should not be surprising and is not an indication that transformation is not real or possible.

Lastly, judging a practice by its practitioners also suffers because it is inherently impossible to measure a practitioners' inner experience. Two people may come to work every day, smile, treat others in similar ways, and so on. Yet, one of them is deeply happy in life and the other one faces internal struggles.

The extreme example of suicides that come as a complete surprise to friends and family illustrate this harshly, but more subtle and common examples abound. This is why the first-person experience is crucial: each of us must experiment for ourselves the effects of these practices on our deeper happiness and well-being.

## Experience

While the scientific approach deals with objective reality from a third-person perspective, and spiritual practice is about cultivating first-person subjective states, the two are neither inherently at odds nor lacking in overlap. The kind of spiritual practice I've been describing is not one of faith-based belief. Rather, it is one whereby the practitioner is placed in the role of experimenter.

The Buddhist Kalama Sutra instructs the practitioner not to believe or accept something because of tradition, authority, scripture, superstition, etc. but because they have experienced for themselves whether it is true and effective. Both the scientific method and this kind of instruction overlap in placing experience and experiment at the center of acceptance of claims. Note that the latter case is different from an *external* experiment on the brain activity of meditators or the like. Because we are talking about cultivating individual subjective experience, each practitioner must conduct experimentation from inside their own private mental laboratory to confirm efficacy. Because all persons and brains vary, we should expect to see some variability in which kinds of practices have superior results – and because we share many traits we should expect to see many commonalities as well. This kind of procedure is not altogether foreign to science. For example, research on pain medication must include the subjective reports of subjects because pain, though it has physical correlates, is also a subjective experience.

**And so it is from experience that I, and many others, can report that spiritual transformation of the kind described above is not only possible, but profoundly life altering.** Before

I describe this in detail, let me first address the inevitable and valid skeptical question of (a) how this differs from the *ad populum* of testimony from many people about bigfoot, angels, or aliens, and (b) how this differs from the testimony of people who claim their subjective experience of God or Jesus is evidence of the objective existence of these beings.

Whether or not certain realms or entities exist is a claim about objective facts. But no matter how 'convinced' I am by a subjective experience, that alone can never be sufficient to prove an objective fact. For this, corroborating objective evidence must be demonstrable and sharable between others. Thus, we cannot use a *subjective* experience to prove an *objective* fact.

In the case for spiritual transformation, however, the intended results are inherently subjective. Therefore subjective experience of them is sufficient to constitute knowledge of the result. If a practice makes me happier, more at peace, or more content, then the claim that the practice results in happiness is – for me – self evidently true. If the claim were, "Jesus makes me happy" this requires an intermediary external fact to be true (there is a living entity that exists who makes people happy). If, however, the claim is "belief in Jesus makes people happy" this can be supported or undermined by studies of reports of happiness compared to the corresponding belief. Likewise, the claim "meditation makes people more at peace" does not depend on an intermediary fact. That would be more akin to something like, "meditation pleases Buddha who lives on an immaterial plane, and blesses those who meditate with peace of mind" – which is certainly not the naturalist approach. The mention of the number of people reporting the same experience with spiritual practice is meant, not to lend weight to an objective claim, but to show a high consistency of subjective reports, suggesting the reader has a reasonable likelihood of similar experience with practices.

# My (Continuing) Transformation

As with most of us, my transformation began with learning. My days of looking at philosophy as merely some intriguing academic mental exercise are long behind me, but this is how many of us innocently slip into discovering what lies deeper. Socrates always fascinated me, so it may have been inevitable that I would find my way to the later Socratic schools. The Epicureans are a favorite of Humanists, but it was Stoicism where I began to notice really amazing effects on my life. Even in some of my earliest stages of learning about Stoicism, I found that just a few 'drops' of it went a long way.

It wasn't long before things I was reading about Taoism and Buddhism would begin to show fascinating overlaps and similarities. That began a multi-year process of comparative study whereby I would analyze their commonalities and their respective strengths. These were not mere collections of claims about the world or its creation, or proclamations of ethical edicts. They consisted of real insights into our minds and our lives. These insights made me reassess many things in my life and began to affect how I responded to them. Yet, all of this was mere intellectual learning, helpful though it had already proven.

Many of us have had what I call *profound experiences* (also known as 'religious experience' or 'peak experience'). In *"Embracing a Natural Life"* I explained some things about profound experience (as far as I could with words), and in our member educational archives the Society has an essay specifically about the nature and function of profound experience.

These come in many forms and have many different effects for us. But without connection to some philosophic perspective, they can often mean little more than an awe-inspiring event – simple entertainment. Perhaps they are moving to us for mysterious reasons and before long we are back to our ordinary lives.

For me, as I continued to read, discuss, and learn, the occasional profound experiences served as epiphanies that helped me on my way. They were direct perceptions of amazing truths about the nature of our world, the nature of my own mind, and the nature of life – things which I had already agreed to intellectually, and thought I'd understood. But until I had these experiences it didn't really 'sink in'. These kinds of experiences helped me to internalize certain bits of wisdom on a more intuitive level. The experiences and the learning fed off of one another. The learning helped spark the experiences; sometimes at unexpected moments. And, the experiences inspired me to investigate and learn more.

One of these profound experiences happened while reading about complex systems theory; another happened while listening to the birds awakening in the trees in the morning. More profound experiences happened on an airplane, petting my cat, listening to music, sharing experiences with friends, seeing films, in solitude, at temple, and so on – each of them different, yet each helping to 'grok' that for which language is so often a poor vehicle.

Simple assent to intellectual concepts is not spiritual transformation. That happens only when the wisdom becomes a deep part of how we intuitively see the world and react to it (and the content of that wisdom is too much for the scope of this essay to seriously address). Profound experience is not the only way the intellectual becomes the intuitive, but it often can provide abrupt plateaus along the gradual transformative climb of transformation.

More common are the everyday practices that help to condition our perspectives and ways of being. Meditation is one of the more common and foundational of spiritual practices. Although I am by no means a master and still have much to learn, my experience with meditation has been remarkable. It has increased my focus, my mindfulness (of both my surroundings and internal states), and my peace of mind. These skills are essential to further spiritual practices. The effects I have experienced from meditation have led me to want to explore it further, but it takes time practicing regularly.

Many other practices and rituals have been very helpful and transformative for me. These include journaling, negative visualization, vision quests, drumming, mindful walking, and what I like to call *demeanor practice*. Each of these have specific purposes and, in the proper philosophic context, can affect deep change over time.

This change has been pronounced, and has had effects in my life. One odd consequence that has come to my attention recently is that I *seem* to no longer be capable of embarrassment or any other form of social anxiety. This may be a subset of a near absence of certain kinds of deep fears, in general. While I admit this is an extraordinary claim, and that I may be experiencing them at undetectable levels, that perception in itself is significant. There have also been some personality changes over time, which seem correlated to my intentions to shift in that direction.

During one period I had been specifically practicing in a manner designed to increase my empathy and compassion. After a time, I noticed I was having problems. It seems I had so changed my responses that I was experiencing disturbing levels of distress whenever I became aware of the suffering of others (including media reports, etc). I went to see a monk about this (since the practices I were employing had been Buddhist) and he informed me that there were other aspects to Buddhist thought I had been missing; namely *wisdom*, which is meant to balance compassion. Specifically, he meant the wisdom of non-attachment and the acceptance of impermanence. Thus began my process of moving toward greater balance. During these periods, it was not only my practices that changed in their general direction, but *who I was* had actually shifted over time, and in direct relation to a designed program.

The most notable example of transformation has been how much I was helped during the time my mother passed away. I explained this in more detail in the *Embracing* article, but in short

I was fortified and sustained in ways that would not have been possible before. It was clear that I was not merely someone who had learned a few nifty ideas or techniques, but that I had become a *different kind of being* than the person I had been before – in my value systems, my responses, my reactions, etc. And, more importantly, the philosophic reading and learning would not have been enough to have affected me or my experience during that time. It was the *practice* that made the difference. The first of these surprising effects happened relatively early in my practice.

Today, I am coming into new challenges, such as concerns over becoming so different in character that I may seem too alien to relate well to others – an important thing for being supportive and doing good in the world. Even making public this concern may have the negative effect of sounding conceited, and surely I must caution myself against that. I am still very much a learner and still have my fair share of challenges and difficulties. Yet, I can't deny that my practice has had an effect on how I see the world and how I relate to others who may not be on the same path (or, in some cases, *any* path). I mention this only to demonstrate how undeniable the reality of transformation is for me.

In fact, if *profound* spiritual transformation is not possible via naturalistic practice, then it is unclear why one would even engage in any spiritual tradition, other than seeking a community in the manner one might join a social club. Yet, my experience of this kind of transformation and the knowledge of what it can do for others is why the mission of the Spiritual Naturalist Society is so important.

## Wisdom and the Role of Science

If we accept that self-directed transformation over time is possible, and that such transformation can result in deeper happiness, equanimity, inner fortitude, and so on; we may look to the next question. We might then ask, what exactly is the content of this wisdom we are supposed to internalize, and how do we know it is advice that results in the kind of change that will be most helpful?

Unfortunately, the past few centuries have set up a strange opposition between science and religion that does us a disservice – especially we naturalists who are looking for a meaningful spiritual practice. Even among Spiritual Naturalists, the culture has lead us to view science and religion or spirituality – *even philosophy* – as 'non-overlapping magisteria' at best, competitors at worst. But if we look to how all of this started out, we get a clearer picture of what's going on.

Although the modern formalized scientific method did not emerge until the Enlightenment, there were certainly rational approaches to understanding our world many centuries before this. These rational approaches, though imperfect at times, often contained many elements of the scientific method. More importantly, these were approaches that valued experience, observation, logic, reason, and peer review (in the form of discourse). When Heraclitus spoke of the transformation of materials to and from one another, it is impossible not to think of him sitting alongside a river, carefully observing his environment. When Socrates debated the nature of the soul (mind) with Simmias, it is obvious from their arguments that these were men who were carefully considering observations they had made and the implications of those observations. One would not have gotten far with Socrates by proposing any knowledge on the basis of 'faith'. The same can be said of the Buddha who, as I've mentioned, specifically rejected faith as a source of knowledge.

These thinkers approached the same universal struggles and torments we all face in life even today, and in their wisdom, arrived at many profound realizations. And, while they may have lacked much of the technical details, or even had many of them wrong, a surprising number of those realizations still hold remarkably true. This is why, for example, Stoicism was such an inspiration to modern cognitive therapeutic techniques.

Prior to the extreme specializations of today, philosophers were not only moral guides and logicians, they were scientists. In fact, no good philosopher would not be scientist and vice versa. It was not too long ago that science was referred to as 'natural philosophy'. This makes sense when we consider that philosophy is the love of wisdom and wisdom must include the accurate collection of facts (though goes far beyond). Thus, any time we are asking: (1) what *is,* (2) what *ought to be,* or (3) how do we *know* those two things – we are doing philosophy. Religion is philosophy, science is philosophy, ethics is philosophy, logic is philosophy. It is all a part of 'wisdom' and its pursuit.

Later, some philosophers decided to focus on the 'what is' portion, and they became what we call scientists. Other philosophers decided to focus on 'what ought to be' and they became our ethicists and moral leaders. Still other philosophers focused on 'how do we know' and they became our mathematicians, logical analysts, linguists, and so on. Although each of these professionals needs to conduct themselves in their jobs such that the integrity of their respective methodologies are maintained, we as individuals have broader needs and concerns. The problem is that we've forgotten all of these folks are doing philosophy and all of this philosophy needs to play a role in our wisdom and our spiritual path if we are to be effective at achieving happiness.

When we realize the original role of philosophy, it should be clear that sciences such as social and cognitive psychology, for example, are not some new alternative to these traditions – they are the modern *refinement and continuation* of a centuries-long investigation. For instance, in Buddhism we are invited to learn more about how our minds work, and experience that through introspective observation in meditation and mindfulness. For the modern naturalistic Buddhist, the latest cognitive theories should inform our practice. As for methods of self-transformation, we are invited to experiment with these and studies on these methods are merely a continuation of the studies that have been conducted on practices by practitioners themselves since before we had a rigorous scientific method. A foundational integration of scientific knowledge and spiritual practice must be a distinctive characteristic of naturalistic spirituality if it is to be relevant and effective.

## The Importance of a Sacred Approach

Yet, I should add a caution here regarding the role of science in our spiritual walk. While the technical terminologies and methodologies of science are critical for the integrity of its process and purposes (the 'what is' part of philosophy), there are two things of which we should be aware: (1) spiritual wisdom requires more than a collection of raw facts and theories, important though they are, and (2) the technical framing of these phenomena is not fully effective for cultivation of inner transformation.

By this, I mean that reading all the articles in all the scientific journals about practices, psychology, and happiness will *never*, on its own, result in spiritual transformation. Further, this is not due to a lack of scientific knowledge yet to be gained. If you had access to God's library on Truth, you could come to memorize it all and this too would not result in spiritual transformation. At the same time, complete knowledge is not required for spiritual transformation, and is not a prerequisite to enlightenment.

As described, transformation of our character, disposition, perspectives, and responses comes not from intellectual knowledge, but from a series of rich experiences that penetrate many different aspects of our minds, emotions, memories, feelings, and so on. This is how the non-intuitive becomes the intuitive. These kinds of experiences happen naturally in life from time to time, and we can harness them if we have the proper wisdom on hand. But as I've mentioned, these are only signposts. The longer more enduring process of transformation comes from intentional participation in practices and rituals that facilitate deep experience of this nature. This means they need to have a moving aspect, and inspirational aspect, and so on. Technical language and mere knowledge are insufficient to generate such experience.

Further, the 'third-person' nature of scientific description is limited for these purposes, even if the data gained is illuminating and useful in its own way. Learning about the effects of meditation on a brain and why it has those effects will never be a substitute for meditating, and so it is with all other practices and rituals.

In our member archives, I have written an essay on what I call *Sacred Tongue*. There I make the case for the legitimacy of sacred and spiritual ways of framing the same facts – not merely as something to make us feel good. Rather, I argue for the legitimacy of this lexicon as a vehicle for truth, and communication of real aspects to phenomena that are not conveyed via technical lexicon. This is just one example of why a sacred/spiritual approach, as opposed to merely a technical psychological one, is important. Other important elements include music, physical procession, focal objects, human interaction, narratives, myth, iconography, and so on. This is what I mean when I speak of spiritual transformation and why it is relevant and central to a Spiritual Naturalist practice.

# Working Ritual with the Center

*B. T. Newberg*

Recently, in honor of the Pagan festival of Samhain, I created a ritual script which experimented with a new technique for creating special time and space (i.e. sacred space): working with the Center. In short, participants circumambulate a chosen focal point. Sounds simple enough, right?

Now, let's explore that a little deeper. Why create special time and space? Why propose new techniques? What is the Center?

## Why create special time and space?

The ultimate goal of ritual is to reaffirm or change patterns of perception and behavior. Creating a sense of special time and space is useful to that end.

Whatever the nature of time and space in an absolute sense, our *experience* of it is malleable. Time can seem longer or shorter, space can seem larger or more vital, and both can acquire a sense of heightened significance, depending on our state of consciousness. Time and space can at times appear special.

At those times, routinized behavior patterns are disrupted as the unconscious mind reevaluates the situation. They are thus prime times for inputting new information into the system. In short, the function of achieving a sense of special time and space is to signal to the unconscious mind that what is about to occur is significant, so that it privileges it henceforth in memory and behavioral decision-making.

To put this in theological language, it is to create space that is *sacred*, meaning "set apart." Ritual time and space is set apart as special and significant.

# Why a new technique?

But wait… what's the point of experimenting with new methods to do this? Aren't we re-inventing the wheel?

There are already several well-developed techniques for creating sacred space in the Pagan community, such as casting a circle or opening the gates. They usually speak in some way of moving between "the worlds", and naturalists can easily read this as moving between states of consciousness. Becoming familiar with these techniques is valuable for naturalists because it allows us to take part in rituals of various traditions, side-by-side with other Pagans in the larger community. And if it works for you, then hey, why not use it?

At the same time, these techniques may leave something to be desired. Their theoretical backings are highly metaphysical. For example, the purpose of a circle is purportedly to keep hostile energies out or desired energies in. Opening the Gates (a technique of ADF and its offshoots) is meant to enhance communication with deities, spirits, and ancestors.

While such theory need not intrude on practice, it leaves me wondering what it would be like to experiment with an entirely naturalistic technique, home-grown and inspired by patterns in nature. Hence, I present: the Center.

# What is a center?

Wherever you look, *centers* (small "c") pervade nature. There are literal centers, such as the atomic nucleus circled by its electrons or the star by its planets. There are also figurative centers, like the watering hole encompassed by herds or the giant redwood by a mini-ecosystem of life. At the most domestic, there is the hearthfire of the home. At the most cosmic, there is the omnicentric origin point of the Big Bang (which is everywhere). Centers are all around.

Crucially, a center only exists relative to what gathers round it. Apart from that, it is meaningless. Centers are inherently relational.

Thus, the distinguishing characteristic of a center is that it is a center *of something.* It unites that something around a shared focus. It is the nexus, source, or heart of a community. And that is what makes it interesting as a pattern for ritual.

## What is the Center?

The *Center* (big "C") is liturgical language for a real and symbolic focus of ritual activity. It is real insofar as it really is what all participants are focused around, symbolic insofar as it reproduces greater patterns of nature. Its role in ritual is to alter consciousness, calling forth the individual ego's relation to the group and the cosmos.

Like all good liturgical language, the *Center* is suggestive more than indicative, evocative more than precise, so that each person can discover themselves in it. Virtually anything can be discovered to be a center if you look closely enough, and that is the point: it's everywhere, but *it takes a shift in perspective to see it.*

## How do you work ritual with the Center?

The basic technique is to choose an appropriate focal point, mark it as the Center, and mindfully circumambulate it three times. This may be supported with appropriate gestures, phrases, and/or hymns.

While the technique is simple, a lot is built into it.

### 1. Appropriateness

The choice of focal point should be *appropriate,* and this is twofold.

First, it means that it should be a real center of actual activity, which requires that participants think about the local ecosystem. In what sense is the focal point a center? Is it a tree around which diverse creatures gather, a well from which a community derives sustenance, or the pole star around which our earthbound perspective turns?

At the same time, appropriateness also means it should fit the intentions of the ritual. This requires that participants link their intentions to the center. For example, a ritual of new beginnings may circle round the starting point of a path, or a ritual of death round a field of crops recently cut-down.

When planning a ritual, you may spend hours, days, or even weeks getting to know the local area and finding the perfect spot. Thinking about the land in this way will ground you in it, get your inspiration flowing, and make the ritual more concrete and meaningful. Moreover, it will begin to shift the ordinary perspective of objects and interests toward a holistic perspective of relationships and symbols.

## 2. Marking

When the ritual is about to begin, the chosen focal point is marked as the Center. A rope may be girded round a tree, a stone set up in a field, a chalk sigil drawn upon the paved path, and so forth. This may be elaborate or spartan, but whatever the marking, it should not eclipse but rather complement the native beauty of the Center.

This serves both practical and symbolic functions. Practically, it makes it clear to all participants exactly where the Center is. Symbolically, it acknowledges your relationship with it, by contributing something of yourself to it. This meeting of self and other further establishes the bond begun by carefully considering the most appropriate location.

## 3. Mindful circumambulation

Circumambulation means moving round the Center. Whether this is done in a solemn procession or a musical dance is up to you. Either way it should be done mindfully, three times. At the end of the ritual, circumambulate once in the opposite direction to signal your mind to return to normal time and space.

Within the imagination, allow *this* center to become *the* Center, symbolic of every center in your life, and indeed every center in the cosmos. Allow it to become a locus of inexhaustible interpretation, a source from which inspiration flows as patterns and relationships suggest themselves to you.

Allow any errant thoughts to pass by unheeded, bringing concentration gently back to the Center.

This may be supported with the use of ritual phrases calling to mind specific relationships while you circumambulate. For example, the Samhain ritual script invokes three relationships of naturalistic transcendence. The first time round, participants raise one arm to the Center and say:

This is the Center, around which all revolves.

It does not revolve around me, I revolve around it.

As I pass round, I affirm my place within the mind.

On the second time round, the phrase is repeated, affirming "my place within the community", and finally, the third time round, "my place within the cosmos."

Traditionally, Neopagans walk *deosil* (clockwise) when creating sacred space. This mimics the motion of the sun as seen from an earthbound perspective in the Northern Hemisphere, where the sun traverses the southern sky. When dissolving the space, they walk *widdershins* (counter-clockwise), which might be taken to represent a new perspective gained during the ritual.

# How does the Center work with psychology?

Repetitive symbolic acts such as these may appear pointless and empty at first glance to some. However, recent research is unveiling how and why ritual appeals to the brain, such that it is found universally across cultures, in both religious and secular contexts. As the following explains, working with the Center takes advantage of embodied cognition, Pavlovian association, and cognitive psychology to effect a change in consciousness.

On the most primitive level, circumambulation creates what historian William McNeill calls "muscular bonding" between the participants – moving together in time. Synchronous movement creates the sense of a group superorganism, and begins the submergence of the individual ego within a larger identity. Through such embodied cognition, the movement of the body shapes consciousness.

On a Pavlovian level, the triple repetition is significant. Three is a number denoting completeness in Western culture, as well as diversity (triplicity as opposed to unicity). These cultural associations, drilled into us since childhood, constellate a desired mindstate by Pavlovian association.

Finally, on a cognitive level, mindfulness monopolizes or "swamps" working memory, leaving no room for mundane or intrusive thoughts, resulting in a slightly altered state of concentration.

Further, the fact that the procedure appears pointless, at least to the uninformed observer, and redundant, circling three times instead of one, is also significant. Lienard and Boyer propose that observing apparently unnecessary steps signals unapparent danger to the unconscious mind, inferring perhaps that the rationale for the steps must be some potential threat known to others but not to oneself.

This activates a mental module they call the "hazard-precaution system," which likely evolved to avoid poorly understood but lethal dangers, such as pathogens and parasites.

154

Following a custom of ritually avoiding corpses or washing after touching blood, for example, has its evolutionary advantages, even if unaware of the real reason why these actions must be performed.

What we're interested in here is not why the hazard-precaution system evolved, but how we can put it to work for us.

Its activation arouses a special attentional state, producing a slightly altered state of consciousness. It directs attention away from goals and toward the specific steps of the ritual, which are typically actions so automatized they become dead to awareness, such as walking. The extra attention paid to walking *in a circle three times* revives the act, makes it fresh again, and thus encourages a sense of vividness and being "in the moment." Ritual cues, such as apparently unnecessary steps, can unconsciously trigger activation. The resulting state of heightened awareness may significantly facilitate the emotional power and inspirational meaning of a ritual.

It is important to note that this system is unconscious and intuitive, part of what Daniel Kahneman calls System 1 thinking. There is also System 2: conscious, deliberative thought, the effect of which is often to inhibit intuitive processes. In this case, for example, a critical thought might question the rational necessity of circling three times, thereby inhibiting activation of the hazard-precaution system and forestalling the desired change in consciousness. The question has merit, but gets in the way in the moment. That's why ritualists often recommend setting aside skepticism for the duration of the ritual. Critical questions can and should be entertained before and after, but not during. It's not to quell criticism, but to allow intuitive systems to function effectively.

If all goes well, the technique should produce what theological language calls a sense of the "sacred."

## Toward naturalistic ritual

Working ritual with the Center can be used as a viable, scientifically-supported method of creating special time and space. It's home-grown from a naturalistic perspective, yet open enough to invite non-naturalist participation without making any feel excluded. It's also untied to any specific cultural tradition, so that Spiritual Naturalists of all stripes may find it useful.

This technique is still very much in the experimental stage, so I remain open to comments and constructive criticisms.

# Spiritual Naturalist Drumming

*DT Strain*

Drumming is an ancient art that has played a ritualistic and spiritual role in different cultures all over the world. Drumming practitioners today may be most familiar with West African and Native American traditions, but there are many others – for example, Taiko drumming techniques from Japan. Why does drumming have a spiritual role in the lives of so many diverse cultures, and what role might it have for naturalists?

In the West at least, new spiritual movements have come to incorporate drumming methods and understandings from a variety of 'mix-and-match' influences. These customized ritual cocktails may vary in their accuracy and allegiance to historically accurate understandings; sometimes intentionally so. In many of these cases, members of the original cultures from which these practices sprang may find offense. So, as we proceed, we should do so with respect for original cultures and be careful that we don't misrepresent them. Even with this approach, however, it should be noted that no amount of respect will prevent offense to some cultures that resent any appropriation of their customs. This is a more general concern with any perennial path such as ours, but we proceed as respectfully as possible while learning from others what we can. The format of drumming rituals varies, but we will primarily look at drumming circles, which have been popularly forming at events and in groups for many years.

Another concern for us, as naturalists, is that one will find a variety of interpretations as to the nature of spiritual drumming in literal terms. That is, there are many beliefs about what is happening with 'energy', healing, bodily centers, and so on. We should not get too hung up on these particulars, as there will always be those with a variety of beliefs. Agreement on these matters is not essential and we should approach them with tolerance while staying true to our own path, which includes a humble approach to knowledge and claims; without the need to force that discipline on others. Mainly, just as we do when reading ancient philosophy, we must be capable of seeing past differences to connect with underlying themes and wisdom, rather than being reactionary to anything we may not agree with and miss an entire area of human activity and its potential benefits. So, some charity is advisable. This would be true even for non-naturalists, each of whom will have their own differences of belief. The famous physicist Richard Feynman is one example of a naturalist who saw great benefits in drumming. So, let us consider these benefits.

## Individual

At the simplest level, drumming is fun. This alone can justify it for anyone, naturalist or not. And, there is additionally an argument to be made for simple fun activity as a healthy part of a spiritual life. But considering some further aspects of drumming beyond simple fun can be intriguing and helpful.

The National Aboriginal Health Organization (NAHO) conducted a series of interviews and collected practitioner journal reports to get a sense of what Aboriginal women practitioners experienced in hand drumming rituals. The general consensus was positive, as one might expect. Some reported their heart rates affected by the rhythm, helping them deal with stress, relaxing and releasing tension. Some even reported finding the activity helpful in dealing with addictions. They generally reported that it helped them maintain a positive outlook on life.

Of course, more research can only help illuminate these effects, but Spiritual Naturalists are encouraged to do their own first-person research, seeing for themselves the effects of participation. Practice, as we have stated, is about more than academic third-person study.

## Community

Obviously, the communal nature of drum circles tends to help participants learn to be in sync with one another in their drumming. This synchronicity can lead to a greater sense of cooperation. Indeed, many armies from all over the world have, prior to modern communications, used drumming to coordinate soldiers on the battlefield and in training. Not only does the rhythm indicate a pace and type of action, but the emotional nature of hearing the drums helped to coordinate their emotions, adrenaline, and attitudes. This concept has carried on into marching bands used to rally fans and players in sports games.

Obviously, this kind of alignment of neural activity can benefit more than a group of soldiers for purposes of war. It can also be used positively to engender a sense of close community for other constructive purposes. In a drum circle, all players are considered equal, regardless of ability and this too has a psychological effect on our relationship with the whole.

## Deeper

All of the preceding has been rather utilitarian or even dry so far; speaking of entertainment, physical effects, and community building. These are worthy things in their own right, but for many, drumming is much deeper and more profound than these dry descriptions can do justice. As even a basic practitioner, I can attest to this, as well as the fact that such is the case even within a purely naturalistic path.

Watching a self-conscious drummer attempt the art is telling. Here, we see that successful drumming requires a kind of 'handing over' of some control and self-consciousness. The analytical side of us, when attempting to helm the ship in drumming, can't pull it off. This is because drumming requires a real-time response. The analytical mind is thinking to itself, "ok, is it time for the next beat now? Now? Now? —ok Now!" and by the time the hand moves to hit the drum, it is already too late. The conscious judgmental mind is getting in the way. It's too busy thinking about the beat. This is not unlike the folk tale about the centipede, when asked how it manages to coordinate all those legs to walk, suddenly loses the ability when it stops to think about it.

This is significant because the 'uptight person' must go through a kind of learning process to 'let go' in order to really enjoy the spiritual benefits of drumming. Here, the hand must already be moving to the drum and must strike it confidently at the right moment, *without* the conscious pre-confirmed knowledge that everyone else will, in fact, follow through with a strike. The dilemma might remind us of the funny example of the person who yells something embarrassing to a friend in the middle of a loud party, just as everyone happens to go silent, making their statement far more noticeable than intended. For all we know, everyone might place the beat in some other place or stop drumming, leaving the self-conscious person whacking a loud drum all by themselves – the horror!

This is somewhat like those exercises in trust, where someone falls backward letting another catch them. We must have a kind of faith that others (or the music) will go along with us in this beat we feel – *we can't wait for confirmation before proceeding or we will fail*. It is not difficult to imagine what this might have to teach naturalists who are used to relying on their intellects and on evidence. It says something about the nature of dealing with reality as it is; often messy, incomplete, and often requiring action without all the answers.

It forces us to get to know ourselves – to learn to trust our instincts, our ways of sensing and acting in a complex environment intuitively and skillfully. This, in fact, could be considered an apt metaphor for what Taoists refer to as 'skillful means' in life. It is this kind of internalization and alteration of our direct responses that we seek in living more consistently with nature and our nature as rational/moral beings. This can potentially shift our attitude in ways that enable us to apply this perspective in other places in our life.

And as we become more accustomed to entering this state of mind, we learn to free ourselves from self consciousness, which could be an aspect of being constrained by the delusions of the ego. We enter that trancelike state of pure experience; without labels; without judgments, and the fictions they often impose upon us. This is, of course, a meditative state, with similar (though not identical) benefits and uses in our spiritual practice. It is also an example of *flow* which is being more appreciated lately as a source of contentment and happiness in life.

And, it is in this altered state of consciousness, that we can become perceptive to things we often overlook. As we give up part of that control, and we trust others to fill in the beats alongside us simultaneously, a network activity builds between these coordinated nervous systems. We begin to operate as a single neurological system, in every way that matters from an information-processing standpoint. This creates a profound sense of shared interconnectedness with others in the group. Importantly, this is not just a 'feeling', but it is a deep *perception* of an external truth: that we *are*, in fact, interconnected with one another in deeper ways than we are typically conditioned to appreciate or capable of directly perceiving.

As the famous jazz musician John Coltrane said, "All a musician can do is get closer to the sources of nature, and so feel that he is in communion with the natural laws". Drumming, like any practice, may not be for everyone, but it is this very real and very natural *enhanced perception* that makes drumming a potential source of spiritual transformation.

It is not, then, too far a stretch for our minds to begin extending this perception of interconnectedness toward other people beyond the drum circle, toward all beings, and toward the universe as a whole. This has implications for cultivation of empathy and compassion and for our value systems, and for the actions that result from them.

# Something Special May Happen

*Thomas Schenk*

Many years ago, I spent a year teaching outdoor education to grade school children. The students would be bused out from the city for their once-a-year instruction about wild nature. In addition to providing the scientifically-oriented subjects that were the core of our outdoor education curricula, I attempted to get students to sit quietly for a few minutes and attend to the sensory qualities of nature. To get them to quiet down, I would tell them: "if we sit quietly, something special might happen." I usually did not have much success getting students to be still, but one morning I had a group sitting quietly when two fawns walked right into the middle of the circle we had formed. Wow, I thought, this is special! Strangely, it didn't create nearly the buzz among the students I expected. Later I asked the teacher why the students were not more impressed. She said, "They think you do this for every group." Oh well!

In the lingo of outdoor education, the technique of sitting quietly in this way is called Seton Sitting. It was named for the naturalist Thomas Seton. It is nothing more than trying to sit very quietly in a natural area until the wildlife forgets you are there. Some people call it "still stalking." Once, while Seton Sitting, a Northern Goshawk landed on a ledge about ten feet from me and graciously ignored me for about ten minutes.

Though its goals are not quite as lofty as enlightenment or attaining oneness with God, Seton Sitting is not too different from the formal practice of meditation. In both Seton Sitting and meditation you have to become somewhat 'ignorant'. Yes you have to ignore the ants that crawl on you, and be unresponsive to a variety of other stimuli. This, I think, is what all forms of meditative practice have in common: to practice them, you have to create a *space* between the stimuli and your response.

In his book *Man's Search for Meaning*, Victor Frankl writes about experiences as a prisoner in the Nazi death camps. Frankl recognized that he had lost control over his activities and his environment. He came to realize, however, that though he could not control the stimulus he was subjected to, he could decide within himself how he would let it affect him and how he would respond to it. Meditation is like this. In meditation, however, it is the very space between the stimulus and response, rather than the response itself that is the focus.

So I invite you to think of the practice of meditation as developing and living within a *space* between stimulus and response. The ordinary mind has patterned responses to various internal and external stimuli. To meditate, a person learns to break these patterns and to be less responsive to these stimuli (though maintaining the ability to respond if necessary). As you become proficient in creating this mental space, you can do two things with it: you can remain in the silence and emptiness of this space, or can choose some object of attention, such as an idea, symbol, or impression, and become deeply immersed in it. Both have their distinctive values. (I call the first *meditation* and the second *contemplation*, but this distinction is not present in ordinary usage.)

In meditation, then, we learn to become less responsive to both external and internal stimuli. The external stimuli cannot be shut out; you need to let them move through. The internal stimuli – thoughts, emotions, desires — can be slowed, but not stopped. Like bubbles in a glass of soda, the meditator lets them rise, pass through, and dissipate. The practice of meditation deepens as we learn to withhold our attention from the stimuli that seeks to engage it.

This is not easy. Most of us have a very strong inclination to give such stimuli our attention and response. In the early stages of learning the practice of meditation, again and again one finds oneself abstracted from the present moment and entangled in a thought, image or emotion. With time, however, maintaining this space between the stimulus and the response becomes easier; as one's practice deepens this space develops into an inner refuge of self control and peace.

In verse 15 of the *Tao Te Ching*, Lao Tze observes that "muddy waters settle and becomes clear." In verse 16 he observes that "leaves fall from the tree to return to the roots." I read these as an invitation to bring all life's muddiness — all the sorrows, distractions and joys of the world — into our meditation. And there let them settle, so that we come forth from meditation with a deeper sense of our being's rootedness in this world and with a clearer mind. This approach, focused on this life in this world, is the approach to meditation I have come to embrace.

The poet T.S. Eliot described the modern condition as being "distracted from distraction by distraction." Our world pulses with disjointed stimuli, pulling the mind this way and that like leaves in the wind. The distracted mind's readiest refuge is in entertainments, which are supplied non-stop by the commercial media. But, these entertainments are just another level of distraction. To gain clarity and rootedness requires a different approach. A formal meditation practice may be the right approach for some, or just sitting quietly with nature might work better for others. One has to try a few things to find what works best. And it is worth it. As I told my students many years ago, "if we sit quietly, something special might happen."

# Distractions to Spiritual Practice

*DT Strain*

I often attend discussions on some aspect of philosophy or spirituality; in our local Spiritual Naturalist chapter monthly gathering, in Humanist events, sometimes Dharma talks, and with friends. I have recently noticed in a number of these conversations some emerging themes which have finally gelled together for me, resulting in the following conclusions. They have to do with things that form distractions to our spiritual progress, or road blocks on our spiritual path.

By '*spiritual progress*', I mean that process of cultivating qualities in ourselves to be more capable of living *the good life*, in both the sense of ethical goodness, and the sense of true happiness and flourishing (which are actually synonymous). And, by 'distraction' I mean something that we might do, thinking we are doing spirituality, when in fact we may be missing the central aims of our spiritual practice. Distractions aren't necessarily bad or something we shouldn't do for other purposes, however. For example, eating a sandwich is a distraction to swimming. Both of these are fine things to do, but we are wasting our time if we think that eating a sandwich is furthering our endeavor to swim. In fact, even important *parts* to spirituality can be distractions if we take them to be the entirety of spiritual practice.

It is my hope that in sharing these thoughts it may be helpful to you in your practice, and perhaps inspire further discussion where I might learn even more from you. I will describe four categories of distraction to spiritual practice though I'm sure these are by no means exhaustive.

## Metaphysical Cosmology

In this first form of distraction, I use the word "cosmology" in the older, broader metaphysical sense – not in the strict term for that branch of science. Cosmology, in general, is an overarching view of "how the world works" – the *ultimate secrets of existence*, one might say. Every culture and religious tradition has its own cosmology, whether that involves migrating souls or heavenly realms and salvation, or animal spirits, etc. Here I mean that which is taken literally as *the true nature of Reality*. Even a purely materialist model based solely on scientific observation counts as metaphysical cosmology when we add to that description a claim that it is all-inclusive of reality. We each, agnostic though many of us may attempt to be, at least have some kind of suspicion of 'how things probably are' even if only in parts. Even as provisional and open minded as we try to be, this exists in us at least to the degree that, when radically different cosmologies are presented, our ears perk and we can be lured into debate.

It can be good fun to discuss the fascinating possibilities and compare our cosmologies, and there is nothing inherently wrong or bad with this subject. In fact, as B.T. Newberg has pointed out in his excellent articles on Big History, our understanding of the world and our place in it not only inspire, but provide important insight to how we might best live. But the really insidious thing about cosmology is that it *feels* like we are *doing* spirituality when we engage in such thoughts and discourse. In fact, cosmology has very little to do with spirituality *as a practice*.

In a story described in the Buddhist Pali Canon, one of the Buddha's students became upset with him because he was silent on a number of questions such as nature of the cosmos and life after death. He threatened to renounce the Buddha's teachings unless he answered these questions. The Buddha, having never claimed to reveal ultimate metaphysical truths, responded with what is called the *Parable of the Poison Arrow*.

In this parable, a man is struck with a poisoned arrow and is brought to a surgeon to remove the arrow and treat the wound. But the man refuses to allow the arrow to be removed until he knows whether the man who wounded him was a warrior, priest, merchant, or worker; what the man's name and clan were;

whether he was tall or short; the color of his skin; his home town; the kind of bow used; from what kind of animal the feathers of the arrow came; and many other questions. The Buddha said this man would die with all of those things remaining unknown to him.

The Buddha discouraged wasting time on metaphysical speculation. He specifically said that these questions *were irrelevant to his teachings and to true religion.*

This is an Eastern parallel to Western schools such as Pyrrhonism, which prescribes withholding assent to non-evident propositions, always remaining in a state of inquiry. In another example, it was Socrates who fulfilled the Oracle's claim that he was the wisest of men because, unlike so many others, he knew that he was unwise.

And that is the real trap of being distracted by cosmology: it is *egotism.* In truth, none of us primates hopping about on this tiny ball of stardust in an obscure corner of the cosmos has access to the ultimate truths of existence. The Buddha, Socrates, the Pope, Richard Dawkins, a caveman, you, and I have precisely the same real *knowledge* of ultimate Reality: which is zilch. When we become engrossed in mental gymnastics and claim-making about these issues, we fool ourselves into thinking we are making spiritual progress when, in fact, we are not even engaged in the endeavor at all. This is why a Spiritual Naturalist can consider withholding assent to claims without evidence to be an important spiritual discipline. In our archives, we describe this practice as *Epoché.*

As a Stoic, I try to remember that knowledge itself is a commodity – an external condition and a resource like wealth; the accumulation of which I do not have ultimate control, and for which no amount will ever satiate my desire. While it is appropriate to my nature, and fitting, that I try to learn and grow in knowledge – one of the axioms of a spiritual walk is that true happiness is achievable and within our control. The key to greater enlightenment and the flourishing life is therefore *not* the mere accumulation of knowledge, and certainly not dependent upon the possession of ultimate knowledge, which appears to be beyond our reach as a matter of principle.

*One of the significant and profound 'advancements' (or re-discoveries, rather) made by Spiritual Naturalism today is the divorcing, or disentanglement, of spirituality from cosmological claims.* If we are to reunite the sacred with the natural, then one of the requirements in this effort is to *let go* of the need to have our spirituality make claims about ultimate reality. To really incorporate modern naturalism, we must respect its space and role in our spirituality. That means leaving claims about the nature of reality up to those who do the hard work of carefully observing and measuring it, and being humble in not trying to fill in the wide gaps in that information with our own speculations. The religious and the non-religious are equally susceptible to this.

## The Ego

Once I was in a discussion and the question asked of participants was, "What areas do you feel you need to learn, improve, or grow in further?" One participant actually responded that he didn't really need to learn anything more, as he was already knowledgeable in his spiritual tradition and was interested in sharing that knowledge with others. It turned out later than the participant was not even aware of some of the most significant philosophers and works from his own tradition.

Yet, we should not take this extreme example of unintentional irony as an opportunity to gloat over how much better we are than to be so egotistical, lest we make the same error. Rather, we should take it as a cautionary example and realize that – just as he was unaware of his own ego – we too are unaware or unmindful of the many shortcomings we most certainly have too.

For example, while I write this article with sincere intentions that it be helpful, and that I might learn from reading your reactions to it, can I deny that my human nature underlies this motivation and some subtle backdrop of egotism exists whereby I think my words superior or worthy to be read by others? Perhaps some part of me seeks the praise of others for having written this, despite my conscious intention to discard concern for the praise or blame of others as per Stoic teaching? To my shame, some residual of this egotism almost certainly exists despite my best efforts. I therefore try to humbly and honestly dwell on this, and try to move beyond my tiny ego to achieve pure motivation. For someone who engages in being a messenger of timeless teachings that far exceed their own wisdom, this is a constant challenge. Yet, we all have stumbled upon wisdom and sharing it with one another is a noble and compassionate endeavor that should be encouraged. If we wait for those with perfect knowledge and wisdom to teach us, then we will be without a teacher. Therefore, all of us students must help teach one another.

There are at least a few ways that the ego can be a distraction to spiritual progress. An egotistical teacher or professor of spiritual wisdom can distract others from the path by allowing their personality to become an object of attention rather than the teachings and practices. As the Kalama Sutra teaches, let us not accept anything simply because a teacher, leader, or authority claims it. Investigate for yourself whether these things are helpful and effective.

But our own ego can also be a distraction to our progress. We must acknowledge that we all have a desperate need to know the path and what lies on every part of it. Leaning more is essential, but not sufficient, and obsession on 'knowing it all' can lead us to anchor ourselves on particular ideas, becoming attached to them. This can blind us, close us off to further possibilities, and limit our progress.

## Academics

Humanity has been seeking wisdom, in all of its cultures over the entire globe, for thousands of years. The wealth of wisdom and teachings available today is truly vast. There will always be more to learn, and even if it were possible to read it all, we would find that the entirety of human thought and wisdom is but a tiny island in a vast ocean of what is yet to be understood.

Again, learning more is an important component of a good life and a spiritual practice. But there is something very important to understand: even if we were to read every text of, for example, Buddhism, we would still not really understand Buddhism if all we did was read. Spirituality is about human happiness and well-being, and this is inherently a subjective experience. Its practices are designed to affect that subjective experience. Therefore, only through first-person *applied practice* of the teachings over time, can we ever really investigate and understand that to which shallow human language is referring.

The Western approach of accumulating data and analyzing it intellectually from the third-person perspective before giving assent is completely inadequate to making progress along these spiritual paths. Just as our spirituality must refrain from making claims about reality, leaving that space to objective investigation – we must also acknowledge the space for subjective investigation and where its proper realm exists.

When we get into bantering about academic philosophic principles and works, name-dropping various thinkers and writers and so on, we can trick ourselves into thinking that we are engaged in spiritual practice. Yet, *without practice, all of this academic knowledge, writing, and discussion is mere vanity.*

## Fixing the World

There are many important and noble endeavors which are, quite simply, *not spiritual practice.* Many of these activities may be very important and even help in our spiritual walk, cultivating various faculties. Yet, they can also become a distraction to our spiritual practice if we confuse them with it.

People who consciously pursue spirituality tend to be caring, loving people and this means there is a high correlation with those who are concerned with the ills of the world and the suffering and plights of others (a wonderful thing!). Yet, this can result in a myopic or obsessive focus on large-scale social issues.

In a recent gathering of the Society's local chapter, we were discussing Taoism, and the question was raised, "What would a Taoist master say as to how to handle the violence in the Middle East?"

While Taoism certainly can have a positive impact on these situations, the question underscores an important point about these kinds of practices as compared to our modern ways of thinking about social problems. We often tend to consider the entire matter from a third-person sociological perspective, as though we were aliens floating above the planet, looking down on humanity. We want to analyze the historical and other underpinnings of the objective situation. Then we imagine that we can come up with 'solutions' which we can – through writing, debating, protesting, or conflicting – convince our fellow human beings to employ (who will certainly follow our undeniable fact-based conclusions), thus correcting the current state of affairs.

This approach is a bit naïve even if admirably optimistic. Spirituality is not sociology. This common approach tends to assume we have more ability to assess the current situation, more ability to foresee the best course of action for everyone, and more ability to control the actions of others than we really do. In actuality, it is more likely that the course of human civilization on the scale of society is a huge cultural tide against which even the most 'powerful' of us have little ability to direct within a significant margin. Even the world's current superpower, with trillions of dollars spent on the most massive military force in history, stretched across the planet with a will to use it to ensure its vision for the world come to fruition is plagued by constant security threats, economic uncertainty, and social ills – a highly precarious position most agree is not sustainable. If we think that a peaceful rather than forceful approach to controlling these externals will be anything but only marginally more successful (vastly more noble though it may be), then we are likely to be similarly disappointed.

So, the very question, "How would Taoism solve the troubles in the Middle East?" is misplaced because it assumes the Taoist master can control the actions of others. Even if we imagine an answer could tell us everything that needs to be done, how then would we make everyone do it? Where spirituality is the concern, this line of thought is a waste of time. But perhaps more importantly, this question is misplaced because *molding the world to our liking (for good or ill) is not the aim of spiritual practice*. Rather than fixing the world, spiritual practice calls on us to fix ourselves. Let me put that more precisely: spiritual practice calls on *me* to fix *myself*.

As such, it recognizes that the only thing I *do* control is *my* choice, *my* actions, and *my* character. It also recognizes that, even the most noble of causes – feeding starving children, helping the sick, securing justice and human rights – are but *externals;* like wealth, health, fame, or many of the less noble externals. They are things not ultimately in our control, and therefore circumstance cannot be a prerequisite for spiritual progress or flourishing. Attachment to 'good causes' is still attachment and will, just as assuredly, be a road block to spiritual progress.

Now to address the predictable and eternal response to this point: please know that this is not a call for indifference or to do less good work in the world. We, in fact, need more of it. This is about our *internal disposition* as we do that work. Doing good is an essential part of the spiritual life, but it is not about the outcome of that work. Rather, it is about our motivation within. If we do good because we want to be the kind of person who does good, because we want to have a compassionate character, then we are, as the Taoists put it, impervious. We are not attached to outcomes, which are ultimately arbitrated by the universe. It is this cultivation of virtuous character which is the spiritual endeavor – not achieving certain conditions in the world. When we forget that, we are distracted from spiritual progress and, ironically, end up harming even those external causes because we can become burnt out, demoralized, or hateful whenever our machinations prove for naught and external conditions do not match our aims.

# What is *Not* a Distraction to Spiritual Practice?

One of the things that is not a distraction to spiritual practice is the one thing most often given as an excuse for not pursuing a spiritual practice; that is, the demands of our schedules and everyday life!

Gandhi suggested that we meditate one hour every day, unless we are busy, in which case *two*. While the length of meditation is open to many views, the implication is that the busier we are, the more centered and spiritually balanced we need to be. But an important thing to understand is that spiritual practice isn't *just* about those official techniques we give names to and set aside time to do those activities. There is absolutely no benefit, *in itself*, of sitting cross-legged silently with eyes closed for any period of time. The real purpose of a spiritual practice, be it meditation or any other, is that we become more capable of *applying* and using what these practices do to us and for us in everyday life; confronting the challenges of the day, each day.

Sitting in a quiet temple with no distractions is the *training wheels* of spirituality. The life of the monk is the life of putting oneself in as *easy* conditions as possible for spiritual progress. Those who face the highest challenges are those who are working jobs, navigating relationships, raising kids, paying bills, and contributing to their communities. Those who choose to undertake a spiritual practice in such conditions are the *high-level practitioners* – playing the game on the highest difficulty setting. Though, to be sure, that isn't to say we are wiser or that we haven't anything to learn from those who have, due to their easier conditions, been able to move further down the path and give us good information about how to walk it and what lies ahead. Such leaders can make excellent guides and we should respect their dedication and knowledge – but we cannot confuse their external lifestyle conditions with the essence of spiritual practice.

Everything we do, from caring for children, to running errands, to cleaning, to interacting with one another, is an opportunity to put spiritual wisdom into practice and further hone our habits, character, and state of being. If spiritual teachings are not applicable to the real life of ordinary human beings, then they are useless. This should help illustrate how off-base are thoughts of real life being an obstruction to spiritual practice. Real life is what spiritual practice is all about.

# Happiness Upon Reflection

*Jennifer Hancock*

More and more I have come to realize that happiness is a matter of reflection. We rarely feel happiness in the moment. We may feel good, or pleasure. But it is only when we take a moment to reflect in the moment that we realize: we are happy. If we seek to have more happiness, we need to make more time for reflection. This is one of the reasons why meditation is so useful. Even if you don't get yourself to a no-thought, just be state of awareness, you are still quieting your mind and giving yourself a chance to reflect, quietly. And there is value in that.

When you are out walking, taking a moment to stop and smell the flowers is an opportunity to reflect on what you are doing while you are doing it and that inevitably brings us a feeling of happiness and contentment and yes, joy in the simple pleasure of being alive.

Whenever we pause to just feel the sensation of wind on our skin, or sunlight on our face, or the deep, ever changing color of our loved ones eyes, we feel that feeling of happiness. Happiness in just being.

Just being isn't enough. You have to take the time to reflect on the fact that you are, to feel happiness. I realize that seems counter intuitive, but it is true. Perhaps this is why we are all told the unexamined life isn't worth living.

Just don't fall into the trap of thinking too much. This is about balance. If all you do is think, you aren't doing. The key is to take a short moment to reflect upon what you are doing, then go back to doing it.

Enjoy.

# How to Stay Mindful

*DT Strain*

Recently I had the pleasure of attending a gathering of spiritual naturalists and similar folks at a local tea house. One in our group recommended we discuss an issue he'd been dealing with: how to stay mindful throughout the day? We all learn and read about various teachings, wisdom, and more but as the day's events take place, we get swept up in what's happening and forget these words of wisdom. Before long we're getting stressed out, not stopping to smell the roses, living in the past or future, and so on.

In our discussion, I decided to present five tips I had come up with, which often help me stay mindful throughout the day…

1. **Meditate regularly:** Breathing mindfulness meditation can be beneficial on a session-to-session basis, but its best effects can be witnessed when we cultivate a practice of doing it regularly – perhaps once every day for at least 15-20 minutes as a good minimum. I am not always on top of my game doing this, but when I am, it's noticeable. A regular practice of meditation really starts to shape our minds and the way they work (and this has been backed up by the latest brain studies). We find it easier to maintain focus, have stillness of mind, and be mindful as a norm. So, the operative term in this is 'regularly'.

2. **Journaling:** Keeping a daily journal of your goals and progress integrating wise thoughts into your way of living can be remarkably effective. Again, it's a habit that requires building. But making the notes at night, as well as reviewing them in the morning helps keep teachings alive throughout the day. We also build a sense of progress in our walk by doing this.

3. **Worn or carried objects:** I sometimes use mala beads to aid in counting breaths during meditation. But aside from this use I have found that when I'm wearing them on my wrist, the tangible object serves as a reminder of my practice and helps me to stay mindful. When I brought this up, a woman at our gathering produced a smooth stone which she said gave her peace by handling it. The object could be a trinket on a necklace, a string on your finger, or anything really – whatever works for you.

4. **Reminder notes:** Sometimes placing inspirational or motivational notes around your home or office can be helpful reminders for staying centered and not getting distracted. These can be simple bullet points, important concepts, or even small koans or poems. While no purchase of a product is ever a requirement for spiritual progress, Thich Nhat Hanh has released a nice little book that comes in a box with a deck of reminder note cards, called *Present Moment Wonderful Moment: Mindfulness Verses for Daily Living,* which I have found very useful.

5. **Mindfulness alarms:** Although you may not wish to do this as a norm, setting alarms to go off at regular intervals throughout the day can be a very effective project to help kick start good mental habits. I have done this before with alarms spaced every 2 hours, but one person in our group told us about reading of someone doing it every 7 minutes! Of course, you will have to consider what is practical for you during a normal day, but trying to remain present, in the moment, and mindful between these alarms can definitely help our progress.

Aside from these little tips for staying mindful, it is also important to note of what we are to be mindful! This is where what the Buddhists refer to as Right Thought and Right View come into play. Often times the things that consume us during the day, like anger, worry, or frustration, come from unwise, delusional, or misguided perspectives and value systems. Having a larger perspective than our own narrow ego is a big help to appreciation of life. My wife has a very effective practice of referring to the issues she deals with at work and on the highway as "first-world problems", which reminds her that while she's dealing with a malfunctioning printer, there are people in the world who don't have access to clean water.

What can this kind of attention practice and mindfulness achieve? For thousands of years, practitioners have reported greater happiness and tranquility when we are able to stay 'in the moment'.

# Daily Fruit

*Thomas Schenk*

There is a folktale from India called *The King and the Corpse*. At the beginning of this tale we are told of a mendicant who appears every day at the king's court to deliver an offering of fruit. Each day the king accepts this fruit and passes it on to his treasurer who carries it away and tosses it through a window into a vault in the dim recesses of the treasury.

This goes on for a decade. Then one day as the mendicant brings his gift a pet monkey, which has escaped from one of the royal apartments, leaps upon the king's arm as he sits on his throne. The king hands the monkey the fruit, and when the monkey bits into it, a jewel dropped out and rolls on the floor. The treasurer runs to the treasury and finds a heap of such jewels accumulated in the vault where he has tossed the fruit. Finally paying attention to this old mendicant, the king gets led into a mysterious and perilous adventure. If you wish to learn of that adventure, though, you will have to read the story*. Here I am only concerned with the mysterious piece of fruit.

The fruit, of course, is a symbol. Though within the total context of the story this symbol gathers ambiguity, I have found richness in what is the most obvious interpretation.

My daily routine is to rise early each morning, put on some coffee, and stretch as the coffee brews. Then I sit for a period of contemplation. I start my contemplation with the thought of that piece of fruit delivered each day by the mendicant. It serves as a reminder that each day is like a fruit containing a jewel, a raw diamond or ruby. The quality of that jewel will be the quality of the attention I bring to the day. What I do with that stone, how I penetrate its natural cleavage to unlock its possibilities, depends on the intentionality I bring to the day. In short, the quality of each day is a function of the quality of attention and intention I bring to it. The symbol of the mendicant's fruit reminds me of that simple truth.

I cannot directly share the jewel of the day with others. The jewel is a gift from Life to me, (Life offers everyone the same). Enjoying that gift to its fullest is to honor the gift, to honor Life. But in addition to the jewel, there is the nourishing pulp of the fruit. I think of the fruit's pulp as the work I can do each day that might be fruitful to others. The jewel is a gift to the invisible realm of my inner being. The pulp is a gift to my body and the tangible world of which it is a part. I can't share the jewel directly, but I can try to share it indirectly through the quality of attention and intention I bring to others and to my work. The jewel and the fruit complement each other.

I wrote this piece recently on the morning of my 60th birthday. People told me I should do something special to celebrate such a momentous day. But if each day brings you a piece of fruit containing a jewel, there simply is no better or more momentous way of celebrating a day than attending to that fruit and intending the shape of that jewel. So I treated my birthday like any ordinary day and it presented me the same generous gift.

* The story can be found in the book *The King and the Corpse*, by Hans Zimmer. Versions of the story can probably be found on the Internet.

# Working Toward Liberation

*DT Strain*

Many philosophies and wisdom traditions have independently come to realize that anguish and emotional suffering is caused by our attachments. Buddhism is perhaps the best known, but Taoism is closely related in this, and many other philosophies touch on it as well. Some philosophies approach the matter by talking about fear, or greed, or false judgments about which things are necessary or beneficial; but these concepts tend to boil down to *attachment*.

Attachment and non-attachment can be difficult concepts because they are incredibly nuanced. Without a subtle understanding, it can be easy to mistake this bit of wisdom. We might wonder how a person can even function without any desires or preferences. Stoicism makes a distinction between "wish" and "desire", each with very specific technical definitions; each not being merely a matter of intensity, but instead arising from different kinds of judgments and impulses, and having significantly different effects on our well-being. Translations of Eastern philosophy sometimes refers to 'unhealthy clinging' and the like, to help make the distinction.

Basically, we become attached to things, people, and conditions when we imagine them to be permanent entities, and we place a value judgment on them such that we cannot be happy in life without them. This kind of attachment can sneak up on us, and we don't realize it until it's too late, the conditions change, and we are devastated. Or, perhaps conditions have not even changed, but we suffer because of a constant fear of losing that to which we have become attached.

This is a vicious cycle of desire that never fully satisfies and results in a life of anguish – regardless of what degree of things or people we accumulate. Yet, for many, this is simply "how life is". They cannot imagine what it might be like to be liberated from such attachments without being some kind of robot or without having a drab emotionless life.

To the contrary, a life with less attachment can be a life of greater joy, equanimity, and peace. We can still enjoy people, things, and situations but we do so in a different manner, from a different perspective. This kind of joy is an appreciation that is more like lying in a soothing river, enjoying the water flowing around us. At all times the water is changing and flowing; parts of it passing away and new parts coming by. Yet, we do not cling to it, trying to collect it all up in our hands. This admittedly vague simile may help to illustrate a little of what the emotional experience of appreciation, love, and enjoyment without attachment is like.

But to achieve this kind of state requires a 'rewiring' of our outlook, from the ground up. This cannot be accomplished by reading an article, but it begins with certain basic information. The following are some means by which we can begin the rewiring…

## Understanding the Aggregate Self

For one, our understanding of our 'self' (or ego) is essential. We are born into an incredibly ego-driven state and we often do not move much beyond that; "All through the day, I – me – mine" as George Harrison sang. But what is this "I" we so worshipfully tend to? I like to use the term "the aggregate self" but in Buddhism it's often referred to as "no self". This is the realization that there isn't some permanent being that *has* emotions, that *has* thoughts, that *has* memories, impulses, sensations, etc. Rather, the self is a system of all these aggregates working together in an ever-changing matrix. Thus, the self is an abstraction.

This may seem rather academic or abstract at first, but deep perception and intuitive understanding of this and its implications begin to change a person's perspective over time, with effort. We begin to realize that the urges we feel are not "us", but a mechanism that evolved for its own purposes. And, more importantly, that these urges include insidious desires to protect the ego and its sense of self preservation. But that rational/moral higher self needn't be a slave to those impulses. These kinds of thoughts matter to our focus and our experience in life.

## Perception of Time

Another perspective-shifting concept is the way we think about time and the timescale of our existence. This may seem contradictory, but in one sense we need to have 'big mind', learning to see all of past, present, and future as one grand tapestry. And, on the other hand, we need to learn to live in the present moment.

How these two work together comes from a deeper understanding of each. Living in the present moment doesn't mean we don't plan for the future or benefit from the past. But it means that we maintain awareness of our present state so as to fully get the most out of our life experience, and so that we aren't needlessly distressing over the past or fretting about the future. These ruminations and spinning of wheels are a great source of suffering, and not necessary to planning within needs.

How, then, can we maintain this hypothetical 'God's-eye view' of time while being present in the moment? When we come to acceptance of the unfolding of events according to natural law, we hand over those things which we never had control over to begin with. We learn to even see the beauty of that tapestry. Thus, a trust is developed. With the rest of Nature left to do what only it can do, we are now free to focus on what we *do* control, our present choices. Ignatian Christians would say "let go and let God" but even naturalists without a belief in such a personal being benefit greatly by realizing what is in their control and leaving the rest up to the Logos (the natural order).

# Conceiving Impermanence and Emptiness

A deep acceptance of the impermanent nature of the universe is essential to this rewiring. More than acceptance, we can come to see the majesty of such a grand flux and understand that everything we appreciate and value cannot exist without it, for without constant change, all you have is either complete chaos or complete order – both lifelessness. As Chuang-Tzu said, "And surely that which is such a kind arbiter of my life is the best arbiter of my death."

*Emptiness* is a translation of a Buddhist concept that basically identifies all of the typical things we give labels to, form opinions about, and have attachments to, are basically abstractions. This is not to deny the reality of an objective universe, but rather to say things aren't what they seem. As naturalists, we realize that the choice to place a label on some particular temporary arrangement of atoms is a convenience of our own choosing, according to a brain that was evolved to do so. The implications of this are profound and when we internalize them, our perspective inevitably begins to shift.

\* \* \*

The real challenge is in the continued application of *practices* that help instill the above concepts into our natural way of being, thinking, and responding. One of the more basic practices is constantly reminding ourselves of these teachings and more deeply exploring them, through continued learning and journaling to ourselves about how they apply to situations in our everyday lives. Marcus Aurelius' *Meditations* is a good example of a book written to himself, with constant reminders of wisdom he found helpful.

Another crucial element is the cultivation of greater powers of attention, focus, and mindfulness; primarily achieved through a regular practice of meditation. Embedding the truths we know intellectually – into a level whereby they can overcome our less sophisticated but genetically hardwired impulses – requires a capacity of mindfulness as impulses arise in real life situations and it is not typical for a person to possess such mindfulness without efforts to improve it.

Engaging in various rituals, large and small, private and public, can help to generate experiences which produce 'ah-ha' moments that bring teachings to life and utilize multisensory inputs that intimately involve more aspects of our minds. Thus is the distinction between knowledge and deeper comprehension. Each individual will react more or less effectively to different styles and traditions, given their own personality, preferences, and past experiences. Exploring this can be part of the fun of a spiritual practice.

In our member educational archives, we have an essay on *Negative Visualization*, an advanced Stoic practice I wouldn't recommend for beginners, but which can be a powerful way to gauge our progress in non-attachment. But aside from this method, the best technique is *persistence*. Over time, one should begin to notice changes that contribute positively to life experience. If not, then guidance may be needed to find effective techniques, since all beings are different.

Here are some excellent external articles on non-attachment that can also be helpful:

http://zenhabits.net/zen-attachment/

http://www.wikihow.com/Practice-Non-Attachment

As is always the case with the written word, this article and the above are merely intellectual concepts. They are also a poor substitute for the more detailed traditions to which the above refers. But, hopefully, this may serve as a stimulant for further exploration!

# PART IV
# SPIRITUAL NATURALISM
# IN TOUGH TIMES

Part of the 'proof in the pudding' of a life practice and philosophy is where it leaves us in times of challenge, hardship, and tragedy. Whether we refer to the 'big' events, or the everyday little stresses of life, Spiritual Naturalists seek a practice that will be more than a series of platitudes; but actually help to move us mentally and emotionally into a place of healthy disposition and inner fortitude. Both traditional thought and modern understanding can illuminate this path, and the essays in this part cover a few high points of them. If you are having difficulties, reading such thoughts can help, but we should not forget the importance of the support and help from others as well.

# The Power of Gratitude

*Jennifer Hancock*

I am a Humanist, which, among other things means I view the world through a natural vs. supernatural lens. Part of my practice as a Humanist is to actively be grateful to the people in my life that make living such a joy.

I realize my time here on earth is limited, and in the grand scope of the universe, my actions are insignificant and will only have a temporary effect at best. But that doesn't deter me from being the best most ethical person I can be here and now.

Why? Because, even though my actions may not matter in the grand scheme of things after our planet has been reduced to its component elements when our sun explodes and dies, my actions most definitely matter here and now to the people I interact with. And yes, that is enough for me. My actions do matter to the people who are alive right now.

This is why being grateful is so important to me. It helps me to actively remember what is good in my life. It makes me feel vibrant and alive and connected whenever I think about how grateful I am to have people in my life I truly cherish and love and who matter to me. I can help make our collective lives easier or I can abandon my responsibilities to existential despair. Since I only have a limited time here, I'm not going to waste it worrying about my eventual death. I'm going to live life fully now.

Unfortunately, supernatural approaches to gratitude such as the *law of attraction*, claim that they will confer magical benefits. This assumes that gratitude is a means to attracting more stuff – but it isn't. That diminishes the power of gratitude and diverts our attention from the real reason to practice it.

What do you see as the benefits of being thankful?

# A Spiritual Naturalist Take on Tragedy

*DT Strain*

A commonly heard response of many religious and spiritual people during times of disaster is, "I'll pray for you". Spiritual Naturalists are a varied bunch and some may engage in some kinds of contemplative prayer. But in our case, we view ritual as a means to help focus our own thoughts and cultivate inner qualities. This means, absent of any confirmed evidence, we don't hold a belief that our prayers will affect the circumstances of others in a supernatural sense, either directly or through the favor of any other entities that listen to and answer prayer.

This begs the question, then, of what Spiritual Naturalists can and should do in response to the suffering of others, particularly in disasters and other tragedies such as the recent Hurricane Sandy which recently struck the Eastern portion of the U.S.

The most significant thing we can do, of course, is to *act*. This can include anything from traveling to the area to volunteer, to giving financially, to helping to spread the word, to simple words of support and encouragement to victims. All of these things really do affect the external circumstances for the better.

However, important though these actions are, action is the *symptom* of spiritual development. Our focus at the Society has been on spiritual practice, and that means ways of developing ourselves to be better people enjoying happier lives, *regardless of external circumstance*.

Fortunately, we do not have to be fully enlightened beings before we can act to help others! In fact, by jumping ahead and performing acts of compassion, this can have an inverse effect to help develop those inner qualities – which makes perfect sense in a universe where mind and body are all part of one, interconnected natural and causally-linked whole.

But, realistically, we also know that there are many cases tragedy strikes others and our ability to do much to help them is severely limited. There is far too much suffering in a world of billions of people to keep up with it all. For those who are on a spiritual path of practice, how then can we respond inwardly – in our practice – in the face of these realities? Certainly ignoring suffering cannot be a path to enlightenment, even when we cannot stop it externally.

## Acceptance

The first step is not to let the great suffering in the world defeat our spirit. If we are in the process of cultivating our compassion and extending our concern for all beings, this will result in great suffering unless we also balance that development with the cultivation of *wisdom*. By 'wisdom' I mean, in this case, the deep awareness and acceptance of the nature of impermanence. In this, we not only recognize the impermanent nature of the universe, but we actually come to see beauty in that whole tapestry of complex activity. Even if we don't like some instances of it which result in suffering and loss, we realize that none of the beautiful things we love would be possible without that ever-changing flow. Here, what is needed is the cultivation of a very subtle and challenging kind of *love without attachment* – a kind of love for others that is like enjoying the soothing waters flowing around us in a running river, but which does not try to stop the flow or desperately grab up all of the water.

All of us are unique and beautiful as we are. We all have our own height, our own looks, our own hair color, and yes, our own lifespan. We live in a certain place, and in a certain time. The time we exist in this pattern is our 'home' on the great timeline of the universe. Everything that happens, happens according to the *Logos* – that is, the same underlying rational order that brings about all things, and in which both death and birth are essential.

These are not the kind of thoughts that will relieve suffering for those undergoing it, who at that time simply need our love and support rather than our philosophy. But it is the kind of wisdom of living in accord with Nature, which we can cultivate in ourselves and – when tragedy strikes us or those with whom we empathize – will greatly fortify us.

## Cultivating Inner Motivation

A friend of my wife is a Catholic, and every time an ambulance passes, he makes the sign of the cross. My wife, also a naturalist, was telling me how there was something about this she found appealing. Especially since coming to an understanding of the practical inner effects of ritual, I too have come to admire this *kind* of practice. I am not sure what supernatural beliefs our friend may have about this activity, but I do believe that the practice of stopping for a moment and performing some kind of physical action when passing a car accident or some other kind of suffering, is a healthy activity.

Outward physical actions connect to our minds. They call upon us to momentarily direct our attention, and this builds mental habits – habits of concern and empathy. For this reason I often try to stop what I'm doing and take a few meditative breaths whenever an ambulance passes or I drive past an accident or learn of some other misfortune. I have even found a more immediate effect: whenever a traffic jam happens, I immediately try to be cognizant that a wreck may have occurred in which people may have been harmed. I try to think about the possible victims as their family might. This concern not only helps to cultivate empathy in the long term, but it also removes any kind of anger or frustration coming from my selfish ego about the inconvenience!

Of course, neither meditative breathing nor familial concern for victims affects them directly. But what it does do is affect *me*. It is a practice whereby, if more people were to engage, would create a more compassionate people and society, and that *will* affect others tremendously. This is the kind of root activity that is, perhaps, the most important kind of endeavor – even more than donating time of funds to any one tragedy – because it affects our world at the deepest level. Human minds are the gateways through which all good and evil enter the world. And, since we can only control our own choices, it is up to each person to engage in their own practice. As Gandhi said, "be the change you wish to see in the world".

When it comes to the victims of Hurricane Sandy, we naturalists, focused on the practical though we are, should not dismiss the importance of taking moments to reflect, focus, and use our imaginations to put ourselves in their place and the place of their families. Let yourself experience on their behalf, if only for a moment and if only to the degree we can. Use the moment to exercise your empathic muscles. This is how the 'duty' of helping others outwardly, becomes a deep *impulse* to do so over time.

## Share Your Empathy

Again, not to dismiss the importance of action, but with the importance of inner motivation also established, it becomes more obvious why we might consider sharing those sentiments with others. Not only can this encourage them to undertake their own practice of cultivating empathy, but it can be encouraging to victims.

Often I will tell people, "best wishes" when prayers and thoughts are sought or seem helpful. This doesn't mean I believe my 'wishes' affect their outcomes. But it is a way of letting them know that I am thinking about them and care what happens. This shouldn't take the place of action to help, but it *can* provide emotional support; much needed since positive attitude can greatly affect our behaviors, our determination, and our recovery. And, if you are the person in need, don't be so offended if someone tells you they are praying for you – whether you believe in prayer or not, the point is that someone cares about you, and that is a beautiful thing!

# Last Hum of the Cicada: Death for Naturalists

*B. T. Newberg*

Deep in the mountains of South Korea, a cicada hummed its last. Walking along the roadside, I saw a spider fall upon it with its venomous mandibles. Caught in the web, it had no escape, and cried:

*hum...*

*hum...*

*silence*

I stood equally silenced as the spider carried off the corpse into the splintered bark of a dead maple. It occurred to me that one day I too would sing the silence of my last song.

Death happens. It's a truth so true it's cliche. Yet, certain experiences have the power to make the truth visceral again. They blow away the dust that obscures it, and make it real again. They force us to confront mortality.

## How do naturalists make sense of death?

Since naturalists avoid supernatural concepts, there is little room for an immortal "soul" that somehow survives death. In the wake of this, there seem to be three principle ways of coming to terms with death.

1. death makes life meaningful

2. we live on through our effects on the world: memories, descendents, and influences we leave behind

3. we live on through that part of us which *is* immortal: the physical constituents of our bodies that disassemble and reassemble into myriad new forms tumbling throughout the Cosmos

## Death makes life meaningful

Brendan Myers writes:

> *Not death, but* immortality, *confers absurdity and meaningless. There is nothing an immortal could do, or build, or achieve, that would outlast him.*

In a somewhat similar vein, a New Scientist article published just last week ("Death: Why we should be grateful for it") maintains that much of civilization's accomplishments have been motivated by an awareness of our mortality.

The first principle may also underlie the Epicurean view of death, which sees the death event as a non-experience (something we anticipate but never actually experience, since we no longer have living bodies with which to experience it), and focuses instead on leading a worthwhile existence while yet alive.

## We live on through effects on the world

Myers places still more emphasis on the second principle, advocating living a life whose story is worthy of being told (whether or not it is actually told). He calls this goal *apotheosis*:

> *...you can be responsible for living in such a way that others* ought *to uphold your life as a model of excellence which future generations can learn from, and perhaps emulate.*

By leaving behind a legacy, be it children, a novel, or the enhanced lives of those known in life, we live on through our effects on the world.

# Immortality as part of the Cosmos

The third principle identifies with the matter of the body, which decomposes and recomposes into myriad new forms.

This was involved in the teachings of some Stoics that upon death our bodies dissolve into the elements and thus rejoin the cosmic *logos*.

A similar, if updated, view is exalted in Oscar Wilde's poem *Panthea*:

> *So when men bury us beneath the yew*
> *Thy crimson-stained mouth a rose will be,*
> *And thy soft eyes lush bluebells dimmed with dew,*
> *And when the white narcissus wantonly*
> *Kisses the wind its playmate some faint joy*
> *Will thrill our dust, and we will be again fond maid and*
> *boy.*

The same principle would also seem to underlie the meaning of death as part of the circle of life, as expressed in Disney's *The Lion King*:

> **Mufasa**: *"Everything you see exists together in a delicate balance. As king, you need to understand that balance and respect all the creatures, from the crawling ant to the leaping antelope."*
>
> **Young Simba**: *"But, Dad, don't we eat the antelope?"*
>
> **Mufasa**: *"Yes, Simba, but let me explain. When we die, our bodies become the grass, and the antelope eat the grass. And so we are all connected in the great Circle of Life."*

## Beyond the individual

What people fear most about death is probably the cessation of the sense of "me." Notably, all three principles cease to dwell exclusively upon the continuation of this "me" in linear time, and reach toward something that transcends the individual personality.

# When Love Seems Absent

*DT Strain*

We all face times when it seems there is little genuine love in the world. Perhaps we've been seeing a lot of depressing things in the news, or perhaps it's more personal. Maybe it's been a long time since people close to us have shown any love to us. Maybe it's a general feeling regarding people we don't even know, but interact with day to day – people in stores, employees at businesses we patronize, neighbors, fellow drivers, etc. Whatever the source or the cause, it can be discouraging when we think of how the world could be – when we think about how we know human beings *could* be toward one another – and then face striking contrasts to that over time or in a single significant incident.

Responses to this can range from anger to melancholy. We might 'toughen up' our outer shell in response; becoming more like the worst we've been noticing. Or, we might simply resign ourselves into a quiet depression and withdraw from interactions; looking down as we pass others, being abrupt, and so on.

Here, we've found ourselves in a dark corner of the world. There seems to be no love present here. But there is another way to handle times like these.

We might feel we are like batteries, charged by love, and who need to exchange that supply with others. So, in times like these, we feel drained of our charge. We look for, and yearn for, others to come along and recharge us. We wonder how much longer we can hold out.

But this view of human beings and love is a little off base. We are not so much like batteries, which store a charge, than we are like power *sources*. All goodness and love enters the world through beings that love. If we feel drained and in need of a charge, it may be that we have forgotten a power that we possess.

Or, maybe we knew we had this power, but we are thinking that our ability to love isn't the issue because that would be an outgoing commodity instead of an incoming one. But this too is forgetting the nature of love and of loving.

I would recommend that, whenever we feel we are in a dark place, that we consider this a sign that we've been tagged by the cosmos – we're "it". Or, if you prefer, we are up to bat. When it seems we have entered a time or place without love or compassion, this means it is our turn to be the source of love for that time and place. I think we would find the results well worth it.

The trick is to make sure that it's real love. Real love is selfless and not based on reciprocity. If we take on only the first part of this, and go out doing a bunch of nice things for people, we might end up worse than we were after seeing them fail to appreciate our actions or return the love. Some people get the idea that the reason we love when we need love is because others will return it (or be more likely to) and we will therefore benefit. When this doesn't happen, they imagine their efforts to get a 'love exchange' going have failed, and more sadness and feelings of futility ensue. Even in cases where love is returned, this is only an exchange of diminishing returns, and inherently unstable as a source of happiness in the long-term.

The truth is that love and compassion doesn't work that way. Rather, it is the *giving* of compassion *itself* which can be the source of our happiness, if we can recognize it and appreciate it as such. As an example, consider making a small animal in a cage happy with food, who may not realize you as its source. Or, consider an ideal mother who is made happier by caring for an infant who, by nature, cannot yet fully appreciate her actions. She doesn't have to wait several years to get a return on her investment. She is happier because she truly loves the infant. Likewise, we can cultivate a true, selfless love for others, and not see them as a resource – a place from which to get love – but an opportunity to practice a love of our own. When we are able to cultivate that kind of empathy and compassion, then in our efforts to gain happiness from giving love we cannot fail. We have been made happier through our acts alone – they are not dependent upon the responses of the object of our love.

As just one example, Dr. Emma Seppala has written an article in *Psychology Today*: "The Best Kept Secret to Happiness: Compassion". There she provides several research projects which have shown how acts of compassion stimulate the same pleasure centers as when we are the recipients, and the happiness can even be greater. She also describes a host of other benefits beyond mere happiness.

So, when things seem darkest, remember that *you* can be a source of love. This, in fact, is how humanity can illuminate all the dark corners – by each of us acting as the light when no others are. Every day is another opportunity to be compassionate when least expected!

# PART V
# APPLIED ISSUES

Spiritual Naturalism, as presented in this book and by the Spiritual Naturalist Society, is primarily an inward journey. Taking to heart Gandhi's recommendation to be the change we seek in the world, spirituality begins with the person in the mirror. But we are, of course, beings that share our world with others, and in this it is undeniable that our spirituality will affect our take on many larger issues. This part features essays that relate to such issues as sustainability, religious freedom, theism, marriage, and even broader issues such as death as a concept and finding wisdom. Yet, unlike many naturalist writings on these issues, we approach them from a distinctly personal angle.

# Religious Freedom from the Inside Out

*Sigfried Gold*

We generally think of religious freedom in terms of coercion by others, political or social imposition of certain religious or irreligious beliefs and practices on people who would choose to believe and practice differently. That's not what I'm talking about here. My concern is with the internal freedom people feel to practice and believe as they are drawn to do and the freedom they offer to others who might believe differently. The two are linked. I wonder if people who are highly critical of others' beliefs can themselves be deeply free to practice and believe in the ways that might work best for them.

We don't invent our own beliefs and practices from scratch. We take them, to one degree or another, from existing traditions. But no one simply practices and believes according to some fixed tradition — we discover traditions, interpret them, give them meaning for ourselves. As much as we may try to adhere to a fixed tradition, we end up mixing in bits we have made up ourselves or have taken from other sources.

The process of elaborating and living our own beliefs and practices is fluid, but it is liable to get blocked up. Aware of it or not, we experience certain restrictions in our ability to take in an external beliefs; or, having taken in an external belief, we get stuck in it, closed off from the possibility of changing it or adding to it in ways that might suit us.

Internal religious freedom involves two contradictory motions:

1. Freedom to believe deeply and completely, to accept received wisdom, an existing tradition, in all its profundity, opening ourselves to all its implications, allowing it to seep into every corner of our being and let us see ourselves and the world anew.

2. Freedom to honor and play with other beliefs and traditions; to hold our own beliefs without denigrating others' beliefs, without closing ourselves to others' beliefs; retaining curiosity about others' beliefs and exploring with an open mind where those beliefs accord with our own and where they do not; maintaining a willingness to question our own beliefs and adapt them to what we learn and resonate with when we expose ourselves to the beliefs of others.

Those who struggle on behalf of the usual idea of religious freedom, freedom from coercion, are to be applauded and supported in every way. The internal religious freedom described here is impossible without a foundation of basic religious freedom in the political sphere. At the same time, as long as some people hold to beliefs in a rigid way, insisting on their superiority to other beliefs we all live in danger of those people gaining political power and imposing their beliefs upon us. Freedom from coercion by others will only be secure when the norm is freedom from internal coercion and from condemnation of others' beliefs. Freedom of belief requires intelligence and sophistication. It is not easy to believe something passionately and also to believe that those who hold contrary views are also right. To people without considerable philosophical sophistication this sounds completely illogical, impossible, or steeped in vacuous relativism. But it is possible and desirable to embrace contrary beliefs in the dialectical way I'm suggesting. I do not myself have the skills to explain clearly how to do this to those who don't already know, but others do — maybe they will help.

# Do Spiritual Naturalists Believe in God?

*B. T. Newberg*

That depends on what you mean by God. Do you believe in divinity consistent with the latest findings in modern science, free of superstition and supernaturalism? Or do you prefer to leave "God" out of the picture, but still lead a spiritual life close to nature? If either is true, chances are Spiritual Naturalism agrees with you.

This perspective, also called Religious Naturalism, embraces the natural universe as revealed by modern science, while cultivating an attitude of awe and reverence toward nature. Supernatural interpretations of God or gods are left behind, in favor of a general reverence toward our breathtaking universe.

From the chrysalis of the butterfly to the destructive power of the black hole, the universe is awesome in grandeur. Some Spiritual Naturalists feel such awe in beholding its beauty, they can find no more appropriate word to call it than "God." Others forego theological language, but are just as moved, and partake in the same experience of the mysterium tremendum described by Rudolf Otto as the characteristic religious feeling.

There are many today in traditional religions as well as outside them who take a naturalistic view. For example, among Christian theologians, Paul Tillich and Bishop Spong both espouse a view of God that is essentially naturalistic. Jewish naturalists include Mordecai Kaplan and Sherwin Wine. Buddhism finds many naturalists, Stephen Batchelor and the Thai monk Buddhadasa being just a few. Taoism has long espoused a philosophy that is basically naturalistic, based on the Tao Te Ching and the writings of Shuang-zi. Contemporary Paganism counts many naturalists in its fold, with some discussing the idea explicitly in the Yahoo group Naturalistic Paganism and on the community blog Humanistic Paganism.

Outside traditional religions, there are also those by-passing God-talk altogether to speak directly of awe for nature. A Google search for "Religious Naturalism", "Spiritual Naturalism", or "Spiritual Humanism" reveals a plethora of sites devoted to precisely that. There are also many authors bringing this idea to life, such as Ursula Goodenough, Chet Raymo, Loyal Rue, Jerome Stone, Michael Hogue, and Donald Crosby.

If you are looking for a transcendent God that stands outside the world and intervenes though miracles, you probably aren't going to be happy as a Spiritual Naturalist. But if what you seek is a God immanent in the world, a God you can see and touch and feel, a God that doesn't demand you believe strange things but rather empowers you to discover the world for yourself, then Spiritual Naturalism may be what you've been looking for.

# Do You Believe in Love?

*DT Strain*

In studying ancient philosophy (the very thoughts that shaped the course of later ideas, culture, and history to come) it is impossible to really understand what you read without setting aside the modern day connotations of the words used. Many of the words like 'spirit', 'gods', 'soul', have been Christianized and taken on meanings that are subtly but significantly different. Instead, to get inside the minds and perspectives of early thinkers you must do as one little green Jedi master suggested, *"unlearn what you have learned"*. When we do this, a fascinating picture of how some ancient people conceived the universe begins to emerge – one that is perhaps far more compatible with our modern scientific and naturalistic understanding than is often appreciated.

I find John 4:8 highly interesting, "Whoever does not love does not know God, because God is love." I've looked at 18 different translations of this verse, and though the first portion is translated slightly different in all of them, they *all* phrase it exactly as "God **IS** love" – not "God is lov*ing*", "God is *the source of* love", "God love*s*", and so on.

The 18th Century cleric and theologian John Wesley noted that God is often called holy, righteous, and wise in the Bible, but he isn't called "holiness", "righteousness", or "wisdom" in the abstract, as he is here with Love. The Jamiseson-Fausset-Brown biblical commentary says of this verse, "God is love – There is no Greek article to love, but to God; therefore we cannot translate, Love is God. God is fundamentally and essentially LOVE; not merely is loving…"

So then, looking at the original Greek, the word used was ἀγάπη or "agapē". This sets it apart from Philia (brotherly friendship love) and Eros (romantic love). Agapē referred to a response to promote well being even when the other has done ill. Thus, it is sometimes translated as "charity". This indicates an intention to refer to a kind of 'motherly' love that is unconditional; that is not dependent upon circumstances or the actions of the recipient ('charity' being the broader concept of giving something you don't 'owe' to the person due to surrounding events or conditions). Agapē is the kind of selfless universal loving-kindness ("Metta") that Buddhists, for example, also seek to cultivate.

**This is what the book of John says God IS – not what God does, or a separate quality that God possesses. A=B and B=A, the two are synonymous according to John.**

This makes more sense when you consider some of the ancient Greek philosophy that greatly influenced Christianity from its earliest incarnations. The Stoics' concept of Zeus was somewhat illusive as far as his/its personal vs. impersonal nature. The Stoics also used the concept of the *Logos*, which originated as a philosophic concept from Heraclitus around the 5th Century BCE.

By Heraclitus' use, the Logos was the underlying rational principle or order by which the universe operated. It also meant "word", as in 'description' or perhaps 'logic'. Later Stoics would consider the Logos to be the divine animating principle pervading the universe; some prominent Stoics' having more of a personal interpretation than others. Today we might consider Logos in these senses as something like 'the laws of physics' or the logic of how nature functions – though with a much more sacred tone. In my own spirituality, I often refer to the Logos, which I find a more effective phrase than speaking of the laws of physics (Society members can read more about the use of *Sacred Tongue* in our member archives). The self-described atheist Albert Einstein comes close to this approach by referring to the subject of his work as *seeking to know the mind of God*. Nevertheless, in both Einstein's case and Heraclitus' the terms seem quite impersonal.

The philosopher Philo would adopt the *Logos* term into Jewish philosophy\*. By the time of the Gospel of John (late 1st Century CE), *Logos* is defined as divine and: *that through which all things are made* (the Word of God). John 1:1 doesn't merely refer to God speaking words, but says "...and the Word (Logos) **was** God". This would seem to indicate an impersonal description of God as the laws of nature. However personal or impersonal Logos has become by this time, it becomes fully personal when Jesus is described in the book of John as the Logos incarnate (the Word made Flesh).

This is not the only example of something that would seem personal, but which the Greeks would use in a broader impersonal sense. "Eros" is commonly described as romantic or sexual love. But philosophically the term was used as a universal law of attraction. That is, **all** attraction that occurred in nature, be it between atoms or between lovers, were manifestations of the general principle of attraction (Eros). This illuminates just how *naturalistic* the ancient Greeks were in conception, even if the details of their exact theories have been refined or replaced since. When we really conceive of all of Nature as One interconnected whole operating by the same laws – including the workings of our minds – then things change. The logic of referring to general concepts that cross the boundary between things with and without human agency begins to make more sense. In integrating the implications of complex systems theory into my own spirituality, I have found such generalized concepts a helpful tool.

It would be no wonder, then, if Agape – like Eros – was also a kind of general natural force. If God **is** the Logos (natural law), and God **is** Agape (universal love), then both of these kinds of statements could be seen as descriptions of the kinds of natural forces or principles which the writers of the Bible may have been associating with the term "God". The more one looks into the lineage of these terms from ancient Greek to early Christianity, the more unoriginal 17th Century Baruch Spinoza's impersonal natural God sounds\*\*.

Early thinkers thought of God as 'the underlying rational order' – the laws of Nature. If love was also described as the principle of the binding of things to one another, this indicates interconnectedness and interdependence. In the 20th Century, Christian philosopher and monk Thomas Merton described Compassion as the "keen awareness of the interdependence of all things". Thus is the bridge between how God can be both physics and love. Spiritual Naturalists will vary on whether they find use of the G-word helpful; some of our members use it and others do not. But this more naturalistic and impersonal interpretation of God is not a new convention. We have good reason to think, in many cases, this may have been the original or earliest philosophic thought of what was meant when the word 'God' was used – and that should be interesting to anyone practicing a naturalistic spirituality.

*Many thanks to Dr. Marian Hillar, Religious History professor at Texas Southern University, for reviewing a draft of this article for historic and academic accuracy.*

*\* Dr. Marian Hillar has contributed papers on Philo's use of 'Logos', available in our member archives.*

*\*\*In fairness to Spinoza, his own take was more appropriately claimed to be a proper interpretation of original concepts, rather than intended to be 'original'.*

# Managers of Human Nature:
# A Job Description for Spiritual Naturalists

*B. T. Newberg*

Job descriptions help us know that we're doing what we're supposed to be doing. So what's the JD for SN?

## Help wanted: Manager of human nature

"The measure of a religious orientation," says Loyal Rue in his book *Religion Is Not About God*, "is not whether it gives an accurate account of divine reality, but whether it effectively manages human nature."

That effectively sums up what SN is all about: managing our human nature. That may not sound very lofty, but it's true. When it comes down to it, we are managers of our own natures.

We manage our responses to our environment, to each other, and to ourselves. In so doing, we cultivate an amazing multiplicity of experiences, from the serenity of meditation to the joy of human bonding and the wonder of beholding the stars in the night sky.

## Why manage human nature?

Why do we need to manage our natures at all? Hmm... well, let's just say being human can be messy. We don't find ourselves perfectly humming machines where all is accomplished flawlessly and without effort.

No, we find ourselves a bundle of impulses, full of conflicting desires and uncertainties. I want this cookie and that sexy piece of meat over there; I want to be loved, to become a respected member of society, and to feel at home in this universe. These goals may pull me in different directions, and the most efficient way to achieve them is by no means clear.

So, managing human nature is necessary as a basic matter of fact. It's natural, in fact. We all do it to some degree; we simply couldn't carry on without doing so. Managing human nature is itself part of human nature.

Like many abilities that come naturally to us, such as maintaining our health or courting a mate, managing human nature is a job that can be done better or worse. Instinct and socialization (which may include religion for some people) give us basic management skills. At the same time, we can always strive to improve beyond these basics. Adopting a personal path of growth is one way to continue learning to manage one's nature better and better throughout life.

SN is a path of human nature management that gives special priority to naturalistic understandings of how the universe works. In this way, we cultivate human fulfillment, while at the same time maintaining an accurate and up-to-date picture of the universe.

## To what end(s) do we manage?

At the most general level, Rue finds that humans have two basic ends or *teloi* that explain why we need to manage our natures. First, we want fulfilling lives full of meaningful experiences. This he calls the telos of *personal wholeness.* Second, we need a functioning society enabling us to pursue those experiences. This is the telos of *social coherence.*

These individual and collective interests often pull in different directions. Thus, in order to achieve these "twin teloi", we must learn to manage our human natures. And the better we manage them, the better we achieve these ends. It's as simple as that.

There is a third possible *telos* to consider: living sustainably within our environment. We can't have either personal wholeness or social coherence if the land cannot support us. This third end is implied in Rue's work, and Michael Dowd makes it explicit by adding *ecological integrity* to the other two.

218

Religions, when they function correctly, help us achieve these ends. They structure our thoughts, feelings, and behaviors in such a way that we gravitate in the right direction. In Rue's words, "It is about manipulating our brains so that we might think, feel, and act in ways that are good for us, both individually and collectively."

## Managers, not bosses

At this point, let's clear up some potential misconceptions: we are not bosses of human nature. We can't be, because we are not in full control of ourselves, if "we" means our conscious, rational, ego-directed selves. If we could just will ourselves to behave as we'd like, we'd have no need of spirituality.

Nor are we the rational charioteer reigning in unruly beasts, as Plato would have it. Often our most brilliant ideas seem to "come to us" as if from beyond. The conscious, deliberative self is neither the chief executive nor the brains of the operation. At best we are middle management (one view demotes us all the way to press secretary).

Rivers and forests are managed. Resources are managed. So too do we manage our own natures.

These are crucial caveats because a fundamental aspect of spirituality may well be that it connects us to something greater – the environment, society, and the vast unconscious.

So let's be clear: SN is not about being the boss or the brains; it's about managing how we relate to what ultimately transcends us.

## Adaptive and maladaptive management

Not all religions manage human nature well. Some become maladaptive. Their pictures of how the universe works may be out-of-date, leading to a crisis of *intellectual plausibility* (in Rue's terms). Or their ethics may no longer fit current social or ecological conditions, leading to a crisis of *moral relevance*.

Many of today's world religions suffer from both of these maladaptive traits.

SN attempts to right the course of our religious evolution. By embracing the naturalism of modern science, and foreswearing supernatural explanations, it addresses the issue of plausibility. By fostering deep affective bonds with each other, our environment, and ourselves, it addresses the issue of relevance.

Such affective bonds rearrange priorities, and ultimately motivate changes in behavior conducive to personal wholeness, social coherence, and ecological integrity. In this way, SN steers a course between supernaturalistic inaccuracy and nihilistic irresponsibility.

## Performance reviews

So now that we have this cushy managerial position, it's time to relax and kick our feet up on the desk, right? Not quite.

As managers, we must produce results. On a very simple level, we can give ourselves a "performance review" now and then by simply observing what we do on our paths and how it makes us feel in response – both in the short term and in the long term. What's working well, and what leaves room for improvement?

On a more complex level, as a community we can constantly work toward ever-more rigorous tests. As a path that values scientific investigation, it only makes sense that we should test our methods for efficiency. If we claim cultivating a relationship with mythology can enrich our lives, for example, we ought to develop ways to verify that hypothesis. That takes time and loads of effort, but it will be worth it if we can pull it off.

Now that we've got a job description, we can rate how well we're doing. What we're supposed to be doing as Spiritual Naturalists is managing our human natures toward personal wholeness, social coherence, and ecological integrity. So, as a final note, let's ask:

Are we making progress toward that goal? How well our we doing? How can we do better?

# What "Death is a Part of Life" Means

*DT Strain*

Often in reading philosophy and wisdom teachings, one has a kind of repeating experience. We see many common phrases or statements by wise teachers. Perhaps we see the same or similar notions from a variety of traditions. And, the first time we see them, we may think we understand them; agreeing or disagreeing. Then we go off, read and learn more, experience life a little more, and before long we come upon the statement again. Only then do we realize that some of the words in it didn't mean what we thought they did, and that the teaching was more profound than we thought. A little more life experience happens and we may have the experience yet again with that teaching, and this may go on an unknown number of times. Here we see a world of complexity, subtlety, and nuance behind the teaching, and we are never really sure if we've fully understood it. As our confidence in our understanding diminishes, our wisdom yet improves and our appreciation for the teaching grows.

One thing we often hear is that "death is a part of life". On the surface, this seems to be a rather obvious statement. When we look at life as a series of events, it quite plainly includes being born, a bunch of stuff happening, and then – inevitably – our death. So, death is a part of life, learning to walk is a part of life, getting a job is a part of life, and so on. As a comfort for the grieving, this seems about as effective as telling someone to "get over it" or "walk it off". We might look at this a little more deeply, and see that learning to accept death is a part of a happier life. But even this does not fully unpack the meaning of this teaching.

Most people look at life and death as opposites. But it seems this isn't exactly right. Rather, the opposite of life is *lifelessness*. Both of these are conditions or states. But death is an event. It is one half of a cyclical process – the other being birth. And, it is this cyclical process of birth and death that we call *life*. So, quite literally, death is a part of the process we call life, just as is birth. To imagine death the opposite of life would be as nonsensical as to imagine birth the opposite of life.

This works not just in terms of human or animal life, but life everywhere, in all systems, and on all scales. Even as I sit here, writing this, I cannot do so without death. My typing hands are living tissue made up of cells that are continually dying and being replaced by the birth of new cells. This is only possible because of the sustenance I consumed. Even vegetarians require the death of the organic materials they ingest in order to live. The similarity of these things to the death of our loved ones and ourselves is not merely analogy. They happen for the same reasons and because of the same universal process of all life.

But now consider what we really mean by 'birth' and what we really mean by 'death'? What is really happening? Let us begin by considering the *Sloan Great Wall*...

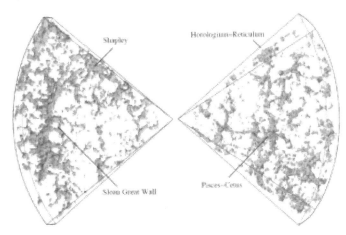

Where are the edges of this thing?

At the time I first learned of it, the Sloan Great Wall was considered to be the "largest object in the universe"*. It is a giant wall of galaxies 1.38 billion light-years in length. My first thought on reading this was that the statement was a cheat! This "wall" wasn't an object at all – it was simply a bunch of galaxies that happened to line up into something we can draw an imaginary line around and give a name to. Sure, they influence one another gravitationally, but to consider them an object? And, what of the surrounding galaxies? They must surely influence the galaxies of the SGW gravitationally, but they arbitrarily don't get to be a part of this 'object'? Earth and Mars influence one another. Can I just draw an imaginary line around the two and give the group a name and now it's an object? It all seemed very fishy to me. It seemed that this name said more about the brains of those who imagined it than about some objective reality in the universe – about as 'real' as the constellations we draw heroic figures over in our night sky.

But if the Sloan Great Wall wasn't the largest object, then what was? Isn't a galaxy just a collection of star systems? And, a star system seems pretty close to my example of drawing a line around Earth and Mars. The recent hubbub about whether Pluto was a planet was more of a philosophical debate than about any of the objective data.

And so it is with all of existence. Our tiny size compared to the Sloan Great Wall might make its true nature more obvious, but in truth *all objects in our world are of this same nature.* Everything you've ever anticipated getting your hands on, every food you've ever desired, every person you've ever loved, and you yourself are different conglomerations of particles. And these globs of particles are surrounded by the same kinds of particles, which move into and out of the named glob. That glob further reaches out and manipulates other globs in a manner not unlike it manipulates its own parts. The more we think about this, the more arbitrary that borderline at the edge of each of these forms we've given a label to seem – just like drawing a large crab or a hunter around a group of stars in the night sky.

And now consider that none of these structures are permanent. They have all come into their current form for a short time, and as their parts continue moving by natural law, will eventually lose their form, much like seeing Mickey Mouse in the shape of a cloud. You could almost say these forms are somewhat illusory – a helpful habit our brains evolved.

*And this is the nature of birth and death.*

As we can see, 'birth' is a much broader concept of the 'coming into being' of various forms, and 'death' is the movement of aggregates to the point where we no longer recognize or label a form (or perhaps now label other forms).

Thus, 'death' includes the dissolution of, not only things we call life forms, but storms, jobs, relationships, planets, nations, and so on. 'Birth' is the coming into being of all of these forms and more, including baby humans. So, in a sense, if these forms are illusory then it begins to look like death (and birth) are illusory. They say more about when our brains identify something than they say about the objective nature of it.

The Buddhists call this realization 'emptiness'. Understanding death in its broadest sense makes us realize how integral all kinds of loss really are to the entire magnificent processes in the universe that make *everything* possible.

Understanding that our ego, our very self, is also illusory – and the implications of that – is a whole other matter!

# Wisdom Hides in Plain Sight

*Thomas Schenk*

I suggest that all the wisdom humans are likely to obtain has already been discovered. Further, I suggest that all of this wisdom can be stated in a handful of aphorisms or proverbs and that most of us are aware of these. If these two propositions are correct, then the problem of wisdom is very different from the problems of science or scholarship where one anticipates the next discovery will bring to light something new. Rather, the problem of wisdom is to understand what is in front of us in plain sight.

For example, "if life gives you lemons, make lemonade" is about as stale and trite as it comes. Yet for all that, some of the most basic aspects of wisdom resides there: i.e. we need not be passive to our fate; we have the ability to reinterpret our existence; we have the power to turn negatives into positives; we have inner resources and the use of these resources can make all the difference between living a sour life or a sweet life.

Another: "ever to admit you are bored means you lack inner resources" — so a mother chides her child in a John Berryman poem. "Inner resources," a term I used above, is seldom heard anymore. When children are bored today, usually they are directed to some product (often with a rectangular screen) or driven somewhere — they are directed to external resources. A book filled with wise sayings is an external resource. The ability to uncover the wisdom that hides in these sayings is an internal resource. A three acre wood is an external resource; the ability to find the beauty and wonder that resides there is an inner resource. One who can find the wisdom residing in a common book and the beauty residing in a three acre wood, will seldom be bored.

Another: "if you don't know where you're going, any road will get you there." The ability to set a goal, develop a strategy for achieving it, and persisting unto success is a particularly human ability: *intentionality*; it is key to both practical and spiritual wisdom. As a practical example, organizations create mission statements to remind them of what they seek to achieve (unfortunately, they often veer anyway). As a spiritual example, "living intentionally" suggests a path toward a richer, more engaging life, and yet also suggests the destination — those who live intentionally are those most likely to find the wisdom and beauty residing in plain sight.

Another: "persistence in a righteous course brings reward." This saying, which appears frequently in the Chinese classic *I Ching*, reminds us of the power of intentionality, as listed above. But it also asks us to consider how much we really care. That for which we deeply care is that toward which we will steadfastly persist. The *I Ching* suggests we ponder carefully how much we really care before we start a venture. To be willing to ponder carefully already requires that we care deeply about the quality of our life and the quality of the lives around us. Caring is at the foundation of inner resources and of wisdom.

Another: "the best things in life are free." Many think this aphorism is merely folly parading as wisdom. To the person who is ever bored, who sees nothing but brush and weeds in the three acre wood, it likely will seem so.

Finally, from Swami Costanza, "always end on a high note!"

# Marriage and Spirituality

*DT Strain*

As a Humanist minister, I have had the honor of conducting the wedding services for many couples. As we work together on the wording of the service and their vows, it calls upon both the couple and myself to think about the meaning of marriage. In this article, I will share some thoughts on the potential benefits of marriage to one's spiritual practice. First, it is important to talk about the commitment integral to marriage, because this plays a role in its effect on our spiritual progress.

## Commitment

It comes as no surprise to my readers nor friends that I am socially liberal, and that extends to relationships. But unlike some social liberals, when it comes to marriage I believe in the importance of lifetime commitments. That isn't to say that there can't be justifiable reasons for divorce. But it does mean a rejection of approaches to marriage that, from the outset, are merely agreements to stick together only so long as "love endures" or, in less eloquent language, until you get sick and tired of one another, or simply feel like a change. There is nothing wrong with that, or any, arrangement between consenting adults so long as both understand one another. But this is called a boyfriend or girlfriend. In these cases, I suggest simply remaining as such.

While the moral obligation to be honest and supportive to a boyfriend or girlfriend is the same as any serious relationship, the distinguishing characteristic of marriage is the *temporal* element – that is, the sacred pledge to be there for one another into the future, in bad times and good. For those who have children, this kind of commitment is what is needed to have mothers, fathers, aunts, uncles, cousins, and all of the stability and support structure most healthy to a child's upbringing. The structure of a family can vary – we aren't stuck with a typical hetero-mono-nuclear model. But what's important are those dutiful bonds of loving commitment. Even for those who choose not to have children, many feel it is still important to have someone in your life to depend upon, to share life's experience with, and who you know will not abandon you when times are tough. The core of the concept is that when we leave our childhood home we leave a supportive family structure, and though we may remain close to that family always, marriage is how we form new families of equal bonds and support.

Of course, we are all free to live whatever kinds of lives we agree upon with others, but this is what I mean when *I* refer to *marriage* in this article. While any relationship offers opportunities to be more mindful, tolerant, communicative, and patient – it is long-term commitment that potentially has the following effects on a more specific spiritual practice.

## A Window into True Love

Most adults come to understand the difference between love and infatuation. What may be less obvious is that further stages of deeper love continue to reveal themselves when in a loving relationship with another after an extended time. We begin to learn the real differences between self-driven love and other-driven love. Given that tough times in relationships over time are inevitable, only a commitment to stay together through those times has the chance to continue for periods long enough for those deeper levels of love to manifest.

Since we are human, we may often mislead ourselves into thinking we can understand what it means to be human from the single example of our own experience. But in a long-term relationship that lasts years or decades, we continue to become more and more familiar with another human being. Even after 13 years, my wife and I continue to surprise one another and I'm told this happens well after 13 years. This makes sense since a person continues to evolve throughout life.

That growing familiarity over time results in an intimate knowledge of our partner 'from the inside'. Just as the discovery of alien life on other worlds would undoubtedly illuminate new concepts in biology as a general field, the intimate knowledge of another person illuminates what it means to be human in general terms. This is a far more profound string of experiences than I can justify with words.

The following is not a continuous effect, but there have been moments in which I see my wife and feel almost as if my subjective view has transported inside her; as if our understanding and perspectives were so intimately tied that I saw the world through her eyes and identified herself with myself. One gets the deep sense of what justice, right, wrong, beauty, humor, and meaning are to another mind. I could never have imagined what this experience was like without being a part of someone else for an extended time. Further, many times it happens in a manner that gets my attention, it has been in more profound ways than before.

The ancient Greeks are often recognized for having had many different words for 'love' which adeptly distinguish between affection, passion, friendship, parental love, and so on. However, the truth we come to find by seeing through another person's eyes is that love is even more varied and subtle than this. Over time, an intimate relationship can help us to learn about seemingly infinitely various kinds and degrees of love. When it comes to spiritual practice, progress is simply not possible without understanding the nature of love more deeply.

## Putting it to Practice

In terms of applied spiritual practice, one important project is that of escaping the ego. That is, seeing beyond our narrow singular point of view toward a broader view. Stoics propose expanding one's sense of self outward to include others. This expandable re-definable vision of the ego is consistent with the Buddhist realization of the 'self' as an illusory construction. In seeing through another's eyes, possible in a deep extended relationship, it is possible to get a first-hand experience of what it means to have one's ego – one's sense of first-person – displaced, expended, and jarred. This can be an important part of learning to expand it further to include all beings. I know the experience has aided in my own efforts along these lines.

Another effect of that kind of connection, is seeing the 'child within' in another person. We all have that innocence – that child we were – still within us. At times he or she comes out in the best sense. Glimpsing this provides a sense of intense affection. In this sense, we come to see the whole person, faults and all, from a sympathetic point of view. This is not too unlike how an ideal mother might see her own child; even the most flawed for which she will yet retain love.

This experience of intimate affection combined with ego-jarring perspectives form two important steps in achieving a more universal compassion for all beings. This is one way in which a long-term loving and committed relationship can be an invaluable aide in our practice and our spiritual journey of transformation.

## Spirituality for the Full Life

Given the incredible experiences of marriage and the remarkable help it has been to my practice, it seems especially odd to me when I think about religious leaders, in the East and West, who take vows of chastity. Regarding those who do this successfully, no one can doubt their commitment and dedication. When it comes to Buddhists monks for example, the absence of family obligations undoubtedly frees such people to pursue wisdom and practices to greater levels than is possible for many of us. These two facts suggest that our respect and attention to their input is warranted.

In the Christian bible, Paul only reluctantly accepts marriage merely as an alternative for those who aren't disciplined enough to be chaste. Even Socrates only jokingly advocates marriage, saying, "By all means marry. If you have a good wife you will be happy and if you have a bad one you will become a philosopher!"

But on how many important aspects of life are celibate spiritual leaders missing out? Given that spirituality should be practical and useful for real people living their lives out in the world, can they really be authoritative on these matters? More importantly, could the lack of deep long-term romantic relationships actually hinder deeper understanding of other spiritual concepts which, on the surface, may seem unrelated? These are important questions, and why I think the active participation of lay persons in guiding, educational, and organizational roles are crucial to a spiritual community.

In any event, if readers take anything from this, I hope it is to consider how their own relationships, rather than distractions or worse, can be opportunities for spiritual growth and development in even more profound ways than perhaps considered previously.

# PART VI
# NATURALIST APPROACHES TO
# SPECIFIC TRADITIONS

Spiritual Naturalism can be practiced in the general sense, used as a primary descriptor for a practitioner, but even in this case, it is wisely informed by a wide variety of traditions, practices, wisdom, religion, and knowledge. There are also practitioners that identify primarily with one or more of these specific traditions, but who have a purely naturalistic take. This part includes essays that describe naturalistic versions of these various traditions. These interpretations can be useful to members of these traditions, but they can also illuminate for the general naturalist how and why the wisdom of these traditions can still be applicable. In the Spiritual Naturalist Society, we encourage all of these forms of naturalistic spirituality, and provide avenues for a diverse community to share ideas and practices.

# Christianity Without God

*Arthur G. Broadhurst*

Regardless of their religious faith there is no serious doubt among contemporary historians that Jesus was a real person who lived in Palestine in the First Century. Historians agree that Jesus was an itinerant Jewish teacher who traveled and taught throughout Palestine gathering disciples around him through the force of his personality and the compelling nature of his message. There is general agreement that Jesus was perceived by the Roman occupiers of Palestine as a dangerous religious radical and a disturber of the peace, in consequence of which he was arrested by the local authorities and summarily executed by the Romans in a public crucifixion, the standard method used by the Romans to deal with political troublemakers.

There is considerable disagreement among historians about how much of the biblical record can be relied upon as history in the ordinary sense in which we understand history–as contemporaneously verifiable events–given the fact that a fairly long time passed from the days in which Jesus lived and taught in Palestine until the traditional stories about him and his teachings that were circulating among the early Christian communities began to be collected from the oral tradition and eventually acquired their present form as the canonical gospels. [To read about the process of collecting the stories see the work of the Jesus Seminar, an organization of leading biblical scholars.]

It is clear from the surviving historical record that something happened following the crucifixion of Jesus that led his followers to take up his message and teachings. When their leader was arrested and executed by the Roman authorities, Jesus' followers were discouraged, disappointed and frightened and they feared for their safety as they contemplated the fact that they too might be arrested and killed. They abandoned Jesus to his fate and ran. However, sometime after his arrest and crucifixion, the crushing sense of disappointment, frustration and defeat the disciples experienced at the death of their leader suddenly gave way in the face of what is called "the Easter Event."

That "something" that "happened" after the crucifixion is described in the Gospels in mythological terms as *Resurrection*. We have learned to demythologize these accounts so that we can understand and interpret their significance to us without resorting to the mythological language in which the early history was transmitted to us.

Once we get beyond the mythological language, it is clear that the disciples had a life-transforming experience that resulted in a re-ordering of their priorities toward a new way of thinking about what was seriously important in their lives and led to their commitment to carry on with Jesus' teachings.

They interpreted this life-transforming experience to mean that the spirit of Jesus did not die with him but was alive in them, challenging them to continue what he had started. For his early followers it was a life-transforming awareness that the spirit of Jesus was alive in them. They understood this to mean two things: they were to model their lives after his life and they were to carry on his teaching about the kingdom of God and what that implied for the people of the region.

Put another way, once we have worked our way through the mythological and theological baggage that has accumulated through the ages, we are left with a fundamentally important truth—those who had met this itinerant teacher and who heard his teaching were sufficiently captivated by his personality and engaged by his message that they were compelled to take up the cause for which he had been killed and to continue his teaching.

At its core, being a Christian today means exactly the same thing for us as it meant to his first disciples: consciously choosing to be an advocate of Jesus and his teachings. It involves what the medieval theologian Thomas A Kempis called *Imitatio Christi*, the imitation of Christ. It means to live as Jesus lived and to teach as he taught, to honor truth and show compassion, to stand with
238

the victims of this world against their oppressors, to stand with the weak and the powerless against the abusers and the comfortably powerful, and to maintain one's integrity no matter the cost. In short being a follower of Jesus meant then and now to be faithful to the spirit of Jesus and his teachings. That is both the meaning and the cost of Christian discipleship.

It is that timeless challenge that continues to captivate and motivate us. It is the challenge accepted by the Peace Corps volunteer, the builder of homes for Habitat for Humanity, the volunteer in the homeless shelters and prisons, the helper in the food kitchens and the driver for Meals on Wheels, those who bring joy and healing to a young child, and the Mother Theresas of the world. There is nothing in that challenge of commitment to the service of humanity that requires us to believe in any particular notion of a divine being or any religious dogma.

This challenge to Christian discipleship seems to have escaped the notice of much of the bureaucracy of contemporary Christianity, particularly the so-called "mainline Christian churches" that muddle along with a comfortable conformist politically-correct Christianity that challenges no beliefs, raises no issues and makes no demands serious enough to change one's life.

This is the fundamental issue over which I part company with those traditional Christians who take the position that being a Christian essentially means having the right theology, that is, believing a particular set of theological propositions. My argument with them is not so much with their particular beliefs or with their confusion between mythology and history, but rather with their premise that affirming a particular set of orthodox doctrinal beliefs rather than striving to emulate the life of Jesus is what essentially defines what it means to be a Christian.

Those who claim they are Christians should be measured against the ultimate test of Christian values – and that means comparing how their words and their actions hold up to the standard of Jesus' words and actions (so far as we can know what they are) rather than whether they hold correct theology. If their claim is to be understood as more than a claim to believe particular propositions about Jesus that may or may not be true and that cannot in any case be verified, their claim is subject to the litmus test of their lives, their decisions and their actions.

We've now come full circle on this issue of whether it is possible to be a Christian without a concept of God; and if so, what that Christianity would look like. We affirm again our premise, that being a Christian does not require a simultaneous belief in gods or theological propositions, in magic or superstition, and that the test for determining whether or not one is a Christian is a simple one: anyone who claims to be a follower of Jesus should be seen standing with the weak against the powerful and the rich, feeding the hungry, comforting the sick, bandaging the wounded, holding the hand of a child, standing with the oppressed against the oppressor. It means humility rather than arrogance and pride. It means becoming fully human.

This is the only view of Christianity that makes sense to me. It is a de-mythologized Christianity, a version without the necessity for god and freed from the theological and mystical baggage of the centuries preceding us, a Christianity that challenges us regardless of our view of god to model our lives after that of Jesus. Being a Christian is not any more complicated than that, but it is at least that.

# Evolutionary Christianity

*Michael Dowd*

These may be tumultuous times, but through it all we can detect ways in which faith traditions are maturing and thereby growing into greatness. Evolutionary versions of each religion— Evolutionary Christianity, Evolutionary Buddhism, Evolutionary Islam, Evolutionary Judaism, Evolutionary Hinduism, and more—are emerging. Why is this happening? Because adherents of each tradition have discovered the same thing: *Religious insights and perspectives freed from the narrowness of their time and place of origin are more comprehensive and grounded in measurable reality than anyone could have possibly dreamed before.* Evolution does not diminish religion; it expands its meaning and value globally.

Understandably, many devout religious believers have rejected evolution because the process has so often been depicted as random, meaningless, mechanistic, and Godless. The growing edge of evolutionary thinking today, both scientifically and theologically, points to a very different understanding of the Cosmos and a far more realistic understanding of God's activity. We encounter a Universe astonishingly well suited for life and our kind of consciousness. Scientists themselves are moving away from a mechanistic, or design, way of thinking and into an emergent, developmental worldview. Evolution from this perspective can be embraced and shared with others religiously.

In this essay I shall outline the key transformations occurring within my own tradition—evangelical Christianity.

## Flat-Earth Faith vs. Evolutionary Faith

On every continent, and within every religious tradition, "flat-earth" theologies are giving way to evolutionary forms of the same faith. By "flat-earth" I am not, of course, suggesting that adherents actually believe that the world is flat. Rather, the term applies to any and all perspectives in which interpretations of core religious doctrines have sailed through the centuries virtually unaffected by an expanding awareness of other peoples, other continents (indeed, other galaxies), and the depths of time.

Flat-earth theologies, thus, cling to ancient understandings that originated in times when people really did believe that the world was flat and that the Sun and the stars revolve around us. For example, flat-earth forms of Christianity today are those that still interpret *sin, salvation, the gospel, the kingdom of God, heaven, hell, the second coming of Christ,* and other core concepts in ways that pre-date the discoveries of Copernicus, Galileo, Newton, Darwin, and all succeeding generations of celebrated scientists.

Flat-earth forms of Christian faith are out of sync with the needs of Christian men and women and institutions today for the simple reason that they needlessly tether our core doctrines to the abstract and the otherworldly—and, hence, to the realm of the imagination. Accordingly, such doctrines have very little to say about how we are to understand and navigate life in *this world, here, and now.*

In contrast, evolutionary forms of Christianity cherish these same doctrines, yet engage each in far more realistic (REALized) ways. The very same spiritual insights are interpreted in light of our modern cosmological understandings—understandings which, thanks to the scientific endeavor, are based on empirical evidence and thus (for all practical purposes) are indisputably real. Thus REALized, Christian teachings offer powerful and practical guidance and support—and not just for Christians.

Here is my prediction: By the middle of the 21st century, Christians everywhere will understand God, our faith, and the nature of the gospel in evolutionary terms rather than flat-earth terms. And they will do so because nothing is lost—and ever so much is to be gained—by embracing both a God-honoring interpretation of cosmic history and an evolutionary view of God's self-revelation.

Those Christians who choose to follow this path will not reject biblical Christianity. To the contrary! Thanks to an evolutionary outlook, God becomes *undeniably real* and the gospel, *universally true*.

## Faith Benefits of Evolutionary Christianity

To my mind, there is *one major scientific advantage* and *eight theological advantages* that evolutionary Christianity has over traditional, biblical Christianity.

The scientific advantage is this: evolutionary faith squares with the facts—that is, it effortlessly fits with what has ongoingly been revealed by God/discovered by scientists about the nature of the Universe, Earth, life, and humanity.

Theologically, evolutionary Christianity offers these benefits:[1]

1. An undeniably real and universally venerable God

2. An experiential and essentially irrefutable view of doctrinal insights

3. A scientifically credible regard for scripture

4. Clearer guidance for living in faith and fulfillment in today's world

5. A faith-enhancing understanding of death that is congruent with modern science

6. An instinctual view of sin and a down-to-earth experience of salvation

7. Greater ease and success in teaching Christ-like, Christ-centered morality

8. A more realistically inspiring vision of the future

## The Nature of Divine Revelation

Many conservative Christians reject evolution. I commend them for their resistance. It compels those of us who do embrace evolution to find ever more inspiring ways of communicating our conviction. Religious believers can hardly be expected to embrace evolution if the only version they've been exposed to portrays the processes at work as merely competitive and pointless, even cruel, and thus Godless. Is it any wonder that many on the conservative side of the theological spectrum find such a view repulsive, and that many on the liberal side accept evolution begrudgingly?

Only when the evolutionary history of the Universe is articulated in a way that conservative religious believers feel in their bones is holy, and in a way that liberal believers are passionately proud of, will evolution be widely and wholeheartedly embraced. Fortunately, that time is now—not 2,000 years ago, not 200 years ago, and not even 20 years ago. Now is when we are awakening to the reality that God did not stop communicating truth vital to human well-being back when scripture was still recorded on animal skins and preserved for posterity in clay pots.

Two thousand years ago, it was widely believed that the world was flat and stationary, and that the entire Cosmos revolved around us. The biblical writers reasonably assumed that mountains were unchanging, that stars never died, and that God placed all creatures on Earth (or spoke them into existence) in finished form. How could they have thought otherwise? The idea of a spherical Earth turning on an axis and orbiting the Sun, or of Polaris as an immense bundle of hydrogen gas fusing into helium quadrillions of miles away, or of mountains rising and eroding as crustal plates shift, or of creatures morphing over time: all these would have seemed absurd to anyone living when the Bible was written. Had God inspired someone to write about such things then, the early church leaders would never have considered the document authoritative. They would have thought it bizarre and dangerously misleading, and would have ensured that any such proclamations were discredited and quickly forgotten.

Many Christians, Jews, and Muslims still regard the early history of the Hebrew people, as recorded in the Torah, to be the history of humanity as a whole. We now, however, know a great deal more about what was happening in the world 3,500 years ago—two centuries before Moses was born—thanks to the worldwide, cross-cultural, self-correcting enterprise of archeological and anthropological science (that is, through what God has been revealing over the last few hundred years through these disciplines).

Although none of this world history is mentioned in the Bible, no historian alive today would deny the following: Before Moses was born and before the story of Adam and Eve was written, King Tut III ruled the Egyptian empire's 18th Dynasty; southeast Asians were boating to nearby Pacific islands; Indo European charioteers were invading India; China, under the Shang Dynasty, entered the Bronze Age; and indigenous peoples occupied most of the Western Hemisphere.

Each of these cultures told sacred stories about how and why everything came into being, why they were special, what is important, and how to survive and thrive in the landscapes and cultures in which they lived. To interpret the early chapters of Genesis—or any of the world's creation narratives—as representing the entire history of the Universe, or to imagine them as rival rather than complementary views of a larger reality, is both to miss the symbolic nature of human language and, ironically, to trivialize these holy texts.

## Private and Public Revelation

We are at a turning point in human history. Catalyzing this transformation is our modern method by which we collectively access increasing knowledge about the nature of reality. New (and revised) truths no longer spring fully formed from the traditional founts of knowledge. Rather, they are hatched and challenged in the public arena of science. This is the realm of *public revelation.*

In contrast, by *private revelation* I am referring to claims about the nature of reality based only on personal experiences— some of which, of course, can be very compelling. Unfortunately, revelations enshrined in sacred texts occurred to people in the past and cannot be empirically verified today. Such claims cannot be proven or disproved because they are deeply subjective, one-person, one-time occurrences, obscured by the passage of time. Accordingly, private revelations must either be believed or not believed. When private revelations reside at the core of religious understandings, people are left with no choice but to believe or not. Thus, private revelation produces religious believers and unbelievers. Only public revelation can produce *religious knowers.*

For example: Is it true that the entire Universe was created in six literal days, as suggested in the first chapter of Genesis? Today millions of people believe so—and millions do not. The result personally: families sundered by theological differences. The result collectively: intense conflict over the teaching of science in America's public schools.

Is it, in fact, the case that devout Jews and Christians will burn forever in hell because they do not embrace as the Word of God the teachings of the prophet Mohammed, as recorded in the Qur'an? Hundreds of millions of Muslims believe this is so. And hundreds of millions of non-Muslims (as well as many liberal Muslims) believe not. The result personally: good people who come to harbor judgment and resentment against other good people, as well as the heartache and estrangement that happens when those "others" are kin. The result collectively: communities and nations are divided and at war.

Is it historically true that God intentionally, purposefully drowned billions of animals and millions of human beings in Noah's flood and instructed Moses to kill tens of millions of men, women, and innocent children, as the Bible literally reads? (e.g., Exodus 32:27–28; Deuteronomy 2:34, 3:4–5, 7:1–2; Joshua 11:12–15) Countless people believe that these stories reveal God's unchanging moral character. Countless others believe they do not. The personal result: millions who leave their religious traditions, unable to worship such a God. The collective result: warring nations, each convinced that God is on their side.

These are the conundrums that worldviews based on private revelation, embedded in unchangeable scripture, inescapably promote. And they are by their very nature unresolvable. That is, short of worldwide conversion to one belief system or worldwide expulsion of all such belief systems, the future of humanity will continue to be compromised by adversities born of conflicting beliefs—especially in a world in which weapons of mass destruction now come in small packages.

Is there, perhaps, another way?

## Facts as God's Native Tongue

Thanks to what is generally referred to as the scientific method, assisted by the wonders of modern technologies (themselves a gift of the scientific endeavor), *public revelation* emerges via a process whereby claims about the nature of reality based on measurable data are proposed, tested, and modified in light of evidence and concerted attempts to disprove such claims. Such a process typically results in a shared understanding that goes beyond belief to broadly shared knowledge that can be considered, for all practical purposes, factual. From this perspective, the history of humanity can be seen as a fascinating story of how God has progressively revealed the nature of reality to human beings, which is tied to how we acquire, share, store, and reconsider knowledge.[2] The discovery of facts through science is one very powerful and inspiring way to encounter God directly. Thus, *facts are God's native tongue*.

- If there are scriptures beyond the holy texts of Earth's various religious traditions…

- If God didn't stop communicating knowledge crucial for humans centuries ago…

- If it is possible for new understandings to arise in ways more widely available and testable than what can be channeled through the hearts and minds of lone individuals…

- Then surely this is it: God communicates to us by publicly revealing new facts.

It is through the now-global community of scientists, working together, challenging one another's findings, assisted by the miracles of technology, and standing on the shoulders of giants (but never blinded by the greatness of past accomplishments)—it is through this wondrous human endeavor that God's Word is still being revealed. It is through this ever-expectant, yet ever-ready-to-be-humbled, stance of inquiry that God's Word is discerned as bigger, as more wondrous, as more this-world relevant than could have possibly been comprehended in any time past.

## The Trajectory of Human Evolution

Human consciousness emerged within a world of powerful and mysterious forces beyond our comprehension and control. As modes of communication evolved—from gestures and oral speech to writing and mathematics, to print, to science, to computers—so has God been able to reveal more and more about…well, everything: God's nature and will, the scale and venerability of Creation, and the meaning and magnitude of humanity's divine calling. An inspiring consequence of seeing the full sweep of history is discovering that human circles of care and compassion have expanded over time.

Early on, owing to genetic guidance honed in a pre-linguistic world, and then supplemented by knowledge that could be accumulated, retained, and shared only to the extent that spoken language would allow, our abilities to cooperate with one another were limited and localized. Anyone outside the tribe was suspect, and probably an enemy. As technologies of communication evolved, our ancestors entered interdependent relationships in ever-widening circles, from villages, chiefdoms, and early nations, to today's global markets and international organizations.[3]

Finally, the emergence of the World Wide Web has made possible collaborations no longer stifled by geographic distances and political boundaries. Throughout this evolution of human communities and networks, an inner transformation has also been taking place. At each stage our circles of care, compassion, and commitment have grown and our lists of enemies have diminished. Our next step will be to learn to organize and govern ourselves globally, and to enjoy a mutually enhancing relationship with the larger body of Life of which we are part, and do so to the glory of God. Traditional religions have played crucial roles in fostering cooperation *within* each tribe, kingdom, and early nation—though not infrequently by provoking suspicion and enmity of those *outside* the group. Emerging now is an orientation that encourages wider affinities and global-scale cooperation.

For religious traditions to fulfill their potentials in our postmodern world, each will be called to harmonize its core doctrines with the evolutionary worldview. This effort will prove far more than an exercise in catching up and making do. Rather, leaders within each tradition will delight in discovering that the evolutionary outlook bolsters their core teachings. Instead of an intrusion on our faith, evolution becomes a precious blessing.

## REALizing God

Evolutionary theology differs from traditional theology in many ways, but none more significant than how real or imaginary God and religious doctrines are understood. From an evolutionary perspective, theological concepts are understood in light of public knowledge rather than private belief. That God's creativity, for example, is *nested* and *emergent* is a fundamental truth that could not have been revealed to the biblical writers in a way they could comprehend—not only because nearly everyone back then believed the world was flat and at the center of the Universe, but also because of the utter necessity of telescopes, microscopes, and computers for understanding the deep-time, developmental nature of God's grace and creativity.

By '*the nested emergent nature of God's creativity*' I'm pointing to the now widely accepted scientific understanding that everything did not come into being all at once, but, rather, developed over great expanses of time and in a nested fashion: subatomic particles coalescing into atoms, atoms emerging into molecules, molecules creating cells, cells creating organisms, organisms creating societies, and so on. Like Russian nesting dolls or Chinese boxes within boxes, each nested whole is also part of larger wholes: societies within ecosystems, within planets, within solar systems, within galaxies, within the Universe as a whole. More, we don't merely believe this is how God created everything; we know it. In many cases scientists can see it happening now and they can measure it. To cite just two of the better known examples: Hydrogen and oxygen come into relationship and create water. Stars create within themselves most of the atoms in the periodic table of elements. So whether we look at the smallest scale or the largest, every nested level is not merely created; it is creative. Divine immanence is real!

From the perspective of evolutionary theology, "God" is nothing so trivial as a supreme landlord residing off the planet and outside the Universe—an otherworldly entity whose main business is engaging in unnatural acts (supernatural interventions). As I and other evolutionary theologians use the term, *God* is nothing less than a sacred, proper name for *Ultimate Reality*—the largest, all-embracing Whole—that One and Only Supreme Creative Reality which transcends yet includes all other realities and makes possible all forms of creativity.[4]

Because human beings are part of the whole and cannot stand outside the whole to examine it, different peoples at different times, living in different parts of the world, reflecting on different plants, different animals, different terrain, and different climates, would inevitably have used different metaphors and analogies to describe the nature of Ultimate Reality. Naturally, they would have told different stories about how to relate meaningfully to that Supreme Wholeness (Holy One) in which we all live and move and have our being. Understanding religious differences is hardly more complicated than comprehending this fact and pondering its implications.

Every characteristic that we attribute to the divine derives from our experience of reality. If we imagine God as beautiful, gracious, loving, awesome, powerful, majestic, or faithful, it is because we have known or experienced beauty, grace, love, awe, power, majesty, or trustworthiness in the world. As Thomas Berry, a 93-year-old retired Roman Catholic priest, cultural historian, and self-proclaimed 'geologian' has said, "If we lived on the moon and that's all we and our ancestors had ever known, all our concepts and experience of the divine would reflect the barrenness of the lunar landscape." Thankfully, we are not confined to a barren moon but can rejoice as part of a flourishing, intensely creative Earth and a vast and awesomely beautiful Universe that call forth our richest images of God.

For example, we can now understand that a "God's eye view of the world" is not merely the objective, transcendent perspective—the view from above or beyond nature. If God truly is omnipresent and immanent, then a God's eye view of the world must also include the subjective experience of every creature. What dolphins and fish see, what bats and birds see, what spiders and dragonflies see: all must be included. God is thus not only Love but also Infinite Compassion. God feels the pain and suffering of all creatures—from the inside. Those who think they can love God and trash the environment, or oppress others, must be blind, utterly, to the immanence and omnipresence of the divine. When we truly *get* the nested emergent nature of divine creativity, we know that our love of nature and our love of one another are essential aspects of our love of God.

- *God is the Mystery at the Center* of our amazement that the Universe is here at all, that it is what it is, and that it is always becoming, yet always somehow whole.

- *God is the Mystery at the Heart* of consciousness, conscience, compassion, and all the other forms of co-creative, co-incarnational responsiveness of life to life.

- *God is the Mysterious Omni-Creative Power* through which the Universe is and ever becomes more intricately and wondrously fulfilled through the interactions of all its parts (each of which contains a spark of the Whole).

## Beyond Evidence: Why I'm Evangelistic About Evolution

Young-earth creationists and others who fail to see God's revelation in the discoveries of science often ask me what evidence I see for evolution. My response generally begins along these lines: "I am not a scientist; thus my evidence begins with this striking fact: well over 95% of the world's scientists and tens of millions of religious people from every faith tradition embrace an evolutionary worldview precisely because of the overwhelming empirical evidence uncovered (revealed) over the past few hundred years. As a species, collectively, we no longer merely believe that the entire Universe has been in a process of evolutionary emergence for billions of years—we know it. And we know it thanks to the mountains of measurable evidence discovered (revealed) in disciplines as diverse as cosmology, astronomy, physics, astrophysics, chemistry, botany, zoology, primatology, microbiology, genetics, anthropology, archeology, evolutionary brain science, and evolutionary psychology."

That is only the beginning, however. Beyond the evidence, I find deep emotional and spiritual sustenance in an evolutionary celebration of my evangelical/Pentecostal faith. I unabashedly celebrate "The Gospel According to Evolution" because a sacred view of the history of the Universe gives me a far more intimate, personal relationship with God and a closer walk with Christ than I had when I was an antievolution creationist. (Yes, in my late teens and early twenties I was vociferously opposed to evolution: I handed out tracts and was eager to argue with anyone who thought the world was older than 6,000 years.)

Now that I have learned *my brain's creation story*—this is, thanks to what God has revealed through evolutionary brain science and evolutionary psychology—I find it infinitely easier to live a life of ongoing victory over my sinful nature. When I interpret the science-based history of everything and everyone in God-honoring ways, and live "in Christ"—that is, in evolutionary integrity: growing in trust, authenticity, responsibility, and service—I experience heaven in this life: here, now, with all my relations, eternally, without fail. Thus, I am *evangelistic* about evolutionary faith because it expands and deepens my understanding and experience of the gospel, intensifies my communion with God, and helps me live a more Christ-centered, Christ-like life.[5]

My heart aches when I meet those who claim to have "accepted Jesus as their personal Lord and Savior," who read their Bible and go to church faithfully, yet who still struggle mightily with their sinful nature or who have sour or less-than-loving relationships with family, friends, or coworkers. For me, steadfast integrity was out of reach until the evolutionary worldview helped me grasp that 'original sin' and evolved 'human instincts' are pointing to the same reality. (Chapters 9-12 in my book *Thank God for Evolution!*: "REALizing 'The Fall' and 'Original Sin'", "REALizing 'Personal Salvation'", "Evolutionary Integrity Practices", and "Evolving Our Most Personal Relationships" are a good way to begin to explore this path.)

# REALizing "the Gospel"

If what we mean by "the gospel" today is the same as what Christians two millennia ago meant when they used the term, we do our tradition a terrible disservice. [6]

The meaning of the gospel is infinitely rich. No generation can possibly exhaust its depths. Every generation has the privilege and responsibility of reinterpreting the core insights of its faith tradition for its own time, as the Holy Spirit leads them.

Thomas Aquinas, one of the greatest theologians in Church history, wrote nearly a millennium ago, "A mistake about Creation will necessarily result in a mistake about God." What Aquinas knew then is even more consequential today. As our understanding of the Cosmos expands, so must our view of God and, for Christians, our appreciation of the meaning and significance of the gospel. Seen as a sacred story of nested creativity in which life becomes ever more complex, more aware, and more intimate with itself over time—this epic of evolution can revitalize the meaning and magnitude of the gospel.

The disciples and early Church leaders, reflecting on Jesus' ministry within the context of their own first, second, and third century political, judicial, religious, and cosmological understandings, formulated creeds and doctrines about the significance of his life and mission. Since then, our view of reality has grown enormously. If the Christian tradition is correct in its assertion that Jesus truly did incarnate God's Great News for humanity, then the meaning, grandeur, and this-world relevance of the gospel today must reach far beyond that which any previous generation, including the biblical writers themselves, could have known. In the words of literary critic and historian Gil Bailie:

> "Those closest to the historical Jesus didn't give the gospel its geographical breadth and theological depth. It was Paul, who never knew him. Moreover, impressive achievements in biblical scholarship have brought our

generation closer to the constituent events of the Christian movement than were, say, the Gentile Christians of the second century. If the life and death of Jesus is historically central, then people living a hundred thousand years from now will be in a better position to appreciate that than we are. When they look back, they will surely think of us as 'early Christians'—living as we do a scant two millennia from the mysterious events in question. They will be right. The Christian movement today is still in the elementary stages of working out the implications of the gospel. The greatest and boldest creedal assertions are in the future, not the past. This flawed and unlikely thing we call the 'church' is on a great Christological adventure. Even against its own institutional resistances, it is continually finding deeper and more profound implications to the Jesus-event."

When we become accustomed to seeing God's will, God's love, and God's transforming power operating on the scale of billions of years and embracing all of Creation, our understanding of the gospel opens and magnifies. Its greater realization, however, will take time and will never be exhausted. The Protestant Reformation, made possible by the printing press, did not happen overnight. Similarly, the "evolution revolution," made possible by advanced telescopes, computers, and the Internet—as well as by ever increasing knowledge of how living systems function—will likely take several more decades before its implications are fleshed out theologically, politically, and economically. Nevertheless, we can say this:

Given what we now know about deep-time creativity and grace, we can no longer in good conscience continue interpreting the story of Jesus' birth, life, teachings, passion, death, and resurrection as primarily having to do with saving a select group of human beings from the fires of a literal hell when they die. Such cannot possibly be the truth of the gospel for our time. That interpretation may still appeal to millions of Christians (sadly, who quibble or fight over just who is in the select group), but it is in no way Good News for most of humanity. Indeed, for all other forms of life on Earth, such an anachronistic interpretation is far more a curse than a blessing. How can we continue to think that this is what God wants?

What we call "the gospel" will be *experienced* as good news only if it is a saving response to the bad news that people are actually dealing with. Said another way, if what we mean by "the gospel" does not address in a hopeful, inspiring way what people themselves regard as their greatest personal and collective challenges, then for them the Christian message will not be salvific. It will be irrelevant. This mismatch, between what people in fact experience as bad news and what our church liturgies present as the Good News, is a big reason why those under thirty are largely unchurched—and why the epic of evolution told in a holy way is gaining wide appeal. To be frank, most young people are not preoccupied with concerns about whether heaven and hell literally exist. The difficulties in their lives today, as well as their concerns for the well-being of the world at large, trump any such otherworldly preoccupations.

From a meaningful evolutionary perspective *the gospel* includes the Great Story of God's love and saving grace as revealed in the Bible, on the cross, and throughout the entire 14-billion-year epic of evolution. The gospel, as such, is transformative on three levels: individually, relationally, and globally. To ignore or discount any one of these is to miss the meaning and magnitude of them all.

*Individually*, the gospel can free a person from addiction to sin and self-absorption, enabling each of us to savor the fruit of the Spirit in the midst of the never-ending challenges of life, and empowering all to be blessings to the world regardless of our shortcomings. It can also enable one to know peace, even in the midst of difficult circumstances and in the presence of difficult people.

*Relationally*, the Christ story shows us how reconciliation is possible with virtually anyone. When I take full responsibility, let go of thinking I'm right and the other is wrong, step into their experience, and communicate with love and compassion from that place, miracles occur. Always.[7]

*Collectively*, the gospel can free us from species pride, arrogance, and human-centeredness by revealing the holy trajectory of evolution, the sacred direction of divine creativity, and how we as a human family can fulfill our role in furthering what God has been up to for billions of years.[8]

## Believing vs. Knowing

I once believed in the literal truth of biblical scripture. I no longer believe; now I *know*. *Knowing* is powerful, it is personal, and it connects me to truth seekers of other faiths and throughout the global enterprise of science. I moved from believing to knowing when I came to accept that a loving God would not have stopped communicating truth crucial to human existence centuries before humankind had the technological capacity to perceive and to understand the vastness of the cosmos, the immense journey of life, and the nearly unfathomable depths of time.

My own spiritual transformation began when I accepted the fact of evolution as yet another revelation of God—albeit a revelation ongoingly discerned and updated by the community of scientists. Equally important, I then took care to nurture a holy (while scientifically accurate) regard for evolutionary history, all the while contemplating how the core doctrines of my Christian faith could be enriched (REALized) by the scientific perspective—not merely reconciled to it. My evangelical roots moved me to set the bar high: An evolutionary form of my faith must move me to sing out praises to God. It must give me the guidance and the practical tools to be successful in pursuing my calling, to live in more Christ-like ways, and to be a blessing to the world. It must deliver me from my sinful nature. It must fill me with hope and fulfill on its promise of salvation.

And so I have come to this:

I no longer merely *believe* in the fall of Adam and Eve, in Original Sin. I *know* that the reptilian and mammalian parts of my brain have drives of which my conscious mind is clueless—and that these inherited proclivities, my unchosen nature, evolved to serve my ancestors in life conditions far removed from those that govern my life today. The story of Adam and Eve reminds me of this.

I don't merely believe that I am saved by grace, through faith, and that someday I'll go to heaven. I know that *every* time I have been enslaved then freed, estranged then reconciled, lost then returned home, it was a gift of God that gave me a peace beyond description. The Apostle Paul's writings remind me of this.

I don't merely believe in the Resurrection. I know that for billions of years, chaos, death, and destruction have catalyzed new life, new opportunities, and new possibilities. I know, both from my own life and from Earth's history, that Good Fridays are consistently followed by Easter Sundays. The story of Christ's death and resurrection reminds me of this.

I don't merely believe that someday Jesus will return and I'll fly away with him, I know that wherever trust, authenticity, responsibility, and service reign supreme, my Lord has already returned. So long as I remain in deep integrity and continue to grow "in Christ"—in these qualities—I experience, right here and now, rapturous joy. The theological promise of the Rapture reminds me of this.

## An Evolutionary Vision of God's True Nature: Christ Jesus

When I suggest that evolutionary theology offers "a more universally venerable God" than traditional images of Ultimate Reality, what I mean is this: When we see God's love, grace, and creativity extending over billions of years, rather than merely thousands of years, we discover a God much less vindictive and tyrannical and far more honorable and praiseworthy than the characterizations of God found in many parts of the Bible, such as the Pentateuch and Book of Revelation. Recent critics of religion, including Richard Dawkins, Christopher Hitchens, Sam Harris, and Michael Earl, are skilled at pointing out gruesome passages in both the Old and New Testaments that portray God as acting or commanding in cruel and unsavory ways. As a devout Christian who holds a high view of scripture, the first time I heard this line of criticism I immediately and forcefully rejected it. My mind instinctively began to come up with justifications. Thankfully, my heart stopped me from going too far down this rationalizing path. Truth won out. Paradoxically, it was only when I allowed this painful information in that I could begin to see the significance (indeed, the magnificence) of the gospel in a postmodern world.

The U.S. Department of Defense defines "terrorism" as "*the calculated use of violence or the threat of violence to inculcate fear; intended to coerce or to intimidate governments or societies in the pursuit of goals that are generally political, religious, or ideological.*" No matter how dearly, even reverently, we may hold scripture, it is an easily verifiable fact that many modern and postmodern people find the picture of God painted in parts of the Bible problematic at best, if not repulsive.

After quoting nearly two-dozen biblical passages, in context, that depict God in a brutal, homicidal/genocidal light, Michael Earl, author of the enormously popular, free online audio program, *Bible Stories Your Parents Never Taught You*, reasonworks.com states:

> "When we look at a horrific story like Noah's flood, or at an event like the conquest of Canaan, with the huge massacres of millions of women and children, we must not lose sight of the fact that these events and actions were carried out by, or done in direct response to orders from, God. The Bible makes that absolutely clear. When we read the brutal Law of Moses, where people's brains are being bashed in with rocks for breaking the Sabbath, for mouthing off to their parents, for having sex with the

wrong people, for believing the wrong things: all of these atrocious laws can be traced back to God. And when we read in scripture about hell, about billons of unbelievers being tortured in fire for all eternity—this is God who is orchestrating all of this. (Given a literal reading of scripture) God, by any stretch of the imagination, is a terrorist. God employs the calculated use of violence or the threat of violence to inculcate fear—and he does it for religious reasons. In anybody's book, that's terrorism."

Many find this line of reasoning difficult to counter from a traditional, literalist perspective. But from the perspective of evolutionary theology—that is, when we realize that facts are God's native tongue, and when we can see the entire history of cosmos, Earth, life, and humanity in a sacred light—not only can we make sense of even the most problematic biblical images of God, but we are also compelled, by both heart and reason, to see God's character and "personality" in Christ-like ways.[9]

## It Matters What We Think About Evolution

It is impossible to understand yourself, your world, or the meaning and magnitude of the gospel in the 21st century without an evolutionary worldview. And when I say impossible, I don't mean just difficult. I mean truly impossible—like trying to understand human illness before we had microscopes and x-ray machines, or trying to comprehend the large-scale structure of Universe prior to telescopes and spectroscopy.

Without an evolutionary theology, when you think about your inner challenges, your relational difficulties, and the trials we face as a species, and when you imagine God or think about what 'the gospel' or 'saving good news' means *for our time*, you'll start with wrong assumptions and end with trivial, and possibly even dangerous, conclusions. It truly matters what we think about evolution. It may be that nothing matters more!

- If you think of Jesus as a cosmic janitor who is going to come back to clean up the mess we've made, then you'll make very different decisions and support very different policies from someone who sees all of us as participants in a divine creative process called evolution. Talk about the right hand of God...it just doesn't get any more real than this!

- If you struggle with addiction, fear, anger, depression, pride, greed, sloth, jealousy, or any other aspect of your 'unchosen nature' or 'inherited proclivities' (and especially if you think your struggles are because your great, great, great, great-grandmother ate an apple at the insistence of a talking snake), though you may console yourself with thoughts of a peaceful afterlife, you may miss out on the heavenly joy and peace that passes all understanding available in *this* life.

- If you think of God as an invisible, otherworldly father/king who dictated all the really important stuff to humans back when people believed the world was flat and that epilepsy was demonic possession, or if you think of Creation as a soulless object devoid of God's living, pulsing presence, then you won't see how naturally and undeniably real God is, nor how generously and faithfully God has been communicating right on up to the present. And you certainly won't see how honorable this planet is, nor what God is up to in the world today!

## The Role of the Emerging Church

While pastoring my first church, in rural New England, I stood under the stars one night with a parishioner, an 82-year-old farmer and amateur astronomer affectionately known as Gramps. Gazing at the Milky Way, Gramps whispered, "You know, Reverend, the more I learn about this amazing Universe, the more awesome my God becomes!"

As we Christians open our hearts to embrace a God-centered, gospel-expanding way of celebrating evolution, we will, in the decades to come, prove to be an enormously positive force on behalf of all life, human and non-human. Our destiny as a species and as individuals is to further God's evolutionary creativity in Christ-like ways that bless the entire Earth community. The role of the emerging Church includes spreading the Great News—evangelizing the nations—and thus ushering the entire human family through a process of cultural death and resurrection, to the glory of God. In this way, like Jesus, the Church becomes a vessel of God's saving grace. We no longer passively wait for Christ's return; we fully participate in it. This is our mission, our calling, our Great Work. And it is why, I believe, the scriptures refer to the Church as the both the body of Christ and the bride of Christ.

**Endnotes:**

1. Much of my book, *Thank God for Evolution! How the Marriage of Science and Religion Will Transform Your Life and Our World* (endorsed by 5 Nobel laureates and 120 other scientific, religious, and cultural leaders) is a detailed discussion of how I see evolutionary theology providing these benefits. For those interested, the entire book can be downloaded for free (as a pdf) or purchased online here: ThankGodforEvolution.com

2. See *Thank God for Evolution!* (TGFE!), Part II: "Reality is Speaking", especially Chapters 4-6: "Private and Public Revelation", "The Nested Emergent Nature of Divine Creativity", and "Words Create Worlds".

3. The evolution of increasing complexity (evolutionary emergence) in the pre-human world occurred along similar lines. Understanding this trajectory clarifies God's will for us as a species and offers unambiguous guidance for our *only* way into a just and thriving future together. See TGFE!, Part I: "The Holy Trajectory of Evolution" and Part IV: "A God Glorifying Future".

The four best resources I know on the question of evolutionary directionality (I highly recommend each) are these: Robert

Wright's *Nonzero: The Logic of Human Destiny*:
<http://www.nonzero.org/>; John Stewart's *Evolution's Arrow: The Direction of Evolution and Future of Humanity*:
<http://www4.tpg.com.au/users/jes999/>; my wife Connie Barlow's *Evolution Extended: Biological Debates on the Meaning of Life*: <http://thegreatstory.org/CBwritings. html>; and Connie's essay "Let There Be Sight":
<http://thegreatstory.org/convergence.html>.

4. See TGFE! Part II: "Reality is Speaking", especially Chapters 5-7: "The Nested Emergent Nature of Divine Creativity", "Words Create Worlds", and "What Do We Mean by the Word 'God'?". This *creatheistic* or evolutionary theistic perspective is distinct from (transcends and includes) previous god-isms, such as flat-earth (pre-evolutionary) theism, pantheism, and panentheism (or dialectical theism).

5. See TGFE! Parts III and IV: "The Gospel According to Evolution", and "Evolutionary Spirituality", as well as my personal testimonial in the Epilogue.

6. See http://ThankGodforEvolution.com/faq.html and http://www.ThankGodforEvolution.com/audio-video for more than a dozen short video clips, as well as a print interview of my responses to the most frequently asked questions I receive related to the perspective outlined in this essay and throughout my book, *Thank God for Evolution!*

7. See TGFE! Chapters 11-12: "Evolutionary Integrity Practices" and "Evolving Our Most Personal Relationships".

8. See TGFE! Part I: "The Holy Trajectory of Evolution", and Part IV: "A God-Glorifying Future".

9. For more on how the evolutionary perspective helps us take a square look at the cruelest of passages of the Bible without recoiling, and how evolution reveals God's Christ-like nature, see TGFE! Chapter 18: "Our Evolving Understanding of God's Will", and Appendix A: "Good and Bad Reasons for Believing" (written by Richard Dawkins) and Appendix B: "REALizing the Miraculous".

# Naturalistic Paganism

*B. T. Newberg*

> *Ours is a path both **inspiring** and,*
> *to the best of human ability, **true**.*

Ours is a naturalistic path rooted in ancient Paganism and contemporary science. This path integrates mythic, meditative, and ritual practices with a worldview based on the current most compelling scientific evidence.

## What defines us?

First, we are *Pagans*. Our spiritual practices are inspired by ancient non-Abrahamic cultural-religious traditions, such as the Greeks, Romans, Egyptians, Norse, Celts, Indians, Chinese, and various native tribes*, as well as corresponding modern traditions such as Neopaganism. We acknowledge there is no way to recreate ancient religions in every detail, nor would we want to. Rather, we draw inspiration from old ways while embracing modernity. We find ancient traditions continue to speak to us just as they did our ancestors, even as they continue to evolve.

Second, we are *naturalists*. This worldview unites our many varieties, and makes us unique among Pagans. Good technical definitions of naturalism are available, but what most Naturalistic Pagans mean by it can be summed up simply:

- only natural causes affect the universe; if there are supernatural causes, there is no reliable evidence yet to support that idea.

To clarify what counts as "natural", we look to contemporary science:

- natural causes are best discovered via the current most compelling scientific evidence

In other words, we adopt an appropriate skepticism toward any supposed divine or magical causes outside nature, i.e. *super-natural* causes, as well as those within nature unsupported by the best evidence.**

While we find little evidence to support most of the *metaphysical* claims made for deities and magic, we find plenty of evidence for the capacity of Pagan myth, meditation, and ritual to affect *psychology*. That is why we find Pagan ways powerful. By shaping human minds, they motivate change through human hands.

As a result of our reliance on demonstrable evidence, a few tendencies emerge:

- We tend to view deities as metaphorical, poetic, or psychological in some sense, and not as causal agents external to and independent of the individual. Thunder is external and independent, but the personification of thunder as Zeus, for example, is not.

- We tend to view magic as manipulating the world indirectly through the individual's own psychology, for example by motivating her or him to action, and not as manipulating "energies" to produce effects with no known physical causal relation to the individual.

- We tend to ground our practices and beliefs in experience, accurate history, and mainstream scientific evidence.

- Our focus on evidence as the primary source of knowledge leads many of us to an awareness of, and gratitude for, the long evolutionary process which has resulted in our existence today.

- Because our worldview doesn't include afterlives or hidden realms, we tend to be focused on this body, this life, and this earth, cherishing each moment and improving the world for all life on Earth.

# How do we practice?

Our style of practice is much like that of other kinds of Pagans. It may or may not be noticeably different, and we work happily alongside other kinds of Pagans. This is often aided by the fact that Pagans usually don't believe in a literal Hell for those who don't hold the "correct" belief.

There is great variation, but some of our most common practices include:

- celebrating the Neopagan Wheel of the Year

- performing rituals

- meditating

- exploring mythology for inspiration and insight

- discovering our world through experience, accurate history, and scientific inquiry

- cultivating insight

- changing ourselves and our society through responsible action

In our practices, we may invoke deities, spirits, and ancestors. If we do, the meaning may be allegorical, archetypal, or cultural. In so doing, we carry on a long tradition going back to ancient times.

# Were there Naturalistic Pagans in the ancient world?

Many assume that Naturalistic Paganism is an exclusively modern phenomenon. However, evidence suggests traditions resembling Naturalistic Paganism date at least as far back as the Axial Age (roughly 800-200 BCE) in Greece and elsewhere. A detailed presentation of research on this subject will be coming out over the course of this year in the *Naturalistic Traditions* column at Patheos.com.

## What is the role of science?

When it comes down to it, there's one simple fact we must all face:

*The universe is as it is whether we like it or not.*

The only question is, when evidence shows the universe out of accord with cherished beliefs, will we be humble enough to accept it?

We take a humble approach to knowledge claims. Faith claims, extra-sensory perceptions, personal visions, and the like have proven unreliable as guides to reality. Meanwhile, scientific method, though imperfect, has proven the most reliable to date. That's why a path based on it may be considered most probably true, to the best of human ability.

Others may differ in their approach to truth, and we wish them well. Meanwhile, we look to the current most compelling scientific evidence.

## What is the role of Paganism?

There is another fact we must all face:

*Everyone experiences reality from a different subjective vantage point.*

While scientific evidence provides our best cue for what's real, there are many valid ways to experience reality and behave within it. Paganism is one way.

First, Pagan myth, meditation, and ritual cultivate a culturally-rooted, nature-based, richly-symbolic subjective experience. Many find this appealing in our age of individualism, environmental crisis, and consumerist alienation.

Second, subjective experience has consequences for behavior. For example, those who come to feel more akin to the environment are more likely to protect it. Pagan myth, meditation, and ritual change behavior by shaping its underlying motivations.

For more on this question, see the recent collaborative list of reasons for why naturalists do ritual in my article, *"Why do ritual as a Naturalistic Pagan?"* at witchesandpagans.com.

Others may differ in their approach to experience and behavior, and we wish them well. Meanwhile, we cultivate connection to our natural roots, wider human family, and our unconscious minds through Pagan practices.

## Why follow this path?

For many of us, the realization that natural forces have resulted in the immense journey of life, over billions of years, shaped by natural selection, parental love, and community bonds, fills us with awe, wonder and gratitude. This overwhelming feeling can be expressed as so many humans have done for thousands of years – through Pagan practices, connecting us to our ancient ancestors, today's human family, and future generations of all life on Earth. Pagan practices have often served to embed people within the wider web of all existence, and still do so today.

A deep and satisfying life awaits. One may even explore a kind of naturalistic transcendence, discovering oneself in relation to nature, community, and mind.

Most of all, this path offers a way to live responsibly in this world.

On the one hand, naturalism grounded in scientific evidence offers a means of intellectual responsibility. Through it, we cultivate right relationship to objective reality.

On the other hand, Paganism offers a means for taking responsibility for one's subjective experience and behavior. Through it, we cultivate right relationship to subjective reality.

Altogether, ours is a path rich with truth, meaning, and responsibility.

*Pagan.* Hitherto, Humanistic Paganism defined *Pagan* by focusing on a Euro-Mediterranean culture zone. This was intended to a) maintain integrity of the term by including a limited range of inter-related cultures, and b) avoid issues of cultural appropriation. Recently, the community has questioned whether this focus may be unnecessarily restrictive, hence the broader definition extending *Pagan* to include all non-Abrahamic traditions. This inevitably begs the question of what so many cultures could actually have in common; on the other hand, it opens the door to naturalistic aspects of Daoism, Confucianism, Carvaka, and so on. Meanwhile, we continue to affirm the importance of cultural appropriation issues. An excellent resource on this is Lupa's *Talking About the Elephant.*

**Outside nature/within nature.* Pagans vary in their acceptance of the term "supernatural." A few consider their deities and/or magic to be outside nature, but most consider them to exist within it. Naturalistic Pagans affirm neither: either deities and magic are outside nature and thus not naturalistic, or within nature but unsupported by reliable evidence. Either way, we find no good reason to affirm either gods or magic in any literal sense. Mis-applied science grants no support either. For example, quantum physics is often touted as "evidence" for magic, but this turns out to be a red herring, since it is highly improbable that quantum effects would ever occur at large enough scales to generate so-called magical effects (for an entertaining presentation of why this is, check out Brian Cox's *A Night With the Stars*). If evidence were to change in the future, magic might become a legitimately "natural" cause, but there is no reason to hold out for such an unlikely development. The same goes for deities claimed to exist within nature, but with no compelling relation to currently known physical laws. Another common red herring is the argument that science is insufficient, because some things that clearly exist, like *love,* cannot be easily tested in a laboratory. This too is fallacious, for several reasons. First, laboratory experiments are only one form of scientific testing; thought experiments, consistency with established facts, and other forms also play a part. Second, love, unlike divinity or magic, violates no known physical laws or facts of biology. Third, love can in fact be tested in the laboratory, indirectly, by measuring associated physical responses. Finally, even if science ultimately could not test things like love, that would have no bearing whatsoever on the truth content of beliefs in deities or magic, which would remain entirely dependent on evidence to support them.

# About Stoicism

*DT Strain*

Stoicism is a philosophy and practice that helps its user enjoy a more peaceful and contented life. Although some think of it as being about being emotionless, what Stoicism actually teaches is how to avoid harmful feelings and enjoy feelings that are healthier.

## Ancient Stoicism

Ancient Stoicism was a philosophy born in ancient Greece. It included an understanding of the universe which has, in many ways, since been scientifically shown to be incorrect. In other ways, perhaps in the more important ways, this understanding of the universe may still hold true.

Beyond just an understanding of the universe (what they called "physics"), Stoicism also included the categories of logic and ethics. Some ancient Stoic ideas may seem dated to us today, but many of them are still very applicable, and help us address many of the challenges all people have faced throughout history. This is why some people today either consider themselves Stoics, or consider much of their perspective to be influenced by Stoicism.

Rather than cover all of the details on ancient Stoicism here, this article will describe some of the core elements of Stoic ideals in a simple format that is compatible with, and applicable to, our modern world. Those who wish to learn more about ancient Stoicism, its history, its founding philosophers, its technical terms, and so on, are encouraged to read other works, many of which are listed at the end of this essay.

## Realizations About Materialism

First, we begin with the understanding that people who view material gain as the ultimate good are doomed to dissatisfaction in life. Surprisingly, this is true no matter what level of material gain a person accomplishes!

There's nothing wrong with material gain itself, and people who are materially prosperous can often be quite happy. But people who focus too much on materialism or wealth and think of it as a primary measure of their success, worth, or happiness will never be satisfied with what they have. Materialistic people are deluded by the belief that "if they just get that one thing" they will be happy. But human psychology doesn't work that way. Once they get what they desire they'll soon grow accustomed to it, and desire something else.

Not only that, but these sorts of people will always be concerned with what "everyone else" has. Materialistic people will tend to judge other people by their possessions as well, and others will pick up on this, usually finding it unappealing. This can make it more difficult to have deep or meaningful friendships. This focus will consume them and they will find themselves in an unpleasant cycle of hunger and jealousy.

The materialistic person may frequently enjoy the immediate thrill of a new item or more money, but often the immediate thrill doesn't last in the long run. These experiences alone rarely add up to an overall life experience of true happiness. More often, when a person looks back over a life of materialism, he or she finds that the periods of jealousy, lack of deep or meaningful experiences, and unfulfilled desire for more goods outweigh the thrills. In conclusion, one can't have a very happy life in this state.

## More than Materialism

While some people live many years of their lives before understanding the pitfalls of materialism and looking back in regret, these warnings are nothing new. Religion, philosophy, and folk wisdom of many varieties have warned against materialism for ages.

But one of the interesting things about Stoicism, is an understanding that the danger doesn't end with materialism alone. All of the dangers that apply to an unhealthy focus on material goods, also apply to an unhealthy focus on many other sorts of things.

Those things include an unhealthy over-attachment to social status, career, and even on the possession of respect, love, or the company of friends and family. As with material possessions, there is nothing wrong with enjoying these things, but an extreme focus on them as a measure of our worth or happiness is unhealthy. Like attachment to material goods, this perspective will also lead to dissatisfaction and frustration in life.

## What We Can Control

What all of these things have in common (wealth, health, friends, family, social status, etc.), is that we ultimately cannot control them. It's true that our actions can affect our chances of determining the state of these things to various degrees. However, the belief that we can have ultimate control over them is a delusion. It is this delusion that leads to our dissatisfaction when our efforts do not result in the effects we desire. For that reason, it is important to recognize the distinction between what we can control (what we can *really* and *totally* control) and what we can't.

When we really think about it, it seems the only things that we have true control over are our priorities, our attitudes, and our decisions. No matter what we undergo physically, no matter how we might be constrained by our circumstances, we still have the ability to decide what we care about, how we think about something, and what sort of choices we make. In fact, even if we try to do something and fail, and even if we couldn't control that, we can still control the fact that we *chose to try*.

## Understanding Good and Bad

The next thing to consider is how we think about good and bad/evil. First, consider why it is that we make the distinction between good and bad in the first place. Why would we call this 'good' and that 'bad'? One reason for doing this is so that we can take appropriate action in response to that recognition.

Whether a storm destroys our home, or burglars steal our possessions, we often say that an "evil" has happened to us. When it's a nice day or when someone gives us a gift, we often say that a "good" has happened to us.

But if we don't really control anything but our own will, then what purpose can there be for considering anything outside our control to be truly good or bad? Why make such distinctions if we can't use those distinctions to ultimately control what happens and what doesn't?

Surely, since we have some influence (but not complete control) over things outside our will, it is best to at least try to avoid the negative things from happening, and try to promote the positive things happening. But remember that it is only the *attempt* to do good or evil that is within our complete control – not the actual *outcome* of our attempts.

But to consider these outside negative and positive things that happen to us as truly 'good' and truly 'evil' themselves is to place an extreme category on them that we can't make full use of. This doesn't match our new understanding that such things are ultimately not in our control.

So, according to Stoic thinking, it is *only* that which we can really control that we need consider good or bad. In other words, from our individual perspective, only our *own* personal priorities, attitudes, and decisions should be considered to be good or bad. We should think of everything else as merely positive and negative outside events – not truly good or bad. Doing this serves to constantly remind us of where our focus should lie. This way we remember that there is no sense in getting worked up over, or overly attached to, things we can't control.

# Caring

This does not mean, as is often misunderstood, that Stoics "don't care" or that they think "whatever" when positive or negative things happen to them or others. Stoics can care about things external to their own will, and can try to act in a way that brings about more positive than negative things. But by understanding that the positive and negative things that happen in our lives are ultimately out of our control, and by not thinking of them as good or evil, the Stoic does not become overly attached to those things.

The Stoic does not place his or her self worth in these outside things and does not invest ultimate purpose, meaning, or contentment in them. This means that a Stoic is more capable of weathering the ups and downs of life with mature acceptance and without an overcoming desperation for better circumstances or fear of worse circumstances.

# Contentment & the Universe

If a Stoic doesn't place his or her sense of self worth or contentment in relationships, status, wealth, health, or possessions, then where does he or she place it? First, Stoics have a reverence and appreciation for the natural universe, or "Nature" for short. As part of Nature, we must also include a reverence for one another and ourselves.

Of course, ancients held certain ideas about the structure of the universe while modern Stoics' ideas are informed by their own beliefs and modern discoveries. But in both cases, Stoics see a vast, amazingly complex structure of interacting parts and forces. These parts and forces are seen as interacting in rational and logical ways.

Some think of this rational element as God and others think of it in a more impersonal sense. However, when it comes to our world, society, and life itself, Stoics agree that this logical structure gives us a balance of creative and destructive, orderly and chaotic, tendencies. The universe, then, is seen as one interrelated whole.

This whole system brings about a Nature where we can never be certain of what the future will bring us. Even if we make our best efforts toward certain things happening, we must be prepared to accept that all of these complex events may not come together as we wish, but will instead come together according to the demands of Nature.

But we also must realize that it is Nature itself that allows all of the positive things in our lives, and even our very existence. By seeing that Nature is the root system that causes both the positive and the negative, Stoics understand that to curse one is to curse the other, for they both are necessary products of the same function. To curse unfortunate events is as nonsensical as trying to open a door by pulling the knob and pushing it with our foot at the same time. Therefore, while we should do our best in life, in the end we should have an acceptance of what Nature dictates. In doing so, we are said in one sense to be "living in accordance with Nature".

This attitude about life doesn't protect us from all harm or pain necessarily, but it does help us avoid overwhelming despair. When it comes to contentment, Stoics choose to focus on those things they can control (their own priorities, attitudes, and decisions).

## How to Choose

If we say that we each should only consider true good and evil to be those choices we ourselves make, this begs the question of which of our choices are good and which evil? Classical Stoicism doesn't seem to spend as much time on what we might call 'ethical deliberation' today.

Stoicism generally suggests that we are often deluded by our obsession with things outside of our ultimate control. This leads
278

us to put value on things we shouldn't. Stoics suggest that if we work on being unbiased and free of these delusions, then our minds will be clear. With clear unbiased minds, knowledge of what is good and what is bad will come naturally to us.

While modern Stoics don't usually deny the need for careful deliberation in complex matters, Stoicism suggests that that human beings have an innate sense of right and wrong, even if it is often distorted by our unclear and biased thinking. Therefore, the first order of business for the Stoic is to try to see things without attachment to what we cannot control, and to simply do what is appropriate to his or her duties and obligations without bias.

For the Stoic, *all* matters are an important part of perfecting 'life practice' or 'living well' and there is no real distinction between what is an ethical matter and what isn't. To a Stoic, virtue is part of our very nature, and should ideally be the primary measure for all of our choices.

## Conclusion

This has been a very brief and simplistic explanation of Stoicism. Throughout, I have tried to phrase everything in very intuitive, common language. Therefore, none of Stoicism's common technical terms and phrases have been used here.

If you would like a more subtle and deep understanding of Stoicism, it is important to learn about these terms and phrases. These include English phrases like "preferred indifferents" and "passions" that have very specific meanings so taking them as you may naturally understand them would lead you to misunderstand what's being said. Other terms include Greek words like "*apatheia*" and "*eudaimonia*".

Here are some good online sources for further learning...

**New Stoa**
http://www.newstoa.com/

**The Stoic Foundation**
http://stoicfoundation.cu.cc/

**The Stoic Place**
http://www.wku.edu/%7Ejan.garrett/stoa/

**Stoicism on Wikipedia**
http://en.wikipedia.org/wiki/Stoicism

**The International Stoic Forum**
http://groups.yahoo.com/group/stoics

And, of course, at the Spiritual Naturalist Society, our articles, topics, and discussions are commonly informed by Stoic ideas among others:
**www.SpiritualNaturalistSociety.org**

# Stoicism as a Spiritual Path

*Michel Daw*

When we hear the word 'Spiritual,' many thoughts come to mind. Some think of a dogmatic approach to belief, almost a blind faith. Along the same lines, others see it as a rejection of rationality, or a trust in myth and legend, often with no connection to the 'mundane' world. Almost by definition, philosophical ideas are to be discussed and debated, and if people think that any ideas are good ones, these ideas are defended and argued for rather than just 'believed'. This is the case with respect to ideas in Stoic philosophy. Stoicism is intended to be an active philosophical investigation (though at all times seeking to support Stoic ideas) no matter where it may lead us. If, as a result of these investigations, a person chooses to adopt the Stoic outlook, this will happen because he or she has decided it is right, and not because anyone has been coerced to do so.

For this very reason, many people would say that there is a spiritual path at the core of Stoicism. In fact, the actual work of practicing Stoicism is referred to by some authors as 'spiritual exercises.' The notion of spiritual exercises in ancient philosophy is meant to emphasize, in the first place, that in the ancient schools of thought philosophy was a way of life. Philosophy presented itself as a mode of life, as an act of living, as a way of being. The practice of Stoic philosophy consists of an invitation to complete personal transformation, a journey along a spiritual path. Stoic philosophy, lived out in this way, is in a very real way a conversion, a transformation of the way of being and the way of living in the quest for wisdom.

Therefore, the actual practice of Stoic philosophy required exercises that were neither simply exercises of thought nor even moral exercises, but rather, in the full sense of this term, spiritual exercises. Since they are aimed at realizing a transformation of our vision of the world and a gradual change of our personality, these exercises have an existential value, not only a moral one. Being a Stoic does not mean conforming our behavior in accordance with some external code of good conduct. Following the Stoic Spiritual path involves all aspects of our being – intellect, imagination, sensibility, and will – essentially our body, mind and soul. Stoic spiritual exercises are exercises in learning how to live the philosophical life, and applying it throughout our whole life.

Ancient Stoic philosophers adopted a range of metaphysical and theological views concerning the nature of creation, providence and fate, the source of our rationality, and Deity. Modern Stoics are not required to do so in order to call themselves Stoics. Like Seneca, a Roman Stoic of the first century C.E., we learn from those who have gone before us, but allow ourselves to find out more about the world as it is, and to change or abandon much that was taught in the past. Ancient writers, even Stoic writers, are not considered masters or prophets, but rather serve as mentors and guides. We do not claim to know ultimate Truth, not even that such a thing might exist, but instead search out knowledge and wisdom wherever it is to be found.

In a more general sense, the notion of 'spiritual path', taken to mean 'way of life', 'outlook upon life', 'personal growth', 'personal healing', is in fact the very essence of Stoicism. Some people accept the Stoic views on moral conduct, but reject the 'wilder' metaphysical and theological views. But you will not be required to adopt any particular beliefs. The actual transformational process is in and of itself intensely personal, holistic and fundamentally spiritual.

The Stoic Spiritual Path calls us to pay attention to ourselves, to take care of ourselves through these inner spiritual exercises. Really knowing ourselves requires a relationship with ourselves that forms the basis of all of the Stoic spiritual exercise. Every spiritual exercise is a dialogue, with others, with the world around us, and most importantly, with ourselves. In this way, it is transcendent in the sense that we move beyond our present and past circumstances, beyond our limited ego-centric perspective, and consider our lives from the view of the potential that inhabits each of us. Socrates is famed for his assertion that '*the unexamined life is not worth living*' (Apology 38a). In the most general of senses, what Socrates wanted to examine is the system of values we adopt to justify what we find of importance. And this is the purpose of this website, and of the Stoic Community.

---

*Originally posted at TheStoicLife.com*

# The Big Deal About Complexity

*DT Strain*

There is a little-known but new and 'emerging' field of science called *Complexity* or complex systems theory. Complexity science has brought together professionals from a multitude of vastly different disciplines. It seeks to study what are called "complex adaptive systems", which as it turns out, tends to be just about everything that is interesting about the universe. Some of the revelations of complexity science are awe inspiring, but there may be deeper implications for modern scientifically-compatible spirituality. Complexity may just change the way you look at the universe.

Furthermore, it seems the study of complex systems theory, mathematical and technical though it may be, is very similar to what Heraclitus was referring to in his descriptions of nature, and what the Taoists were referring to with their concept of organic pattern or "Li" – that which is not entirely orderly, but clearly not entirely chaotic or random. And, unlike retrofits where some religious folks sometimes take the latest scientific theories and say, "hey that's what x is in my religion", in this case the thing being discussed by the ancients and that which Complexity addresses are the same phenomena. So much so, that one might consider complex systems theory to be the modern continuation of the Stoic investigation into the nature of the *Logos* (the rational order underlying the universe), and similar lines of thought in some other traditions. There are also numerous components of Buddhist and Taoist philosophy which observe traits about the nature of the world which are described by complexity science.

A **complex system** is one where you have multiple agents interacting according to their own individual rules and, as a result, this large system operates in a very ornate and even "intelligent" way without orchestration from a top-down hierarchy. Complex systems include things like: the economy, the ecology, individual biological organisms, the weather, some computer networks, flocks of birds, and our brains. Complex systems even include the ebb and flow of cultural traits and other meme-based intellectual concepts which interact with one another over time.

Something that is completely orderly is inert and static, and something that is completely chaotic is random and haphazard. But complex systems lie in balance between these two extremes, maintaining an order that is dynamic.

The fascinating thing about Complexity, and why there can be a single field at all, is that all of these systems operate by the same fundamental principles. The actual science behind this is more mathematically deep than most non-scientists may need to understand, but these various equations can be applied to both neurons in the brain, as well as organisms in an ecology or corporations in an economy. What this suggests is that Complexity is not merely pointing out analogies, but that all of these manifestations portray an underlying order that governs how matter in our universe organizes itself. In his book, *Complexity: The Emerging Science at the Edge of Order and Chaos*, Mitchell M. Waldrop lists the following traits of complex adaptive systems:

- They undergo spontaneous self organization.

- They are adaptive to the environment around them.

- They are dynamic, unlike snowflakes and computer chips, which are merely complicated but static.

- They result in emergent properties.

- Once they reach sufficient complexity, there is no way to mathematically deduce their behavior from the base rules by which the individual agents operate, even using every particle of the universe as a bit in a computer that runs for the lifetime of the universe. The best way to see how they will perform is to simply run and observe the system. They are effectively "indeterminate".

- The smallest of changes in initial starting conditions can lead to enormous differences in behavior of the system.

- They tend to bifurcate into layers of organization, where module-like systems work as single agents in larger, more complex structures.

What Complexity teaches us is how simple components acting on just a few basic rules of interaction, can lead upwards to greater levels of complexity. Waldrop say this addresses divergent questions such as:

- Why and how did the Soviet Union collapse overnight?

- Why did the stock market crash more than 500 points on a single Monday in 1987?

- Why do ancient species and ecosystems remain stable for millions of years and then transform or die out in a geologic instant?

- Why do rural families in a nation such as Bangladesh still produce an average of 7 children, even when the villagers are aware of the ill to society and birth control is freely available?

- How did the primordial soup of amino acids emerge into the first cells?

- Why did individual cells form an alliance into the first multi-cellular organisms?

- How can Darwinian natural selection lead to intricate structures such as an eye, whose components require simultaneous development?

- What is "life" exactly?

- What is a "mind" exactly, and how does a 3 pound lump of matter give rise to one?

- Why is there something rather than nothing?

- How is the cosmic compulsion for disorder matched by an equal compulsion for order?

In fact, Complexity science is now having an impact not only in multiple previously unrelated scientific fields such as artificial intelligence, sociology, and economics, but also in several new business and corporate concepts. Some people think this is all about math and science, and don't see the enormous philosophic implications of what's actually being addressed here. Consider the following from Waldrop:

> *"I'm of the school of thought that life and organization are inexorable," he says, "just as inexorable as the increase in entropy. They just seem more fluky because they proceed in fits and starts, and they build on themselves. Life is a reflection of a more general phenomenon that I'd like to believe is described by some **counterpart** to the second law of thermodynamics – some law that would describe the tendency of matter to organize itself, and that would predict the general properties of organization we'd expect to see in the universe."* (bold mine)

Now, when we consider the words of Heraclitus, he tells us of a process that never rests; an everliving fire in an unceasing process of eternal flux. He speaks of the way upwards (order/peace/harmony) and the way downwards (entropy/chaos/disorder). Paradoxically, the everliving fire which creates this flux also secures its stability. This eternal exchange is the same for both microcosm and macrocosm alike (layers of organization).

Heraclitus seems, in his own way, to address many features of complex systems theory. He was observing the very same sort of activity in Nature that Complexity scientists study today, although not nearly as refined or informed. Even his famous statement that one cannot step twice into the same river, is essentially a description of Autopoiesis (a process where some complex systems are constantly remaking themselves with new material, while keeping the same form). These observations had a large impact on philosophies that built upon them. Similar observations in other cultures also held a connection to the remainder of their philosophies; leading up to meaning, ethics, perspectives on life, and values. Chuang-Tzu's attention to the 'way' of nature in his ethical and lifestyle prescriptions is a good example.

# Taoism and Naturalism

*DT Strain*

Taoism (also spelled Daoism) is a life philosophy and practice of living in harmony with the *Tao*. Tao means 'way' or 'path' – a sort of double meaning, as both the 'way of Nature' and the 'way to happiness'.

The primary source of Taoist teaching is called the *Tao Te Ching*, which could be translated as something like, "Book of the Way of Nature, Virtue, and Empowerment". The book is believed to have been authored by Lao Tzu, the founder of Taoism, in the 6th Century B.C.E. Perhaps the next most prominent Taoist figure is Chuang-Tzu, whose writings in the 4th Century B.C.E. are also considered foundational (A condensed summary of the teachings of Chuang-Tzu are available to Society members in our member archives). There have been several other works and today the Taoist canon, the *Daozang* (Treasury of the Tao) consists of almost 1,500 texts.

While Taoism, by its nature, is highly focused on the individual life-practice, institutions grew up around Taoism over the years. Throughout Eastern history, there has been much meshing and cross-influence between Taoism, Buddhism, and Confucianism with elements of each to be found in the other as they are often practiced today.

With such a long history, and having been an integral part of so many cultures, Taoism is vast and certainly includes many aspects practiced in various parts which naturalists would not find compatible to their views. Some Taoists accept and include such things as exorcisms, ancestor worship, literal belief in myths, divination and astrology, immortality, alchemy, and more. But this is, of course, no different than the many supernatural elements practiced in the supernaturalist end of the spectrum in many traditions which naturalists yet find useful ethical and other wisdom, such as Christianity, Buddhism, Paganism, and more.

Within this complex body of thought and custom lies much deep and subtle wisdom which is fully compatible with a naturalistic worldview. This 'core Taoism' can be found practiced in many places; especially as it often finds itself in the West.

The *Tao* is the ineffable 'flow of the universe' – the true nature of the universe, which lies beyond our full grasp and beyond capture by mere language. Tao is both the source of everything that exists and the driving force behind the universe. It may be cautiously comparable in some ways to the Western Stoic *Logos* (the underlying rational order on which the cosmos operates). The nature of the world, according to Taoism is that all things are flowing and in a constant state of re-creation. There are also orders of magnitude and nested cycles in Nature. Thus, when we understand the ways of Nature, we understand ourselves, and vice versa.

This is remarkably similar to what the originator of the Logos, the philosopher Heraclitus, said of Nature. It is also remarkably compatible with how we understand the complex systems of life and the environment to work today. But intellectual awareness of these facts is different from deeply ingrained intuitive knowledge of the subtle but profound implications of such a universe.

To be 'one with the Tao' means that we have freed ourselves from selfishness and desire – from the binds of our narrow egos, and are living simply, in harmony with the nature of things. Many of the teachings and practices of Taoism are aimed at helping the practitioner achieve this state, and can be tested by those who wish to apply themselves to them.

Taoist ethics includes a concept called Wu Wei or "effortless action". This is the art of moving in unison with the natural flow of events, rather than crudely going against the grain. Its hallmarks are patience, timing, simplicity, spontaneity, attention,

292

and moderation. The "three treasures" of Taoism are: compassion, frugality, and humility.

These concepts can have very practical applications. For example, in facing our fears, Taoism helps the practitioner to internalize a value system whereby irrational attachments that breed fear are released. Taoism can also enhance joy in life through greater appreciation of the world around us. In its assessment of the ego and techniques for seeing beyond the ego, Taoism helps us to bring love more fully into our lives. Through its approach to compassion, Taoism can also aid in more external endeavors, such as conflict resolution. For more on these practical applications, see Diane Dreher's book, *The Tao of Inner Peace*.

One of the things naturalists may find most relevant in Taoism is how intimately linked its prescriptions are with realizations about 'the way the universe works' – along with an outlook on the universe which is compatible with a modern scientific conception. Further, understanding some of the basics of Taoism will be helpful in approaching many other Eastern concepts and practices, especially in Zen Buddhism. In turn, where concepts like these are touched upon by Western philosophers, a wider understanding of these ideas can only add breadth of comparative understanding.

# Naturalistic Buddhism

*Ted Meissner*

Buddhism is a term inclusive of the teachings and practices of Siddhartha Gautama, known as the Buddha or "enlightened one", from the 5th century BCE in the Indian subcontinent. There are three major branches of traditional Buddhism: Theravada ("The School of the Elders"), Mahayana ("The Great Vehicle"), and Vajrayana ("Diamond Vehicle"), with new development of non-traditional secular forms in contemporary society. Within each of the classic branches are many further distinct categories, including schools like various sects of Zen.

With few exceptions, Buddhist traditions share the premise outlined in the *Four Noble Truths* as a core teaching:

1. We are often dissatisfied with our experiences in life.

2. This dissatisfaction is conditioned by our lack of understanding, which can lead us to unhealthy craving.

3. There can be a cessation of this dissatisfaction.

4. That cessation can be nurtured by a practice we can do ourselves.

On the surface, these concepts are often misinterpreted as being analogous to other religious ideological stances, rather than coming from experiences all people can have and see for themselves. Even a light examination into many of the concepts described in Buddhism reveals how conducive they are to empirical investigation:

- We find that things and processes are subject to change, nothing is permanent. Even the universe is expected to come to a close.

- We're subject to cause and effect, and our actions have an impact not just on our lives, but on others as well.

- When we want things to be different than they are, we can experience dissatisfaction: having what we don't want, not having what we do want.

- We're not able to stop change or things happening outside of our control, but we can change how we respond to them.

- There are specific skills that can be developed to attenuate our craving for things to be different than they are.

Through an intentional practice, we can develop the skills we need to loosen our attachments, with a resulting lessening of our dissatisfaction and a more beneficial experience with moment by moment living. This practice can be done by anyone, and is not dependent on any ideological views or supernatural assertions. That process of development is known traditionally as the *Eightfold Path*, which is divided into three main sections:

- Wisdom — we need to know how things work to fix the problem

- Ethical Behavior — choosing more beneficial social interactions has more beneficial results

- Mental Development — we can practice beneficial mind states, improving our ongoing experiences in life

Each of those sections has two or more components of an eminently pragmatic nature, completing the eightfold scope of skillful ideas and practices.

Note that there can be many ways to interpret these foundational aspects of the Buddhist path, and what follows is simply one way of expressing them in alignment with a Spiritual Naturalist point of view.

# Wisdom

**1. Understanding** — There are two aspects of skillful understanding, the first is the recursive inclusion of the Four Noble Truths. That is, the last of the four truths refers to the eightfold path, and the first of the eightfold path refers to the four truths. Such tying of these ideas together may seem redundant, but really attests to the criticality of understanding the problem at hand as an important step in seeking ways to address it.

The second aspect of skillful understanding is that of karma, or "volitional action", which was a significant departure from the predominant view of the Brahmin religion of Gotama's time. Rather than being seen as a ritualistic purification of one's spiritual self by a religiously sanctified intermediary, karma was instead altered to be self empowered pragmatic action to impact one's life.

As we can see in the world, our actions lead to outcomes. Gotama suggested the critical factor in cause and effect was the ethical quality of our intentional actions, and that such actions would come to fruition in like ways. Seen from the naturalist perspective, words and deeds and even mental states of kindness and compassion tend to have more beneficial results than their negative counterparts, and these effects in turn condition further results.

**2. Intention** — In keeping with Gotama's idea of the key role played by intent on the quality of what we say and do, the second part of Wisdom is around the kinds of skillful intention more likely to produce beneficial results. Primarily, Buddhism encourages a less grasping and more generous attitude, positive intent or good will, and a transparent interest in not causing harm. Note that these are not empty admonishments, but demonstrable factors that can create the conditions of a better life.

# Ethical Behavior

**3. Speech** — Perhaps the most challenging steps on the Buddhist path is the first aspect of ethical behavior, that of skillful speech. The most coarse examples of this are speaking truthfully, in ways that foster harmony, with gentleness, and in a constructive and open fashion rather than less constructive ways like gossip.

This is not limited to the spoken word, however, and can mean any means through which we communicate, including the written word, body language, and our very expressions. We should also endeavor to initiate communication when our intention is positive, and do our best to select the right time to speak. The acronym THINK, standing for is it True, Helpful, Inspiring, Necessary, and Kind, is a good rule of thumb.

**4. Action** — The second component to ethical behavior is around our physical acts, building on the theme of positive intent. Again, we see guidance to take no actions that have a reasonable expectation of harmful results. Generous actions rather than taking what is not given or outright theft is also encouraged, as is careful consideration in our sexual engagements.

**5. Livelihood** — The third aspect of ethical behavior pertains to how we make a living, suggesting that we not use the constraints of working in a particular role as an excuse for not adhering to the ideals of leading a constructive and beneficial life. Of course there is a much greater diversity of careers in today's world than in Gotama's time, and one should consider the results of one's job with a critical eye of Skillful Intention as a guide.

# Mental Development

**6. Effort** — The first element of mental development is that of skillful effort around the kinds of mind states we foster, both positive and negative. On the negative side, we should do our best to prevent the arising of new negative states of mind, and abandon those that have already arisen. On the positive side, fostering the arising of new positive states of mind and the maintenance of those already in place is encouraged.

It is important to remember that this really does take effort, that it's a challenging practice we need to continually refresh. The Eightfold Path is a path of significant resistance, on the part of our own mind!

**7. Mindfulness** — Second in the triad of mental development is mindfulness, a practice that is getting a great deal of attention in our culture due in large part to the efforts of researchers like Jon Kabat-Zinn and others who are studying mindfulness in a therapeutic context. Though there are a very wide variety of ways to interpret mindfulness, in classical Buddhism it remains a pragmatic exploration of non-judgmental awareness of our bodies, our initial positive and negative and neutral reactions to that which we encounter, our mental states, and various (and sometimes exhaustive) lists of phenomenon.

Mindfulness is most often associated with insight meditation, though is certainly not limited to the confines of the meditation cushion. With practice, such observation can help us loosen habit patterns and give us more mental room in the flurry of the present moment's distractions, which helps us make better decisions for the benefit of ourselves and others.

**8. Concentration** — The third part to mental development is that of concentration, traditionally associated with various stages of meditative skill. Rather than the wide and expansive awareness of mindfulness, concentration meditation focuses on a single object. This can lead to experiencing a mind free from less helpful mental states centered on greed, ill will, unskillful doubt, lack of energy, and unhelpful musings about the past and future. Instead, we can experience more helpful mental stages of great joy and equanimity, which are much more conducive to creating positive change. Concentration is not separate from mindfulness, but is also an attentive practice for the mind on a narrow rather than wide range.

These steps on the Buddhist Eightfold Path should not be taken as sequential, but should all be practiced as foundational skills the development of which leads to living a more constructive and beneficial life for us and those around us. This is pivotal to the transformation of our contemporary society, and the future of humanity.

# Living Life Intentionally

*Jennifer Hancock*

This is such a repeated and rather cliché phrase. We can all be happy if we just live our lives intentionally. The problem isn't that this advice isn't good. It is. The problem is that we are never really told HOW to live our lives intentionally.

We are also told that the unexamined life isn't worth living. To me, this is the same advice as live your life intentionally. The key to both is to think. Specifically, you need to learn how to think well.

To live life intentionally requires you to have intention. To have intention you have to think. It's as simple as that. You can't run on instinct and achieve this. I'm not saying instinct doesn't have a place, it most certainly does. It's more that wise people check their instincts with their critical thinking skills. This allows them to avoid doing stupid things that had they thought for just a moment before they acted they could have avoided entirely. It also helps them to fine tune their gut instincts that are good to help them figure out how to more effectively accomplish what their gut is telling them to do.

This is why people who think and think well, tend to be so successful. For a Humanist, critical thinking is a central part of our practice. This leads people to think we are emotionally dry, but nothing could be further than the truth. We view our emotions as informative tools. They tell us what we need to pay attention to and to work on. Our intellect tells us how best to accomplish that. To us, it's the best of both worlds.

# ABOUT THE SPIRITUAL NATURALIST SOCIETY

## Our Mission

The mission of the Spiritual Naturalist Society is to spread awareness of Spiritual Naturalism as a philosophy, encourage the further development of Spiritual Naturalist thought and practice, and educate others on the traditional wisdom and contemplative practices that inspire Spiritual Naturalism. In addition, the Society exists to help bring Spiritual Naturalists together for mutual learning, growth, encouragement, and fellowship.

## How Does the Society Fulfill its Mission?

The Society spreads awareness of Spiritual Naturalism by publishing educational materials and articles freely on its website, by advertising its own existence and press releases to bring more visitors to that site, by supporting local chapters that host in-person discussion groups and other events, by seeking to publish its educational articles in other publications and websites outside its own, by engaging with other organizations with compatible missions, and through exclusive educational materials offered to members. It encourages further development of Spiritual Naturalist thought and practices by bringing together authors to contribute new materials, by bringing together members in forums for the purposes of discourse and dialog, and by initiating special collaborative projects. Lastly, the Society aids in fellowship of like-minded Spiritual Naturalists from all traditions and backgrounds through other sections of its forums, comment areas, social media, events, and through encouragement and support of locally-initiated groups.

## Who are our Members?

Members of the society come from a variety of traditions. This is because spiritual naturalism is a new paradigm that cuts across familiar labels. Spiritual naturalists can be found among Buddhist, Jewish, Taoist, Humanist, Pagan, Unitarian, atheist, agnostic, and many other communities. Within all of these traditions there is a rising sense of appreciation for the natural universe, a respect for rationality as the basis for humble knowledge, a desire for a spiritual wisdom that is consistent with the modern scientific understanding of the cosmos, and a return to *compassion* as the core value upon which spirituality should rest. Individuals within many religions and other groups are working to heal the schism between the natural and the sacred. Much like an interdisciplinary community, naturalists from all of these backgrounds are welcome members of the Spiritual Naturalist Society, without the need to leave their own traditions.

## Our Principles

Other than our mission as an organization, we are also deeply committed to several principles and operate in accord with them. Among these are:

1. We believe all human beings are equal in their worth and should be given equal opportunity and rights, regardless of their race, sex, gender, ethnicity, nationality, religion, disability, or their sexual orientation or identity. Each individual is deserving of treatment as an individual, based on his or her character and choices, rather than any of these group identities or characteristics.

2. We believe in treating others as we would be treated. We believe in practicing loving-kindness toward even those who do not return it. We believe universal compassion for all beings and unconditional love is the best answer to our conflicts.

3. We try not to criticize the beliefs of others, be it in a respectful academic sense or in a bashing or flippant manner. We instead try hard to focus on what we believe and hope that it will help others find happiness, whatever their tradition. We believe being a living example of our

values is a better way to spread them than criticism and conflict.

4. We believe in acting ethically in both our personal lives and organizationally. This includes great care with the private information we handle on behalf of our members and subscribers, ethically handling all money and funds of the organization for the purposes they were given, and being honest in all things to our volunteers, members, and the public.

5. We believe in the compassionate use of reason for solving our problems. This includes a humble approach to knowledge and the claims we make. It also includes respect for the scientific method, used responsibly and ethically for the betterment of all.

6. While we are not a political or activist organization, we support a more peaceful, charitable, tolerant, just, and democratic world. We also support greater access to education, the necessities of life, and environmental responsibility. We encourage our members and subscribers to take up worthy causes with activist organizations as a part of their personal practice. Ultimately, we believe that change in the world begins with change in our heart, which is where the mission of our Society is focused.

## Are We A Religion?

People have many different definitions of 'religion' and think of the word in different ways. For some, Spiritual Naturalism is a religion because of its inclusion of ritual and contemplative practices that have been associated with other religions before. In fact, some prefer the term *Religious Naturalism* and they are equally welcomed members. For others, Spiritual Naturalism is not a religion, but a philosophy, because it has no supernatural or faith-based aspects. The official position of the Spiritual Naturalist Society is that it is up to each individual to decide for themselves whether to call (or not call) their views or themselves 'religious', 'spiritual', 'philosophic', or otherwise.

## Statement on Politics

The Spiritual Naturalist Society is an apolitical organization. While political participation can be a noble part of a healthy life, and a means to help make the world a better place, the focus of Spiritual Naturalism is on a *personal* life practice – working first on the person in the mirror. Ultimately, it is contemplative practice, inner development, and cultivation of a compassionate heart and rational mind that serve as a replenishing source of wisdom and strength for individuals to make positive change in the world. As an organization supporting a spiritual practice, we seek to be a refuge from the rhetoric, sectarianism, and partisanship common to politics. To those ends, the Spiritual Naturalist Society does not engage in political activity, protests and demonstrations, take political positions, or support parties or candidates. Further, we welcome people of all parties and economic views.

## The SNS Logo

The logo of the Spiritual Naturalist Society is a tree, referring to many metaphors at once. In one sense, it represents the slow but steady cultivation and growth of our character and good life through continuous practice. In another sense, it represents the wisdom taught under the Bodhi tree by the Buddha, as well as knowledge, as represented by the Tree of Knowledge referred to in the Christian Bible. The branches of the tree can also represent the evolutionary paths along which all life develops. In yet another sense, the tree represents nature – or the natural universe as revealed by rational exploration. All of these meanings touch on different aspects of Spiritual Naturalism and are therefore suitable to our Society and its mission.

# AUTHOR BIOGRAPHIES

**Arthur G. Broadhurst** has a B.A. degree from the *University of Richmond*, a B.D. and M. Min. degree from *Colgate Rochester Divinity School*, and a background in philosophy of religion and literature of the ancient world. An ordained minister of the United Church of Christ, he has served as Chaplain and Chairman of the Religion department at a college prep school in New Hampshire and minister of several churches associated with the *Unitarian Universalist Association* in Vermont, Connecticut and Florida. In later years he was active in business, retiring as President and Chief Executive Officer of *School, College and University Underwriters, Ltd.*, a reinsurance company based in Bermuda. He runs the website *The Christian Humanist* and is the author of numerous publications including *The Possibility of Christian Humanism, A Humanist Notebook* and *Stories, Folk Tales and Legends from the Bible*. He lives with his wife Sue Hamilton Broadhurst in Florida.

**Susan Blackmore** is a writer, lecturer and broadcaster, and a Visiting Professor at the University of Plymouth. She has a degree in psychology and physiology from Oxford University (1973) and an MSc and PhD in parapsychology from the University of Surrey (1980). Her research interests include memes, evolutionary theory, consciousness, and meditation. Sue writes for several magazines and newspapers, blogs for the Guardian newspaper and Psychology Today, and is a frequent contributor and presenter on radio and television. She is author of over sixty academic articles, about eighty book contributions, and many book reviews. Her books include *The Meme Machine* (1999), *Conversations on Consciousness (*2005), *Zen and the Art of Consciousness* (2011), and *Consciousness: An Introduction* (a textbook, new editions 2010 and 2011). Her work has been translated into more than 20 other languages. She practices Zen, campaigns for drug legalization and plays in her village samba band, Crooked Tempo.

**Sharmon Davidson** is a visual artist. Her artwork has been shown professionally throughout the eastern United States, receiving awards in both regional and national juried exhibitions since 1994. Solo show venues include the Frable Gallery at ArtSpace in Richmond, Virginia, and the Miami Valley Cooperative Gallery's space at the Dayton Convention Center. Several pieces of her art toured the country for two years in the national traveling group exhibit A Patchwork of Women's Art. Her work has been published on magazine covers, appeared in Art Calendar (Professional Artist) magazine, and has been selected for inclusion in Art Buzz: The 2009 Collection, a premier showcase of top quality, contemporary visual art from around the world. Sharmon earned two Bachelor's degrees in Drawing and Art Education from Northern Kentucky University while raising her children. She furthered her education at the Art Academy of Cincinnati and has taught in Kentucky public schools. She is currently represented by the Promenade Gallery in Berea, Kentucky, and is a member of the Kentucky Guild of Artists and Craftsmen. You can learn more about her and her work at www.sharmondavidson.com.

**Michel Daw** is a modern Stoic, reviving the ancient philosophical and spiritual path. He has been jointly hosting monthly Stoic Workshops with his wife, Pamela, in the National Capital Region and has spoken at festivals and conferences on Stoic Spirituality. Together, they also manage TheStoicLife.org, a Stoic website and resource center, as well as *Words of the Ancient Wise*, a daily Stoic blog. They discuss and teach Stoicism to others through social media, online materials, and from their home in Ottawa, Canada.

**Michael Dowd** is a religious naturalist, evidential mystic, and *big history* evangelist. He is the author of the bestselling book, *Thank God for Evolution: How the Marriage of Science and Religion Will Transform Your Life and Our World* (Viking/Plume), which was endorsed by 6 Nobel laureates and other science luminaries, including noted skeptics and atheists, and by religious leaders across the spectrum. Michael and his wife, Connie Barlow, a science writer, have devoted their lives to sharing the inspiring side of science in ways that offer practical tools for living and realistic hope for the future. Since April 2002 they have traveled

North America and have addressed more than 1,600 religious and secular groups. Michael and Connie's work has been featured in numerous national and local print, radio, and TV media, including The NY Times, LA Times, Washington Post, Newsweek, Discover, CNN, ABC News, Fox & Friends, etc. He also recently delivered a TEDx talk.

**Sigfried Gold**, born-again atheist and author of tailoredbeliefs.com, invented a non-existent God to serve as his higher power in a Twelve-Step recovery program. He prays fervently, consults his non-existent deity for guidance, respects religious people, and does other things that, in his words, "unfortunately and unintentionally mystify and piss off many non-spiritual atheists". He agitates for a world in which every person, no matter how skeptical or idiosyncratic, can find a suitable community to help her live according to her own values, and where religious difference sparks curiosity, not animosity. Professionally he designs information visualization software to help people understand complex data. He has a Master of Fine Arts in Creative Writing and a Master of Arts in Biomedical Informatics. He lives in Takoma Park, MD with his wife and two children.

**Jennifer Hancock** is author of *The Humanist Approach to Happiness: Practical Wisdom, Jen Hancock's Handy Humanism Handbook*, and *The Humanist Approach to Happiness: Life Skills Course*. She writes a freelance column about Humanism for the Bradenton Herald newspaper and publishes the *Happiness through Humanism* blog and podcast. She is also a speaker, specializing in Humanism, ethics, morality, and what motivates us to be better humans. Jennifer Hancock describes herself as unique in that she is one of the few people in America who was actually raised according to Humanist principles. Her upbringing gives her a distinctive approach to the promotion of Humanism. This has led people like bio-ethicist and author Torben Riise, Ph.D. to claim that she is "one of the finest minds in Humanism" today.

**Rick Heller** facilitates the Humanist Mindfulness Group, which is sponsored by the Humanist Community at Harvard University. His writing has appeared in Buddhadharma, Free Inquiry, UUWorld, Tikkun, the Boston Globe, and Lowell Sun. He is the creator of *Seeing the Roses*, a website that presents videos demonstrating meditation and mindfulness techniques in a secular context.

**Ted Meissner** has been a meditator since the early 90s, with training in both the Zen and Theravada traditions as well as more contemporary teaching methods. He is the Executive Director of the Secular Buddhist Association, and host of the SBA's official podcast, The Secular Buddhist. Ted's background in skepticism, science, and critical thinking informs his examination of the evolution of contemplative practice in modern culture, and he is a regular panelist on interfaith discussions regarding the complex issues facing our global society.

**B.T. Newberg** is an author, editor, teacher, and husband. Since 2000, he has been practicing meditation and ritual from a naturalistic perspective. Upon leaving the Lutheranism of his raising, he experimented with Agnosticism, Buddhism, Contemporary Paganism, and Humanism. He now blends all these experiences into his life as a Spiritual Naturalist. After founding the community blog *Humanistic Paganism*, he currently writes the column *Naturalistic Traditions* at Patheos and contributes writing and course design to the Spiritual Naturalist Society. Professionally, he holds a master's degree in education and teaches English as a Second Language. Having lived in England, Malaysia, Japan, and Korea, B. T. Newberg currently resides in the place of his birth, Minnesota, with his wife and cat. As Education Director of the SNS, he is responsible for the Society's educational programs, such as course design and collection of supporting materials in both the archives and courses. This also includes helping to select and manage mentors.

**Thomas Schenk** says he has no credentials besides having lived for 50-plus years. He calls himself a space-age Taoist, Black Sheep Catholic, Perennial Philosophy Pantheist, and Dharma Bum, which suggests he is not inclined to commitment. Tom maintains a largely unread blog called the *Golden Hive of the Invisible*, which can be found at hiveoftheinvisible.blogspot.com.

**DT Strain** is founder and Executive Director of the Spiritual Naturalist Society. He is a Humanist minister, speaker, and writer on the topics of ethics, spirituality, and ancient philosophy. His background includes leadership experience and strategic marketing for major corporations and non-profit organizations. DT Strain is the founder of the *Humanist Contemplative* concept and group, which has since helped inspire a similar group at Harvard University. He is former president of the Humanists of Houston, founder of the Houston Freethought Alliance, and has served as vice-chair on the Executive Council of the American Humanist Association's Chapter Assembly, on the Education Committee of the Kochhar Humanist Education Center, and as a member of the Stoic Council at *New Stoa*. He attends the Jade Buddha Temple, and has spoken for their English Dharma Group. He writes for the Houston Chronicle Belief page and Patheos.com, and his work has appeared nationally in other magazines, newsletters, and in the journal "Essays in the Philosophy of Humanism". He is occasionally a guest at panel discussions for universities and organizations. DT Strain has also appeared as a panelist on the Houston PBS television program, *The Connection*, discussing religious belief and non-belief, and speaks at other venues upon request.

The following articles originally appeared at www.humanisticpaganism.com: *Real Religion?, Big History: The Heart of Spiritual Naturalism, How Do You Understand Nature?, Saving the Marriage of Science and Myth, Three Transcendents, Working Ritual with The Center, Last Hum of the Cicada: Death for Naturalists, Managers of Human Nature: A Job Description for Spiritual Naturalists, Naturalistic Paganism.*


*Do Spiritual Naturalists Believe in God*? originally appeared at www.blogcritics.org.


*Christianity Without God* originally appeared at www.christianhumanism.net.


*Evolutionary Christianity* originally appeared at www.evolutionarychristianity.com.


*Stoicism as a Spiritual Path* originally appeared at www.thestoiclife.com.


All other articles originally appeared at www.spiritualnaturalistsociety.org.

To learn more about Spiritual Naturalism or to become a
member, please visit us at

**www.SpiritualNaturalistSociety.org**

CPSIA information can be obtained at www.ICGtesting.com
Printed in the USA
LVOW08s2139250315

432067LV00001B/147/P